COMPLEXITY SIMPLIFIED
LEADING INNOVATION & CHANGE
FOR 21ST CENTURY LEADERS

WOLFGANG RIEBE

1st Printing 2016

Publisher:
MindPower Publications
www.mindpowerpublications.com

Layout, Drawings & Cover Design: Elof Gribwagen

ISBN-13: 978-1530787975
ISBN-10: 1530787971

DEDICATION

I dedicate this book to all those leaders that want to pull their hair out daily at the restrictions imposed upon them by non-sensical regulations within their organisations that have resulted in over complex policies, procedures, red tape and bureaucratic processes that now smother productivity.

TABLE OF CONTENTS

Contents   Page

Contents   Page

Contents   **Page**

Contents   Page

FOREWORD

Welcome to this book on complexity thinking simplified. As a magical keynote speaker (someone that speaks, trains and uses magic tricks to bring across messages) I have noticed a steady increase in complexity within companies over the last few years. As someone that uses logic to develop magic tricks with which I info-train my audiences, this corporate complexity started intriguing me. Why? I think logical and use the most basic logical concepts to fool and audience and I have noticed that it is becoming easier to fool people. In fact my first book and keynote called 'Discover Your Magic' I open with a simple trick based on logic where I fool the audience and then show them how simple the secret is. I base the whole keynote's premise of logical thinking on this one trick.

In a similar vein, this book and it's accompanying keynote has simplicity as its premise. Initially I wanted to call the book, 'Think Like A Magician', however the title sadly didn't appeal to the current 'business thinking' trend, so 'Simplify Complexity' it became. In the end I still feel my first title is way more true to the drive for writing this book, as most of the complex and impossible tricks you see magicians perform, are usually based on the most simplistic principles ever. It's just that we all have grown up in such a fast paced changing world that these simple concepts, in my opinion, are discarded by our subconscious minds and hence we end up with so many complex interpretations of events that has led the world to where it is today.

As someone that has spoken to companies throughout the world, I began to notice that more and more leaders are struggling to cope with this ever-changing world, plus are being caught up in the complexity of policies and regulations, red tape, bureaucracy and political correctness. Hence I saw this need for leadership today, to begin simplifying and thinking out of the box. This in turn led me to embark on a postgraduate dissertation with the York St John University in the UK in 2014 in leading innovation and change where

I decided to formally research whether complexity thinking inhibits innovation amongst leadership in multinationals.

What a fascinating journey it was investigating the academic research available and embarking on my own case studies. In the end, I feel I had an incredible enriching experience at this late stage in my life. In fact, even though I completed the degree with merit, my dissertation supervisor did comment that my academic work read more like a book, than an academic treatise of the subject. Little did he realise that this was my full intention!

It is all good and well to put together a linguistically proficient research paper based on academic insight only, but where does the real life practicality of what really goes on in business come in? Furthermore, people in my mainstream target market would struggle to understand it, and after all – that's the market that I want to change. Hence my intention was to create a book and a keynote, tackling the topic of complexity thinking and finding simple solutions to combat complexity that remains academically sound, yet is written in such a way that most people will enjoy reading it.

In a nutshell, this book is my dissertation, with a few added notes and anecdotes. If you are not into heavy reading and the 'how and why' behind complexity thinking and changing leadership patterns, then the final chapter is a simple short summary of solutions to complexity, based on Lee Cockerell's book on Creating Magic and Jim Collins' views in his book, 'From Good to Great'.

In order to discuss complexity and its origins, I need to start with a few background chapters to build a foundation for my argument.

Chapter 1 is a short, light-hearted poke at complexity thinking... although I believe it contains more truth than most will realise.

Chapter 2 deals with critical review of theories of innovation, change and associated leadership as a good basis for the following chapters.

Chapter 3 provides more insight through a literature review of key theories, and the relationship between strategy, innovation and change.

As leadership plays a vital role in the origin, as well as the final solution to solving complexity, Chapter 4 provides A critical evaluation of the role leaders play in influencing innovation and change in organisations.

My personal favourite is Chapter 5, and in my opinion, the leading cause of complexity within organisations today that deals with culture and innovation within organisations today.

Chapter 6 is then finally the resultant research dissertation and case studies questioning whether complexity thinking in fact does, or does not inhibit innovation amongst leadership in multinationals.

Finally as an afterthought, Chapter 7 is a brief summary of possible solutions to bring simplicity back into the workplace.

I trust you will find this a fascinating read and find the path back to simplicity again.

"Whether you make the effort to accomplish a dream or not, the time will pass by regardless. So why not make the most of the time that you have, and do it as simply as possible?"

(Wolfgang Riebe)

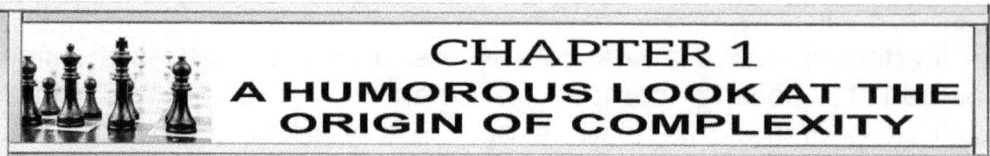

CHAPTER 1
A HUMOROUS LOOK AT THE ORIGIN OF COMPLEXITY

Before I begin with the academic research, let me share my personal and light-hearted views on where complexity thinking originated. Factually, we all think differently, cross culturally, religiously, across the sexes and of course across varying business sectors. Some not particularly politically correct, but still containing an element of truth even if many don't want to accept this. Of course this has additionally led to a plethora of issues amongst the sexes that have no logical explanation for either man or woman.

As I will be covering a number of business frameworks and models I felt it apt to begin the book with a fairly simple model based of female logic and thinking.

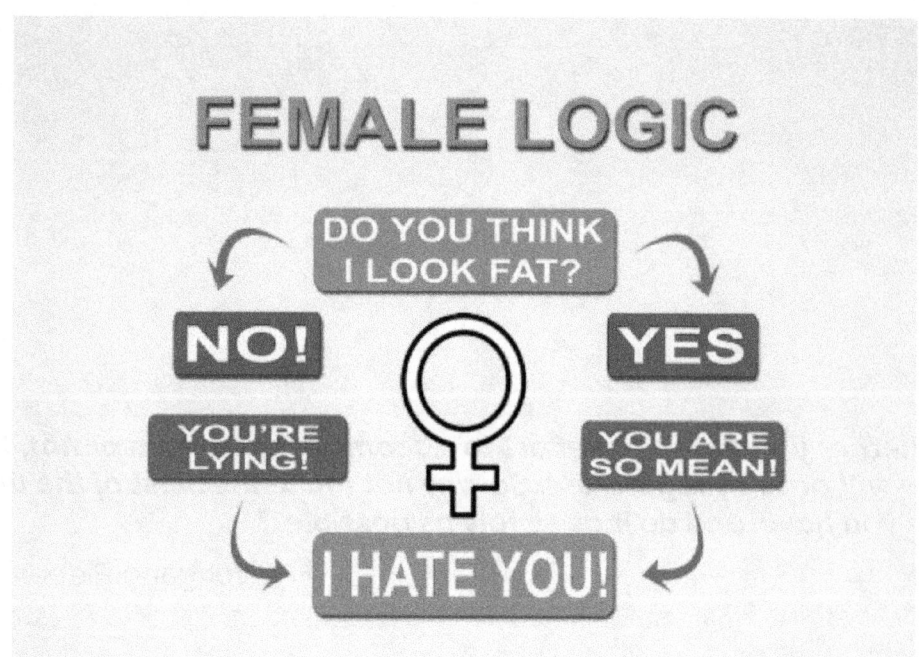

And here we have the beginning of complexity thinking! If this doesn't make sense to you, one can take it a step further with another diagram...

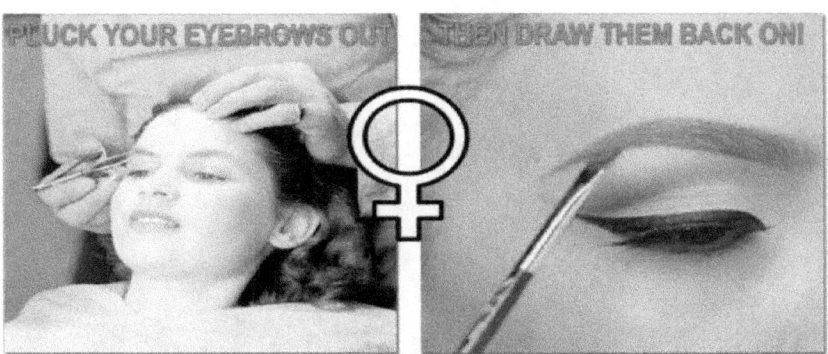

With equality in the workplace finally starting to become a reality, these two examples could possible explain the stress and confusion that men are feeling within larger corporations today towards their female counterparts.

However, in all fairness, and before I get labelled as sexist, research, whether quantitative or qualitative,   always needs to remain objective... so for the ladies, let us consider how men think...

Yes I clearly realise that no woman understands this logic at all. Even worse, when it comes to shopping, there is an even bigger divide between the sexes...

Now that both sexes have had a good chuckle at each other, let me move on to the real 'problem logic' in the world, starting with how governments think. So as not to offend anyone, I believe the below example puts it nicely into perspective.

So the next time you put on your seat belt, think about this non-sensical but very real example. It is important that you realise that illogical thinking is not something new, in fact it has been around for decades. If anything, logical thinking has been a a challenge for many leaders, even back in the 70's for those of you who remember the Star Trek TV shows.

LEADERSHIP LOGIC
IT STARTED YEARS AGO!

Funnyjunk (2014)

Strange, even today I meet companies where the entire 'c' level structure all fly on one plane or sit on the same bus to the same event? Haven't they learnt the lesson yet? What happens if there is an accident? Suddenly the entire leadership is gone! Weird how no one thinks of that?

So where do we start to look for solutions?

Having brought up two children and believing to understand how children think, I believe we can learn a lot from young kids, especially when it comes to simplifying our thinking processes. On the next page is a classic social media post by an unknown author explaining a logical answer to a logical question... would you have come up with his too?

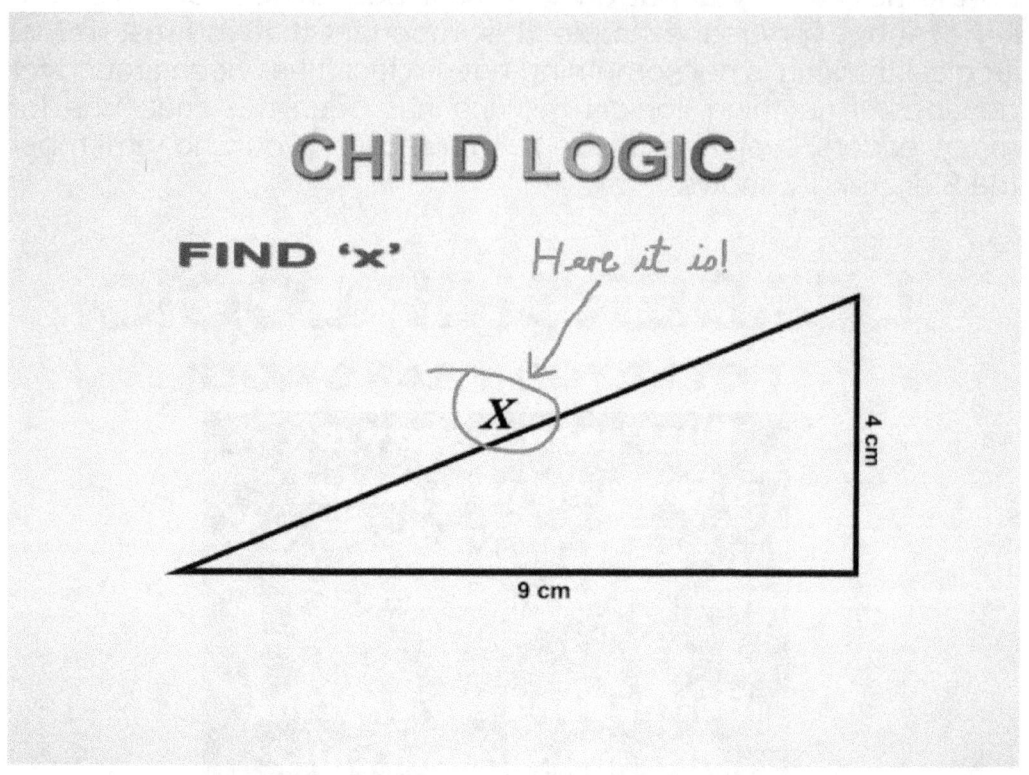

Many studies will reveal that the first 7 years of a child's life are the foundation of future thinking and that through psycho-social, socio-cultural and behaviouristic influences, children start developing complex thinking patterns. In fact I believe this to be the foundation of St. Francis Xavier's quote, "Give me the child until he is seven, and I'll give you the man". Although I agree with Xavier that basic value systems ingrained in these formative year will always remain, it has become more and more apparent that as a society today we can however be manipulated and brainwashed to loose that childhood logic as we move on into adulthood. Don't you believe me? Ask a child to take the scrabble block letters below and come up with a word...

 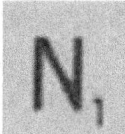 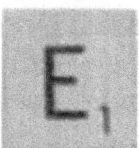 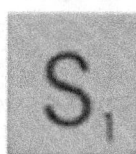 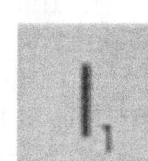

What word do you immediately see?

Children see...

 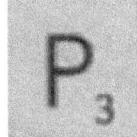 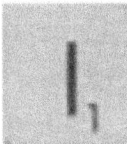 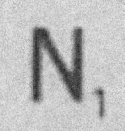 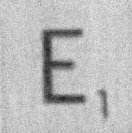

Guess you are chuckling now! Yep they haven't been corrupted yet! In all seriousness though, here is in my opinion the ultimate example of logical thinking and how difficult it is to apply it in today's world. Below is a picture of a bus – I simply want to know in what direction do you think the bus is traveling?

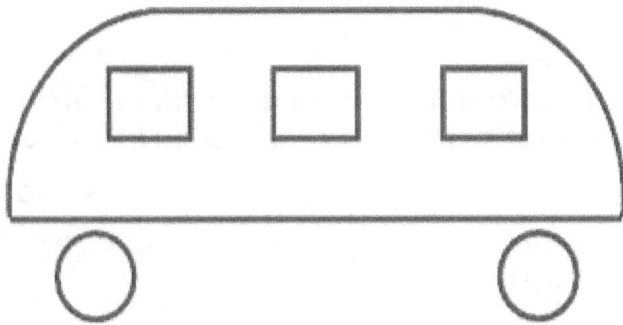

There are only two possible answers and I am amazed at the reasoning behind each possible solution that people have shared with me. The logical answer is incredibly simple, but dependent on where you live. If you live in Europe or the US the bus is traveling from right to left.

Why?

You can't see the door! It is on the other side – so obviously the bus is traveling from right to left.

If you live in the UK, India and Australia, it would be the other way around.

*"**Don't confuse my personality with my attitude.**
My personality – that's me. My attitude, well, that depends on you!"*

(Wolfgang Riebe)

CHAPTER 2
LEADING INNOVATION & CHANGE

INTRODUCTION

"Most of the things worth doing in the world have been declared impossible before they were done."

(Louis Brandeis, 1856 – 1941)

The global village landscape of the modern world has completely re-wired the way in which we do business. From speed of access to information and resources, to global capital, cultural diversity, political upheaval, and cross border competition – the playing field in this new millennium has forever changed. Therefore these resultant new opportunities have brought about new challenges, risks and unexpected consequences for leaders in the struggle to remain constantly innovative and keep up with the change. *(Waite 2014)*.

This chapter will explore and review innovation, change and its leadership, plus critically analyse the theories, models, approaches and strategies utilised in business today.

By referring to various relevant theories in innovation and change, I will also share 'real-life' examples of a successful and less successful innovation/change and finally conclude the chapter with a case study on performance as a leader of innovation and change.

1. A CRITICAL REVIEW OF THEORIES OF INNOVATION, CHANGE AND ASSOCIATED LEADERSHIP

1.1 INTRODUCTION

The aim of any business should be realistic, measurable future growth and profit, while staying ahead of competitors. To achieve this, leadership must constantly create and sustain innovative value propositions that change with the times in order to stand above the crowd so as to gain maximum market share.

1.2 PROBLEMS ASSOCIATED WITH THESE THEORIES

In 1957, according to the S&P 500 average company life expectancy was 75 years. Today it ranges between 35 - 40 years and is waning. Sustainable continuous innovation appears to be declining *(Kuhlmann 2010)*. Examples of failed businesses include the likes of, Pan American Airlines (USA), Orion Pictures (USA), Commodore Computers (USA), Polaroid Corporation (USA), Bugatti Automobili SpA (Italy), Fokker Aerospace (Netherlands) and Nationwide Airlines (South Africa).

Interestingly, *Tidd & Bissant (2009)* derived from the Communist Manifesto of Karl Marx and Frederich Engels in 1848 that the innovation challenge is not new, as companies have always had to deal with shifting targets. Even with established recipes, it needs to be understood that the risk always remains that the rules of the game will always change.

1.3 INNOVATION

Many contrasting definitions have been suggested over the years. According to *Leonard & Swap (1999, p. xiii)*, *"Innovation is the embodiment, combination, and/or synthesis of knowledge in novel, relevant, valued new products, processes, or services."* Elaborating, and adding to this, is *Razeghi's (2008, p. 24)* view that , *"Innovation is not the result of thinking differently. It is the result of thinking deliberately (in specific ways) about existing problems and unmet needs".*

Although these two definitions offer a satisfactory broad understanding of innovation, *Holbeche (2006)* more importantly added that the success of an innovation within any organisation is dependent on a clear vision and well planned stable strategy.

Additionally, *Goffin & Mitchell (2010)* asserted that managing innovation differs from one company to another. The challenge being that one cannot adopt general best practice across all industries, rather one has to adapt suitable ideas to a particular company's needs.

Their Pentathlon model has a simple framework and covers 5 focus areas (**Ideas, prioritisation, Innovation strategy, people and organisation** and **implementation**). However, being phenomenal in one area is not enough to ensure success. Critically, very few, if any organisations can be an expert in all areas, thus outside intervention is required which is likely costly and involves lengthy processes. Moreover, this model focuses on products and new services rather than processes and the practice of doing things (*Goffin & Mitchell 2010*).

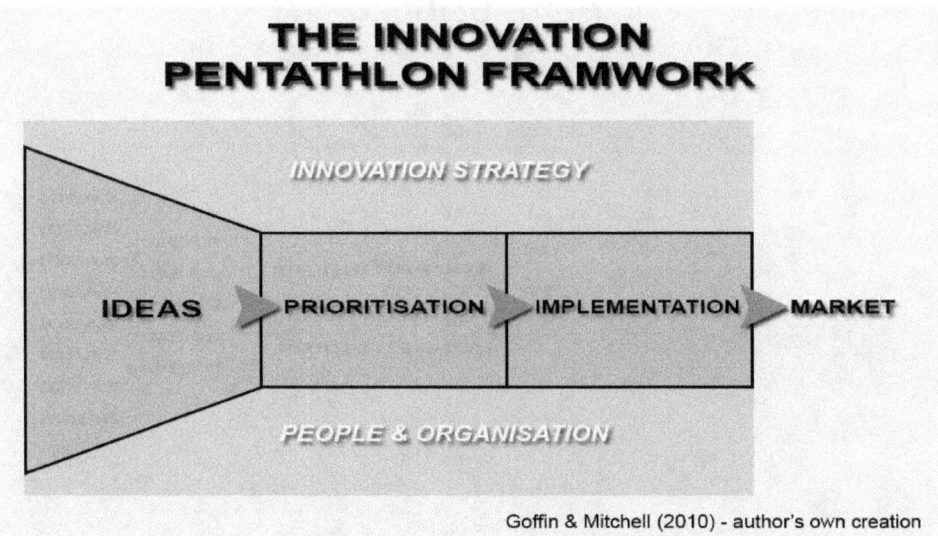

Goffin & Mitchell (2010) - author's own creation

Despite technological advances, changing customer needs and intensified competition as innovation drivers, in an interview with the Cranfield School of Management in 2007, Goffin discussed the initial Pentathlon Framework. He shared that in a second edition of his book he would place larger focus on problem recognition within organisations. He felt that innovation management lacks motivation, as there is no penalty associated with a missed opportunity. The reason being that many companies never comprehend what they are missing out on (*Goffin 2007*).

On the other hand, according to *Isaksen & Tidd (2006)* well-aligned business strategies lead to success. However, they felt that small changes could be seen as a safer progression within a company (incremental), whereas totally new out-of-line (radical) innovations would be better suited for market considerations.

Subsequently *Tidd & Bessant (2009)* maintained that innovation could be viewed as a safer approach to defending key issues and be seen as a potent means of acquiring competitive leverage. They do however not believe that this will necessarily guarantee success. Motorola's satellite handset enabling calls anywhere on the planet is a great example. Although novel at the time, the masses required phones in cities rather than the middle of the desert.

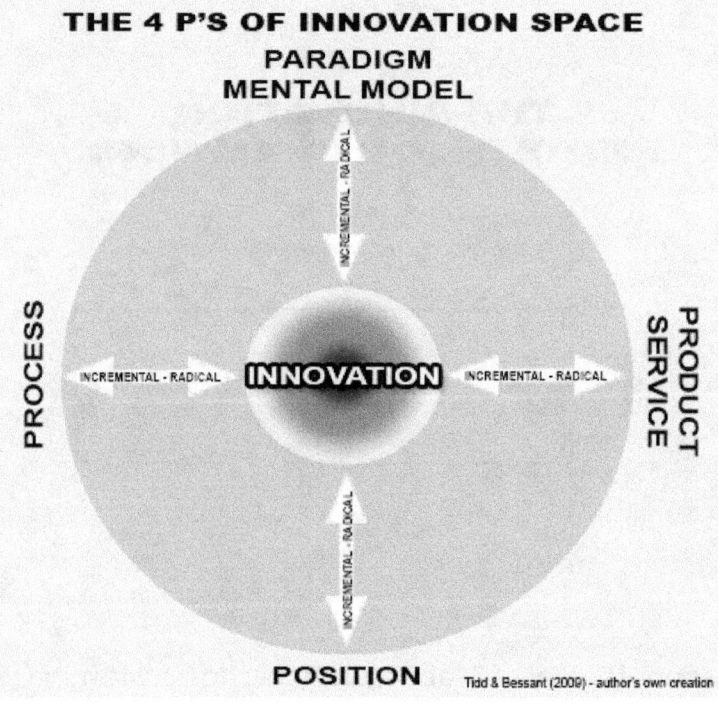

Hence the failure of this innovative concept. Conversely, I was fortunate to host the Europe Nokia launch of the N8 in September

2010. It was the first phone with a 12-megapixel autofocus lens. Suddenly tourists did not need to carry a bulky SLR camera with them, hence adding to the appeal and success of the N8.

Depending on the type of innovation, different paths are suggested in Tidd's 4Ps approach. One can see that disruptive innovation would require a contrasting management style to routine innovation. If one looks at Tidd's four dimensions of innovation space, to deliver new or enhanced products, organisations combine a mixture of extant and new knowledge, known as product innovation.

Organisations that want to improve services by becoming more flexible and efficient are often challenged to use limited resources more productively, known as Process Innovation. To target a new market and change the context of an old product is known as Position innovation. A move from regular to Internet banking can be seen as a paradigm innovation where a client's mental attitudes towards and organisation has shifted. For this theory to be truly successful, a combination of all four approaches needs to be implemented *(Tidd & Bessant 2009)*.

Although, innovation, invention, creativity and change are closely linked, the definitions of creativity and innovation are more comparable - hence Professor Amabile's theory of the organisational influence on creativity and innovation could also come into play. She believed that the contemporary approach (where all humans with normal abilities) can be influenced by the social environment to produce at least a basic creative work in some domain is important.

It is only with comprehensive knowledge and all the ins and outs of a subject that one has the capacity to follow a set of cognitive pathways in order to solve a specific issue. This model clearly indicates that creativity produced by individuals and teams are the leading origin of innovation within an organisation *(Amabile 1996)*.

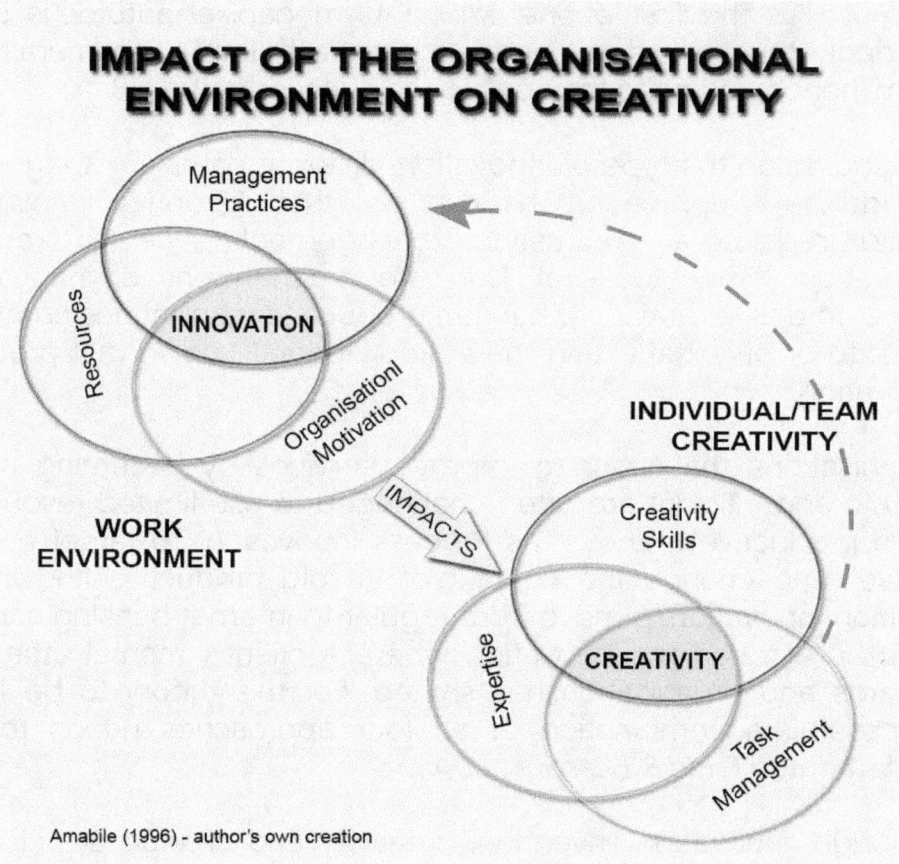

IMPACT OF THE ORGANISATIONAL ENVIRONMENT ON CREATIVITY

Amabile (1996) - author's own creation

1.4 CHANGE

As a speaker on Change Management, my favourite quotation by *Robert Louis Stevenson (1850 - 1894)* is, *"Life is not a matter of holding good cards, but of playing a poor hand well."* This aptly applies to change. However, it's not so much about the change, if you consider *Heraclitus (535 BC – 475 BC), "The only thing that is constant is change,"* but what you do with that change and the strategies you implement to make that change successful.

Before reviewing various change models, consider the definitions of change. It can be defined in terms of its magnitude and whether it is frivolous or considerable *(Dibella 2007)*, incremental or discontinuous *(Nadler & Tushman 1995)*, to transformational - from enterprising to a formal structure; the regeneration of a current business; the major re-evaluation of the company's core focus *(Flamholz & Randle 1998)*.

All innovation involves change, but not all change is the result of new ideas or breakthroughs *(Boak 2010)*. Why? Because innovation needs to transcend the theoretical realm before any real change can happen. Without change, it is simple innovation without a result and has no meaning to an organisation *(Carnell 2007)*. Furthermore, the change may be occurring solely for the purpose of survival for a particular company, hence innovation would not be the driving force in this instance.

Holbeche (2006) felt that change cannot be bought, and that it should be seen as a mindset, or culture that lights a creative spark within an organisation where leaders influence others to change old established practices and transform them into effective new, refined, competitive and even revolutionary profit making strategies embraced by the entire organisation.

In addition, *Holbeche (2006, p. ix)* said, *".. change has become the constant. Add globalisation to technological shifts, multiply by today's volatile economic climate, and you have what D'Aveni (1994) called 'hypercompetition' to describe the disorder and unpredictability facing 21st-century organizations."* Similarly, *Senior & Flemming (2006)* saw change happening due to continual swings in demand & supply, alternating end-user needs and fluctuating employee expectations.

If anyone, *Holbeche (2006)* insightfully highlighted that this new era has become a completely new playing field from which no company is immune. Complete and fast restructuring while managing 'dynamic stability' is the norm due to global customer choice and competition coupled with higher efficiency and low-cost products and services. It would appear that radical change in order to survive is becoming the norm over incremental change. However, *Holbeche (2006, p. 253)* also said, *"Change does not have to be driven by crisis. It has the potential to unlock and improve organizational effectiveness."*

Beer & Nohria (2000) spoke about Theory E (based on economic value) and Theory O (based on organisation capability) changes. Theory E is considered the 'hard' approach, involving economic incentives, layoffs and restructuring and more common than the 'soft' Theory O in the USA.

A COMPARISON OF THEORY E & THEORY O
BEER, M & NOHRIA,N (2000)

DIMENSION OF CHANGE	THEORY E	THEORY O	THEORY E & O COMBINED
Goals	Maximise shareholder value	Develop organisation capacities	Explicitly embrace the paradox between economic value and organisational capability
Leadership	Manage from top down	Advocate participation from the bottom up	Set direction from the top & engage the people below
Focus	Emphasise structure and systems	Build staff behaviour, attitude and corporate structure	Simultaneos focus on hard (structures & systems) and soft (corporate culture)
Process	Plan and establish programmes	Experiment and evolve	Plan for spontaneity
Reward system	Motivate through financial incentives	Pay is fair exchange for committment	Incentives used to reinforce change, rather than drive it
Use of consultants	Consultants analyse problems and shape solutions	Consultants support management in shaping own solutions	Consultants are expert resources who empower employees

Hart (2003)

Additionally, *Cable (2012)* felt that today's workforce is more skeptical and inquiring; therefore the focus should be on smaller changes that ultimately conclude in the large change. This has led to a new leadership challenge as these multitudes of smaller changes can result in differing perceptions of the reason for the initial change, hence resulting in confusion. This view corresponds well with *Holbeche (2006)* where she identified the biggest challenge in managing change being, management of the people in order to affect their willingness to take part in the change.

In the past, *Shaul Oreg (2003)* investigated this 'resistance to change' phenomena in individual personalities. He concluded that comfort in a particular routine; differing individual reactions to a change; lack of long-term vision and reluctance to change thinking all effected an individual's resistance to change. In later years *(Oreg, Vakola &*

Armenakis 2011) completed a 60 year review of 79 studies focusing on the role of the individual's readiness in accepting organisational change and added that various anticipated factors, either beneficial or harmful also play a vital role in the acceptance of that change. These studies were further validated in the findings of *Maria Vakola (2014, p. 195)*, *"The results show that perceived impact of change mediates the relationship between the pre-change conditions and work attitudes and individual readiness to change."* From these findings it can be concluded that only once employees shift their thinking in tune with that of the company and its decision makers, can the organisation benefit from the full impact of that change.

2. LEADERSHIP OF CHANGE & INNOVATION

2.1 UNDERSTANDING THE DIFFERENCES BETWEEN A MANAGER VERSUS A LEADER

Before one can analyse the various change models, one needs to clearly identify the role of a leader, versus a manager in leading innovation and change. *Zaleznik (2004)* in an article first published in 1977, described leaders as visionaries with entrepreneurial spirit and managers as planners focusing on a process who prefer to avoid risk. Interestingly, back then he argued that even though there were differences, companies could not survive without these two types of people. Years later *Kotter (2001)* explained that in today's changing world, even though leaders focus on change and managers on stability, they have different roles and cannot operate independently of each other. *Macoby's (2000)* views were in line with Kotter, as he saw leaders as change agents, while managers as the administrators. The latter two views could even be offshoots from *Capowski (1994)* who described leaders as visionary and the initiators of change, and managers as rational problem solvers.

Yukl (2012) defined leadership as consisting of two components; securing an agreement as well as supporting everyone in the change process. Simultaneously he also recognised that it often takes many people to bring about change. Therefore it is no longer simply the work, or sole responsibility of one individual.

Building on this, *Cable (2012)* referred to a new leadership where employees have to be inspired and given a purpose to follow through on the change. He further clarified that leaders need to acknowledge that the change can be a struggle and not always make sense immediately – this calls for a new management approach where leaders have to continually encourage the employees and guide them through the tough times.

These views are fittingly summarised by *Straker (2013)* on his Changing Minds website where he describes managers as characteristically authoritarian and transactional with subordinates reporting to them, compared to leaders who have followers due to their more charismatic and transformational leadership.

Therefore the roles of leader and manager are interdependent and interconnected and both play an important role in managing change.

2.2 OVERCOMING RESISTANCE TO CHANGE

The change process is dynamic and continuous, and not static as implied by various change models *(Kanter, Stein & Jick 1992)*. Even though *Horwitz & Klontz (2013)* maintained that the leader creates the resistance, many other views exist, from communication breakdown, violation of trust *(Ford, Ford & D'Amelio 2008)*, lack of vision, lack of management support and workload stress *(Holbeche 2006)*. The underlying problem is that uncertainty and fear can lead to resistance to change as described by *Umble & Umble (2014, p. 18)* where they explain that organisational leaders need to *"...peel away three broad layers of resistance, ... as with the layers of an onion"* in order to actualise a buy-in from all affected parties. They describe three broad categories divided into seven clear-cut layers of contention that need to be solved in a logical sequence:

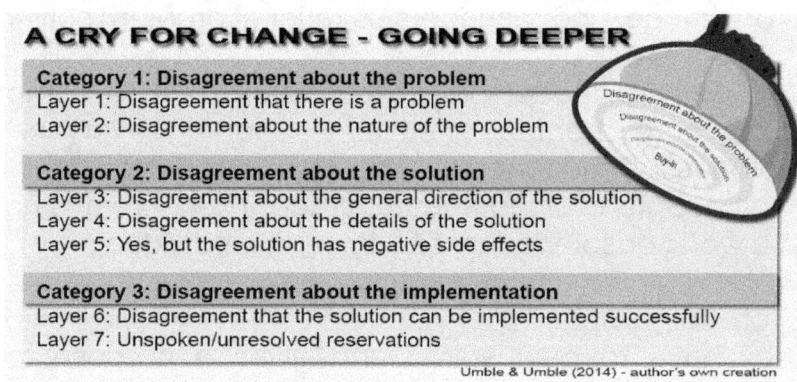

A CRY FOR CHANGE - GOING DEEPER

Category 1: Disagreement about the problem
Layer 1: Disagreement that there is a problem
Layer 2: Disagreement about the nature of the problem

Category 2: Disagreement about the solution
Layer 3: Disagreement about the general direction of the solution
Layer 4: Disagreement about the details of the solution
Layer 5: Yes, but the solution has negative side effects

Category 3: Disagreement about the implementation
Layer 6: Disagreement that the solution can be implemented successfully
Layer 7: Unspoken/unresolved reservations

Umble & Umble (2014) - author's own creation

As many people in an organisation have little or no say in changes, leaders must accept that this is an emotional ride for employees, hence empathy and clear communication is a must in order to maintain a balance between reason and emotion *(Holbeche 2006)*.

2.3 CHANGE MANAGEMENT MODELS – A CRITICAL REVIEW

A shifting social zeitgeist has resulted in diverse and plentiful change models being developed over the past few years. Three mainstream models will be assessed *(Lewin, Kotter & Rogers)*, in conjunction with three supplementary models *(Bridge, Kübler-Ross & Prosci)*.

In 1996 Kotter's research found that only 30% of change models worked. In 2008 McKinsey's survey of 3199 executives found similar results in that only a third of transformations prevail. On these grounds *Lawson & Price (2003)* and *Aiken & Keller (2009)* identified four requirements that are needed for staff to change behaviour and which can be used as a foundation before employing any of the current change models.

a.) **A compelling story that they can identify with and relate to**
Problem - often employees do no care about the same motivators as their leaders. Research has indicated that when staff can write their own story and add a taste of personal ownership, their motivation increases substantially.

b.) **A respected leader role model who lives the change**
Problem - many leaders don't believe they need to change and see themselves as above their staff.

c.) **Reinforcing mechanisms in terms of systems and processes**
Problem – money is an expensive solution. Focus should be on systems & processes that are fully functional.

d.) **Capability building as staff so that they are skilled to bring about the change**
Problem - formal barriers have not been lowered for staff to practice new skills. Similarly, *Boak (2010)* agreed that various

changes in organisations have differing effects and need appropriate approaches.

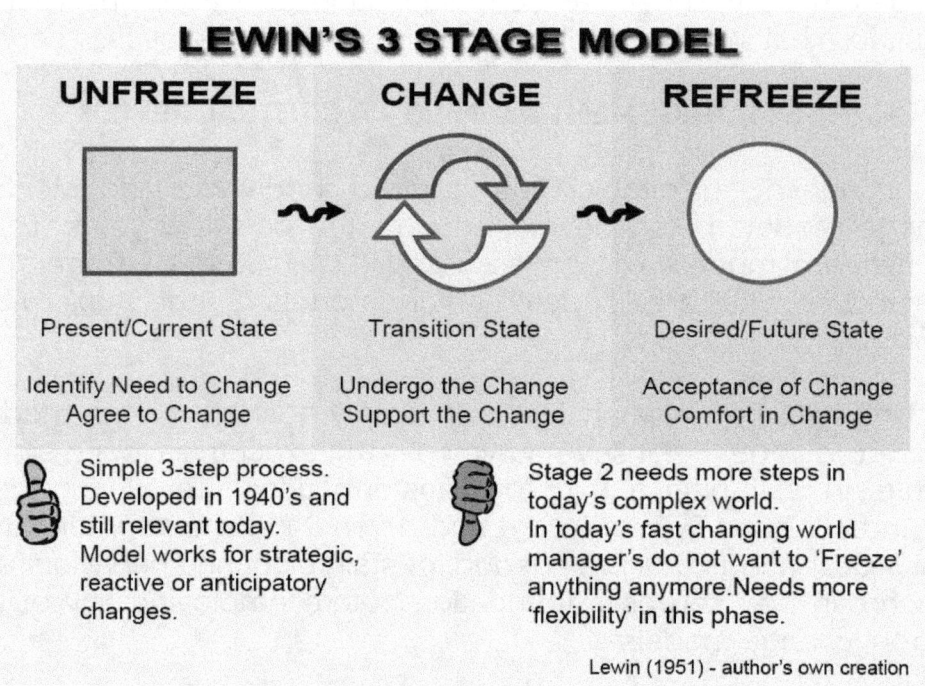

One of the foundation models of change management is Lewin's *(Lewin 1951, Burnes 2004 & Mayfield 2014)* simplistic three-stage Unfreeze-Change-Refreeze process. First there has to be a need and agreement (unfreeze) for the change. Secondly the old mindset has to be changed - also seen as the 'transition' phase. Finally reaching the refreeze stage where acceptance and comfort of the new is accepted. Although it takes time to implement, many organisations still prefer this model due to its ease of use.

In 1995 while advocating his 8 Step approach, *Kotter (1996)* stated that successful changes must go through a lengthy series of phases over a considerable time period. Leapfrogging over a phase only creates a false illusion of speed, while bungling, or a miscalculation in any phase can have calamitous results. In the interim, and after researching numerous organisations *Kotter (2002)* found that larger strides and successes are associated when sizeable leaps in change are implemented. This view is on par with *Holbeche (2006)* where she saw radical change as a necessity to survive, as a norm in today's changing world. Kotter also acknowledged that modifying individual's behaviour is a core challenge in each of his eight stages, while stating, *"People change what they do less because they are given analysis that shifts their thinking than because they are shown a truth that influences their feelings" (Kotter & Cohen 2002, p. 1).*

Although Kotter's model includes uncomplicated steps in a linear process in order to prepare and accept change, it may be more advantageous to view these steps as a continuous process rather than individual stages, insomuch lessening the disadvantages of skipping a step. This would also make the buy-in of staff easier to achieve.

Although conforming well into the culture of classical hierarchies, the model is distinctly top-down, thereby limiting employee participation and relying on the leadership to identify the needed changes in time (Step 1). Our rapidly changing world gives rise to challenges in selecting a competent leader group with identical shared goals, especially in large complex conglomerates where swift decisions hinder proper exhaustive research (Step 2). Developing a doable vision is strategically important. Step 3 fails when employees are not convinced of the feasibility of the new vision. It does not stop here. In step 4 a buy-in can only be achieved by thinking out of the box and using a vast array of methods for staff to understand and commit to the change. Another hindrance is that companies often do remove all the barriers to move forward. In step 5 the introduction of new incentives, systems and performing appraisals can significantly increase the success of the change vision.

For step 6 to succeed, staff sacrifices need to be rewarded quickly in order to keep the process moving along. These short-term wins also thwart criticism and cynics. The downside is that careful planning is required while time is often limited. Couple this with increased work pressure, and incentives had better be appealing! By consolidating successes, transformational leaders can launch further projects to drive the change deeper into the company for step 7. In the final 8th step, the new approaches and shared values are anchored into this new culture. An advantage of reaching this step is that employees have successfully shared and lived the entire process and these new norms and values are then easier to reinforce with new people joining the team *(Kotter 2002).*

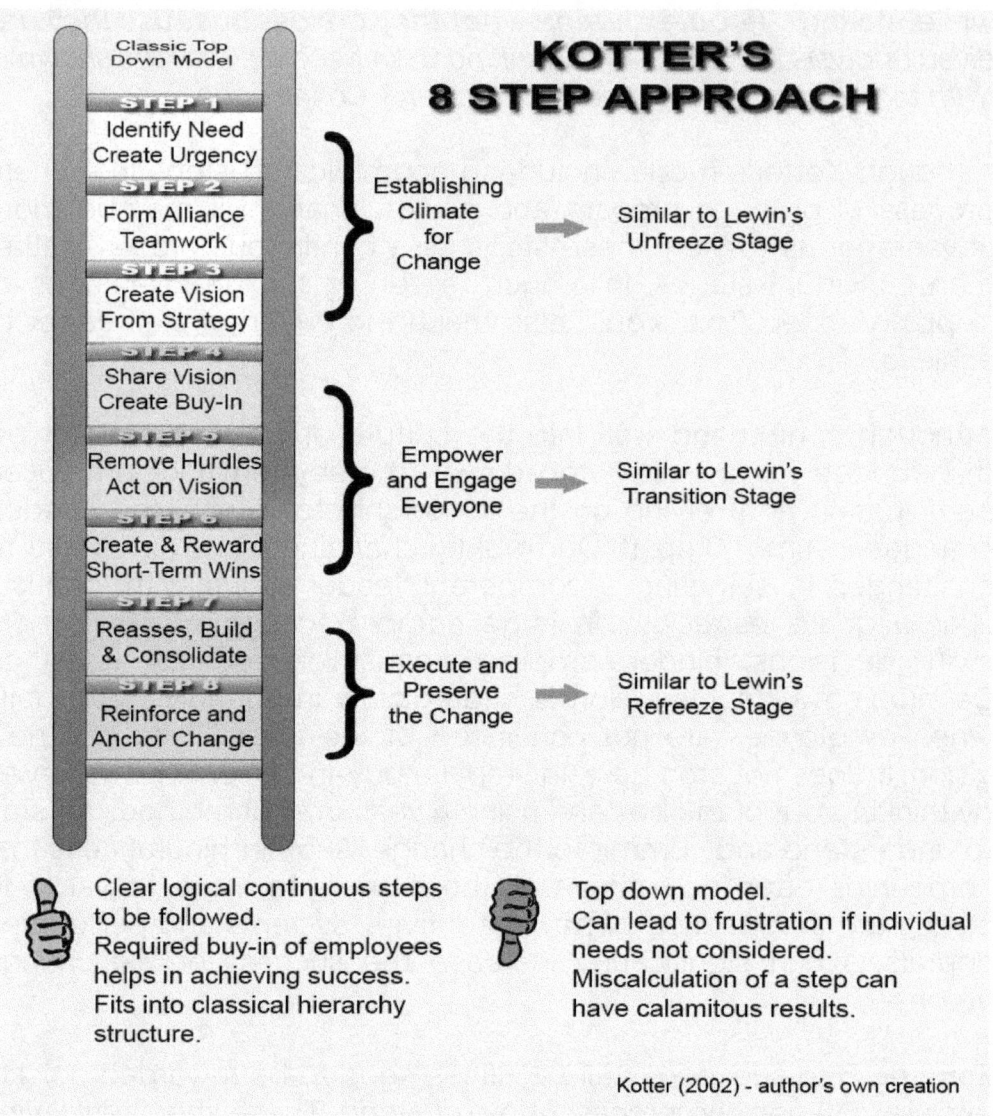

Kotter (2002) - author's own creation

In contrast, Bridge's transition model differs from Kotter in that he focuses on transition, rather than change. Hence this model is helpful in implementing change, but cannot be used as an autonomous substitute change management model. According to *Bridges (2009)* change occurs even when people are not In agreement with it. Therefore it can occur rapidly, while transition which is internal, can take longer. The benefit of his model is that it strives to clarify the psychological effect of the change in three stages; ending, neutral zone and new beginning. Note the similarity to Lewins' model.

BRIDGE'S TRANSITION MODEL

Bridge's sees change as situational and without people necesarrily tranistioning. This model clarifies the psychological effect of the change.

NEUTRAL ZONE

NEW BEGIN

ENDING

Letting go of the Past	State of disorientation	Acceptance and New
Acknowledge the Loss	Anxiety, Confusion &	Sense of Purpose
Accept the Emotions	Resentment are Normal	Signs of Success
Clearly Define What is Lost	Good space for creativity and Innovation	Energy Rising

Similar to Lewin's 3 phases, but focus on Transition, rather than Change.
Ending Phase similar to Kotter's Steps 1-3 (Establishing Climate for Change)
Neutral Zone similar to Kotter's Steps 4-6 (Engaging Everyone)
New beginning similar to Kotter's Steps 7-8 (Execute & Preserve Change)

 Learn to comprehend feelings of all involved.
Anaylses psychological effect of the change

 Not a substitute for other change models.
Cant' be used on it's own, but in conjunction with other models

Bridge (2009) - author's own creation

The challenge in the first ending stage is to overcome the resistance caused by the emotional upheaval of letting go of the past. Strong listening and communication skills, coupled with excellent training and resources are essential in order for them to accept this new sense of loss. The neutral zone can be seen as a bridge between the old and the new – similar to the change phase with Lewin. However in Bridge's model this neutral zone is often characterised by confusion, anxiety, impatience and skepticism. Leaders need to constantly provide feedback, boost morale, and promote short-term wins as in Stage 6 of RossKotter's model. The new beginning stage 3 is supplementary to Kotter's Stage 8 as both stages represent a renewed norms and values *(Bridges 2009 & Kotter 2002)*.

Bridge's model can be arranged alongside Elizabeth Kübler-Ross' Change Curve, as both highlight the feelings humans experience as they go through a change. Although the Kübler-Ross' 5-stage model *(Kübler-Ross 2003)* only represents exiguous possible emotions a human experiences during major life changing events, it nevertheless acts as a sound base for establishing communication strategy. The drawback is that it mostly assumes negative reactions to change (Denial, anger, depression, bargaining & acceptance) that are challenging to implement in a large group. Prof. George Bonanno from Columbia University claimed that without grief, there would be no stages to pass through. His research contradicts Kübler-Ross in that he found that the absence of grief can have a healthy outcome *(Bonanno 2009)*.

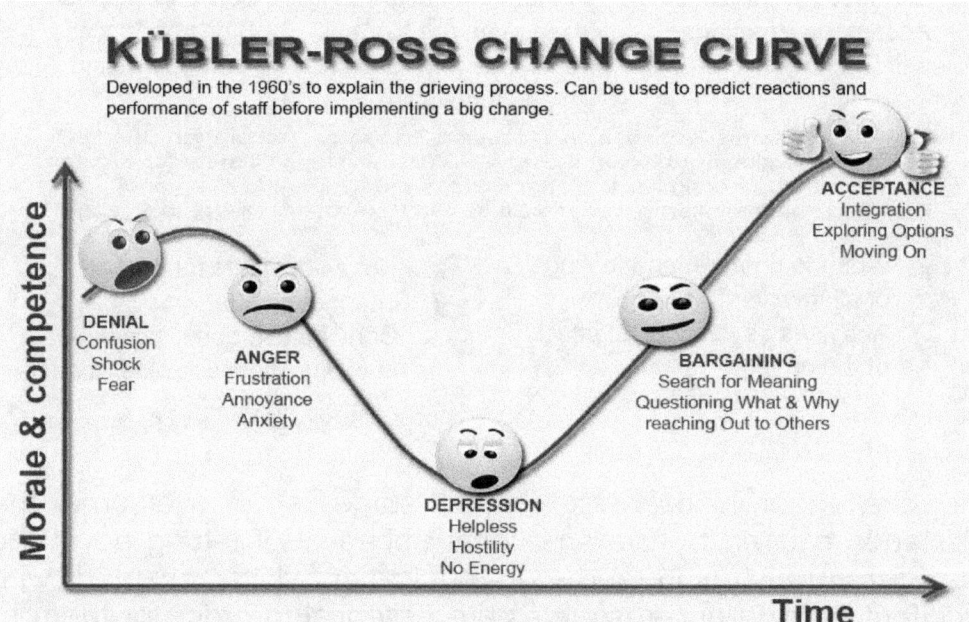

KÜBLER-ROSS CHANGE CURVE

Developed in the 1960's to explain the grieving process. Can be used to predict reactions and performance of staff before implementing a big change.

Morale & competence (vertical axis) / Time (horizontal axis)

DENIAL Confusion, Shock, Fear

ANGER Frustration, Annoyance, Anxiety

DEPRESSION Helpless, Hostility, No Energy

BARGAINING Search for Meaning, Questioning What & Why, reaching Out to Others

ACCEPTANCE Integration, Exploring Options, Moving On

Bridge's model can be arranged alongside Elizabeth Kubler-Ross' Change Curve as both highlight the feelings humans experience as they go through a change.

Highlights feelings experience by humans as they go through change.
Acts as a sound base for creating communication strategy.

Only represents limited range of emotions.
Only assumes negative reactions to change.
Challenging to implement in a large group.

Kübler-Ross (2003) - author's own creation

In addition, *Hiatt (2006)* discussed the ADKAR goal-orientated change management model developed in 1998 by Prosci who researched over 300 companies undergoing large-scale change. This model focuses on the way that information (communication and training) is shared and whether these have the desired effects during the organisational change. Therefore it should be seen as a supplementary model that aligns traditional change management activities to a specific goal by creating a checklist. As a leader this model assists in highlighting disparities/holes in the change process by determining staff resistance to change and by guiding them through the change. Personal and professional development during the change is managed through the creation of an action plan that is reinforced in the long term. The power of the ADKAR model is apparent in its ability to identify where the process is breaking down and which components are being neglected. *Jeff Hiatt's (2006)* research indicated that the most frequently voiced reason for change failures is the 'people dimension'. Hence the focus on managing five basic key goals in the ADKAR model;

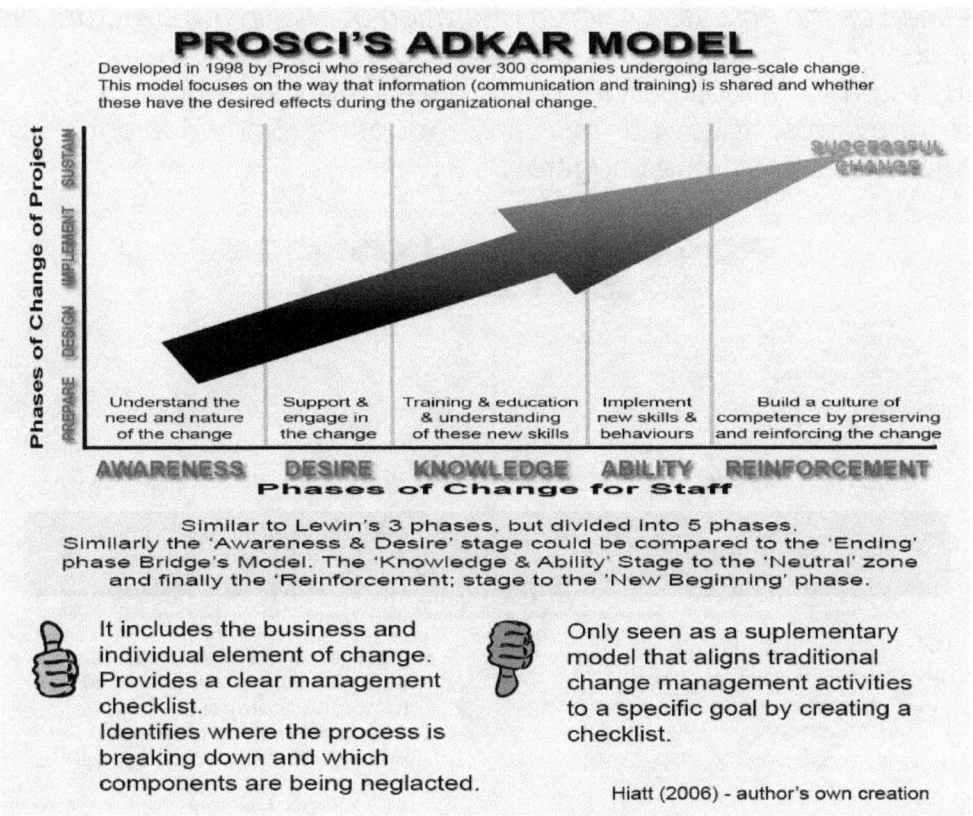

Awareness - understanding the need and nature of the change.
Desire - to support and engage in the change.
Knowledge - of how to change and what the change looks like.
Ability - to execute the change daily.
Reinforcement - to preserve the change

In their book Change Management: The People Side of Change, (*Hiatt & Creasey 2012*) views can be concisely summarised as; the outcome of changes in an organisation are essentially linked to staff members carrying out their professions individually. The link between a successful workable solution and final achievement of the final change, is dependent of how well the employees accept and endorse the change.

Roger's Technological Adoption Curve is a sociological model originally based on a diffusion process model developed by *Beal, Rogers and Bohlen (1957)*. In his book Diffusion of Innovations – 5th edition he explains how people embrace or acquire a new product or innovation through diffusion; *"Diffusion is a kind of social change, defined as the process by which alteration occurs in the structure and function of a social system"* *(Rogers 2003, p. 6)*. This process can be illustrated via a 'bell curve' and identifies the first people to change as Innovators, followed by Early Adopters, Early Majority, Late Majority and finally the Laggards.

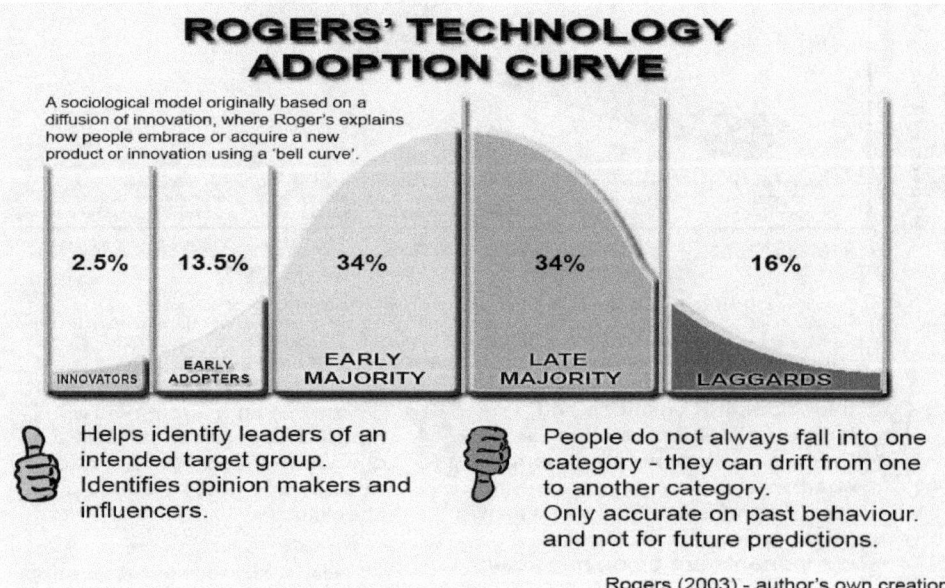

ROGERS' TECHNOLOGY ADOPTION CURVE

A sociological model originally based on a diffusion of innovation, where Roger's explains how people embrace or acquire a new product or innovation using a 'bell curve'.

2.5%	13.5%	34%	34%	16%
INNOVATORS	EARLY ADOPTERS	EARLY MAJORITY	LATE MAJORITY	LAGGARDS

Helps identify leaders of an intended target group. Identifies opinion makers and influencers.

People do not always fall into one category - they can drift from one to another category.
Only accurate on past behaviour. and not for future predictions.

Rogers (2003) - author's own creation

Although this model was initially applied in the agricultural sector, today it can be implemented in various industries. However, it does foster an understanding of, as well as identifies the leaders of the intended target group. Leaders, risk-takers and brave people - those falling into the first 'innovator' group tend to be glorified. On the downside, this group takes all the risks and can only learn from their mistakes – however when successful, this can lead to evangelising these individuals by the rest of the organisation. This in turn metamorphosis's into a mighty motivator for the next group (Early Adopters – respectable leaders, but more careful) to follow suit, while still learning from the mistakes of the innovators and thereby reducing rick in the change. From the Early Majority stage (thoughtful, yet accept change faster than others) technology and service standards have developed sufficiently to initiate mainstream adoption. The Late Majority stage (skeptics) enjoys reduced risk from past learning and a solid establishment of standard process. Finally the laggards (traditionalists) may be left with little, or no opportunity for reward and even less emotional excitement for the change. Therefore no justification remains to deny the change, and hence the change occurs faster within this category *(Rogers 2003)*.

2.4 RECOGNISING THE NEED FOR CHANGE

Tushman & Romanelli (1985) found that as an industry sector grows, change is not constant, but grows in a sigmodial (s-shaped) pattern as described below.

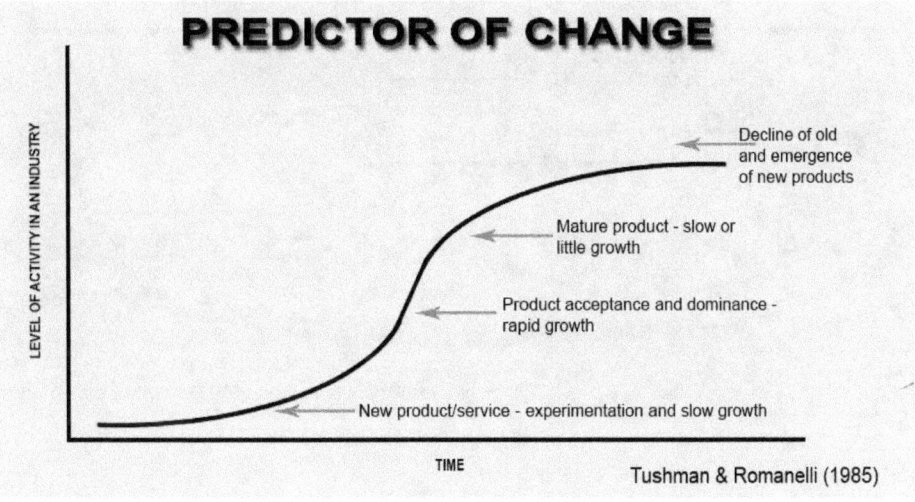

Tushman & Romanelli (1985)

In this widely known 'predictor of change' tool, one clearly sees that the initial phase is slow, before the rapid growth phase kicks in. *Hayes (2010)* attested that companies who identify and plan for this change in time, (ideally in the slow growth phase) can develop an effective strategic plan and respond to the change accordingly. However, those that fail to anticipate the need for change (in the rapid growth and/or decline of old products phase) need to react expeditiously and effectively in order to implement a long-term survival plan. Not all attain this outcome, and they fall into a Death Spiral *(Nadler, Shaw & Walton 1994).*

Reasons include complacency in success, coupled with an internal focus where the decline in performance is followed by a belief that the *"solution is to do more of what led to the success of the past"* *(Hayes 2010, p. 64). Nadler, Shaw & Walton (1994)* referred to this as an organisation becoming "Learning Disabled," as illustrated in their Trap of Success diagram below.

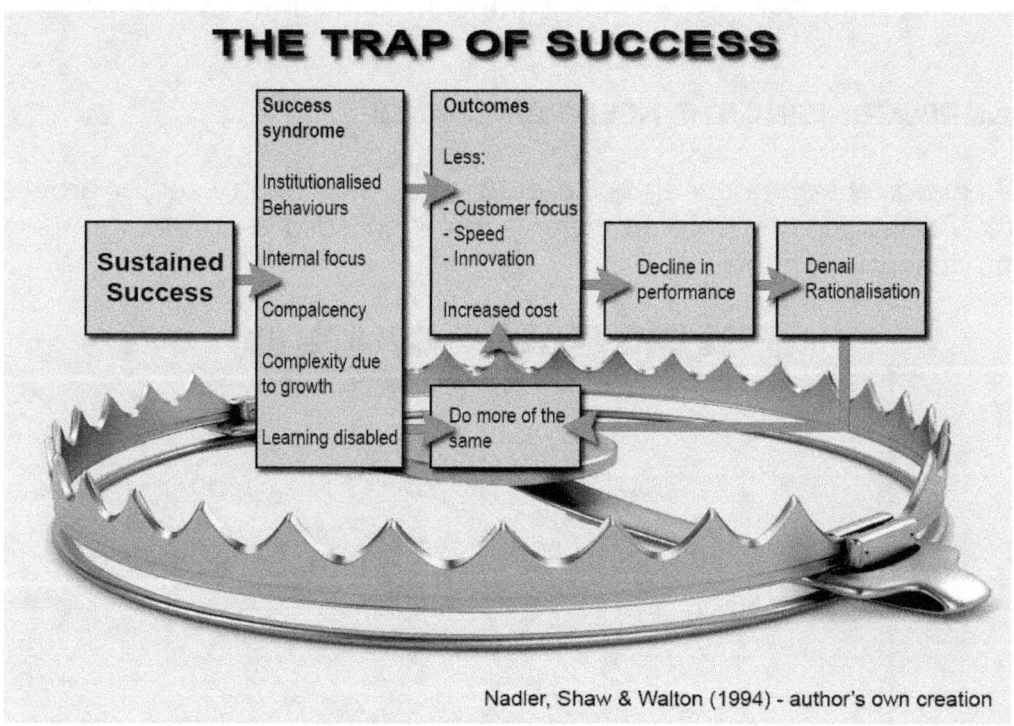

Nadler, Shaw & Walton (1994) - author's own creation

A pertinent additional point is that individuals who perceive this need for change may not always be in the 'chain of command' hierarchy to do anything about it *(Hayes 2010; Gravenhorst, Werkman & Boonstra 2003)*.

2.5 ANALYZING THE NEED FOR CHANGE

Senge (2006) identified the 5 Disciplines (Personal mastery, mental models, building shared vision, team learning and systems thinking) needed to determine shortcomings in attitudes. In an interview in 2008 he stressed that individuals will only accomplish things that are important to them and for which they care *(Senge & Crainer 2008)*. Hayes additionally referred to quality of 'change-agent' relationships, whereas *Mayfield (2014, p. 68)* effectually stressed the importance of 'stakeholder engagement' and argued that the misguided philosophy of *"people just distract and get in the way of working the right processes"* is the biggest mistake organisations make. Mayfield built on Kübler-Ross' 5-stage model when he highlighted that leaders have to break down the emotional obstacles to change. This is all in line with *Kotter & Cohen's (2002)* view that the core challenge is modifying individual's behaviour. *Estaban (2014)* concurred that helping and guiding employees, is the most challenging aspect of the change process. In a similar vein *Oreg & Berson (2011)* acknowledged that too much attention is given to the 'content' of the change, rather than the 'process'.

Furthermore, in their study of schools and the principal's influence of changing teacher behaviour, they highlight that an individual's value system affects the importance of that change, i.e. one person may believe in the acceptance of new ideas, whereas another may seek comfort in tradition and stability. Interestingly, on being questioned whether the economic downturn will further freeze enthusiasm to change, *Senge (2008)* responded that people are beginning to comprehend that this is only the start of inevitable larger economic changes to come and that everyone seriously needs to work together to create a sustainable world. Therefore, more and more it is imperative to foster conditions that will drive change *(Kanter, Stein & Jick 1992)*.

Their 'Big Three Model' covers many levels of analysis and cross-level research. The Macro-evolutionary level focuses on the relationship between a company and the environment, e.g. where the company changes from a family-run, to a publicly held company. Micro-evolutionary level of change refers to internal changes affecting the size and culture, e.g. downsizing. Revolutionary change which influences the 'power relationships and structures' that affect the regulation of resources *(Kanter, Stein & Jick 1992)*.

2.6 LEADERSHIP SKILLS DURING THE CHANGE PROCESS

Research indicates two distinctive schools of thought here. First the classic 'here and now' view, i.e. *Esteban (2014)* shared known tips on effective change leadership. However, one stood out; employees should not hear about the intended change in the hallway, it must be communicated direct from the leader. This is a focal element of engaging effectively with your team. *Schachter (2014)* placed the emphasis on the CEO, referring to him as the *"CCE – Chief Change Evangelist"*. He added that one needs to assess the team's current 'change elasticity' by comparing past challenges, and to share responsibility for the change.

John Kotter on the other hand appeared to have moved towards the second more futuristic school of thought, starting in 2001 *(cited in Bereel 2009)* where he stated that leaders do not produce plans, clear up obstacles, or coordinate people - they prepare companies for change and guide them through this process by aligning the behaviour and attitude of the staff. Ten years later *(Kotter 2011)* in a video interview, described a change leader as a skilled driver in a powerful car with a large powerful 1000 horsepower engine. *"It's about 'big visions and masses of people who want to make things happen."*

In 2013 he called for a *"new kind of leadership" (Kotter 2013, p. 6)* as rapid technological advancements, international free trade and global competition has now completely changed the business platform. Improving 5% on the previous year's performance is not adequate anymore. In addition *Cooper (2005)* included the implementation of new business processes, outsourcing and a shift from a product to a service culture. However, he predicted a rapid downsizing of companies resulting in smaller staff and short-term contracts aimed at completing specific projects.

In addition William Starbuck in *(Cooper 2005, p. 21)* cited four great conflicts of the 21st century;
- The Conflict between the Affluent and the Moderately Poor
- The Conflict between Companies and Nations
- The Conflict between Top Managers and other Stakeholders
- The Conflict between the Short-Run and the long run

Hamish McRae, also in *Cooper in (2005, p. 273)* saw this new generation as characterised by 'variety' with no favoured models, and no single processes to success. He focused on 'human capital' where leaders must attract able specialists and guide them in augmenting these skills.

2.7 CHALLENGES FOR LEADING INNOVATION & CHANGE

Hayes (2010) insightfully stated that in all levels within a company there are a range of complicated circumstances, and the synergy between these components influences the operational effectiveness of the organisation. In order to evaluate and assess efficiency diagnostic models are created that commonly focus on circumscribed crucial aspects that appear to offer a broad portrayal of the 'real world.' However these models are mostly developed from personal experience that often results in a subjective, or biased recommendations for change. Hence the need to identify whether individual models adhere to the demands and/or dilemmas, that need to be dealt with *(Hayes 2010)*.

Iles & Sutherland (2001) research on organisational change focused on the health care industry, particularly within the NHS, using the Total Quality Management (TQM) approach. Like *Hayes (2010)* they promote the classic models that act as diagnostic checklists *(Iles & Sutherland, 2001)*. Results indicate difficulty in methodical evaluation, with 'piecemeal' implementation focusing on inessential and administrative activities *(London School of Hygiene & Tropical Medicine 2001; Iles & Sutherland 2001)*.

Hammer & Champy (1993) believed in Business Process Reengineering (BPR) where only organisations willing to take the risk of complete radical change and 'rethink' their entire strategy using current 'know-how' can remain competitive. Their comprehensive & tantalising case studies on Taco Bell, Hallmark, Bell Atlantic and Capital Holding make a powerful argument in favour of BPR *(Hammer & Champy 2001; Sullivan 1993)*.

3. A CASE STUDIES

3.1 SUCCESSFUL INNOVATION/CHANGE

A real-life example that was experienced first-hand, has been used below, but the company and people involved have been kept anonymous.

CASE STUDY 1 SUCCESSFUL

The leadership team of Africa's largest financial company, decided to establish a new department, based on a network marketing system. They needed someone with experience in this field, and appointed Subject A to head the venture. *Leonard & Swap's (1999)* definition that innovation is an amalgamation of knowledge resulting in unique new services fits perfectly, as the leadership had identified a gap in the market by expanding on knowledge gained over 169 year history.

Razeghi's (2008) view that innovation is the outcome of studious contemplation on current issues and needs, is spot on. The insurance industry was in a down swing, and they needed a new mass market revenue stream. This fell exactly in line with *Senior & Flemming (2006)* who see change happening due to continual swings in demand & supply.

As a result of political and economic changes in South Africa, a lack of suitably qualified financial advisors, including the current downturn in insurance sales, the first goal of Awareness in Prosci's ADKAR model had been identified and understood. The executive leadership team had looked at Network Marketing/Multi Level Marketing as a possible solution and identified an entire new lower income, mass market, target group. On examining Kurt Lewin's Force Field Analysis *(Lewin 1951; Burnes & Cooke 2013)* the driving forces overshadowed the restraining forces, unbeknown to Subject A, the new department head.

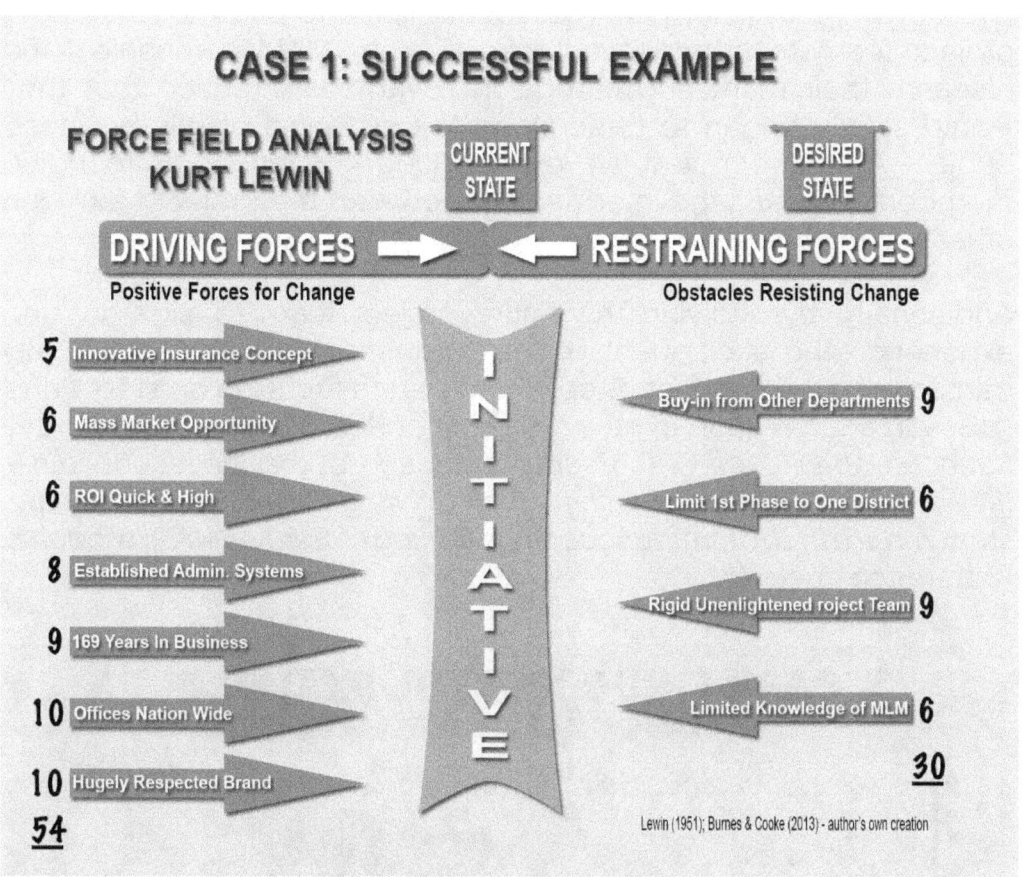

CASE 1: SUCCESSFUL EXAMPLE

FORCE FIELD ANALYSIS KURT LEWIN

CURRENT STATE

DESIRED STATE

DRIVING FORCES ➡️ ⬅️ **RESTRAINING FORCES**

Positive Forces for Change   Obstacles Resisting Change

INITIATIVE

5 Innovative Insurance Concept

6 Mass Market Opportunity

6 ROI Quick & High

8 Established Admin. Systems

9 169 Years In Business

10 Offices Nation Wide

10 Hugely Respected Brand

<u>54</u>

Buy-in from Other Departments 9

Limit 1st Phase to One District 6

Rigid Unenlightened roject Team 9

Limited Knowledge of MLM 6

<u>30</u>

Lewin (1951); Burnes & Cooke (2013) - author's own creation

The company had fallen into the Trap of Success with institutionalised behaviour. *(Nadler & Shaw 1994)* Lewin's three-stage model was viable, as a current 169-year ingrained mindset had to 'unfreeze'. There was a six-month goal to launch the product, hence the transition phase needed to run smoothly. The buy-in from older established departments was presented as challenge, as their ingrained financial mind-set saw this new department as competition, and wanting to poach their current portfolios. However, the biggest challenge was the direct project team. They viewed network marketing as a pyramid scheme and in contravention of the ethical brand of the company. In fact, prime candidates to *validate* the Kübler-Ross model, as all their reactions were negative! Hence a strong focus on Kotter's Step 2 to win over the staff and goal 2 of the ADKAR model of creating the support. Subject A literally had to *"...peel away three broad layers of resistance..."* Umble & Umble (2014, p. 18).

By applying a transformational leadership style and motivating the project team to attend events from other MLM companies and research their marketing campaigns, with the intention that they would slowly began to understand the potential of this business. Subject A also recruited five experienced networkers as founding members to act as the intermediary between the project team and other stakeholders.

Additionally, by allowing the entire project team to 'sign-up' and experience the excitement of the business, Subject A eventually transformed the mindset (Step 3) and began focusing on step 4 and 5 (Buy in and creation of new systems) of Kotter's eight step model. *Kotter & Cohen (2002, p. 1) "People change what they do less because they are given analysis that shifts their thinking than because they are shown a truth that influences their feelings."* See ADKAR model & Kotter Steps below:

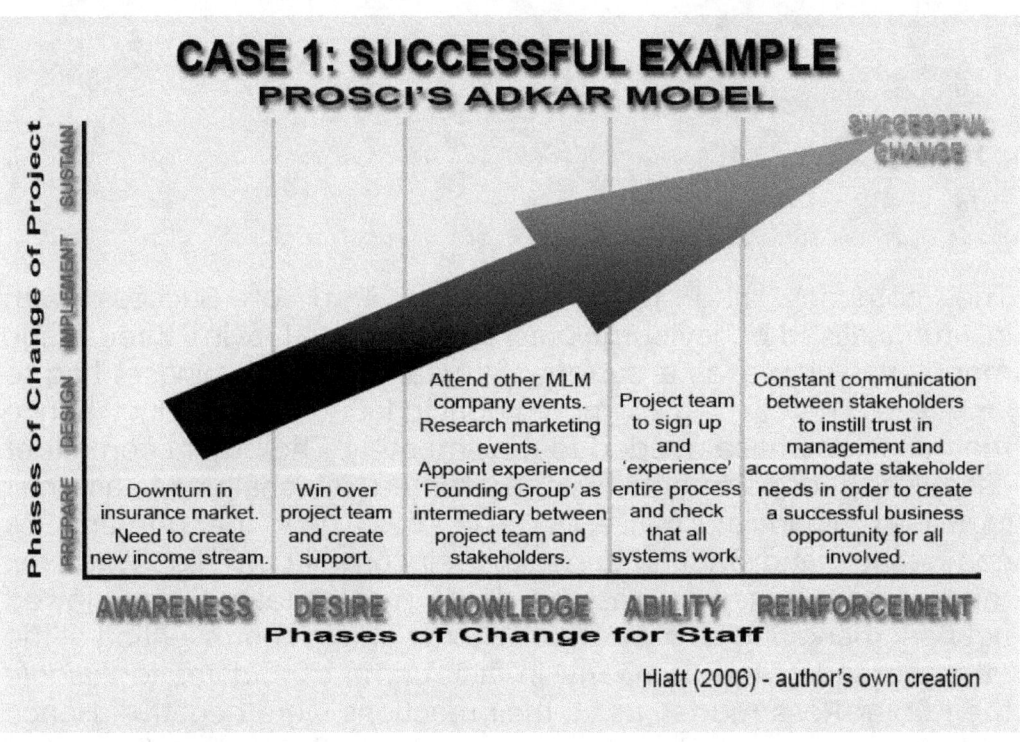

The company had years of research to back-up conversion of sales figures within the broker and agency space. Within the first three months the closing rate on policies surpassed all predicted forecasts and came in five times higher than any previous figures – Kotter Step 6 planning short-term wins. This resulted in converting the laggards *(Rogers 2003)* and this the new 'flavour of the month' department of this financial powerhouse – Kotter's final steps 7 & 8.

CASE 1: SUCCESSFUL EXAMPLE

KOTTER'S 8 STEP APPROACH

STEP 1
Identify Need
Create Urgency

Slow down in insurance market and identification of network marketing (Multi Level Marketing MLM) opportunity. Urgency created by being the first mainstream player to enter this market.

STEP 2
Form Alliance
Teamwork

Foster 'buy-in' from other departments in firm, as well as project team by appling a transformational/Democratis leadership style and involving all stakeholders in the process

STEP 3
Create Vision
From Strategy

Workshops with project team and creating of Founding Members with experience in MLM to share, assist and strategise future vision with project team.

STEP 4
Share Vision
Create Buy-In

Invite project team to MLM company events so that they fully understand the excitement and potential of being innovative within a 'rigid' financial sector. Have Founding Members educate and clarify all issues.

STEP 5
Remove Hurdles
Act on Vision

Sign up entire project team so that they personally experience how the opportunity works, earn referral commissions and check that all systems work.

STEP 6
Create & Reward
Short-Term Wins

Sales figures 5 times higher than projected and ahead of any other departments in terms of return on investment. Also offering added incentives and prizes to top performers.

STEP 7
Reasses, Build
& Consolidate

Constant dialogue between project team, founding members and network members (stakeholders) to address all issues and improve service levels.

STEP 8
Reinforce and
Anchor Change

Weekly startegy sessions with project team and founding members. Monthly training sessions with network. Bi-monthly rallys, Regular weekly presentations at head office. Creation of website for personal monitoring of busines. Creation of clubs, quarterly incentives and annual holidays.

Kotter (2002) - author's own creation

3.2 UNSUCCESSFUL INNOVATION/CHANGE

CASE STUDY 2 UNSUCCCESFUL

Using the previous example from a different perspective, consider a new department head, Subject B. He erroneously underestimated the individual readiness *(Vakola 2014)* for the project team and other departments to support the change. Therefore his Force Field Model *(Lewin 1951; Burnes & Cooke 2013)* should have included more restraining forces with a much higher rating.

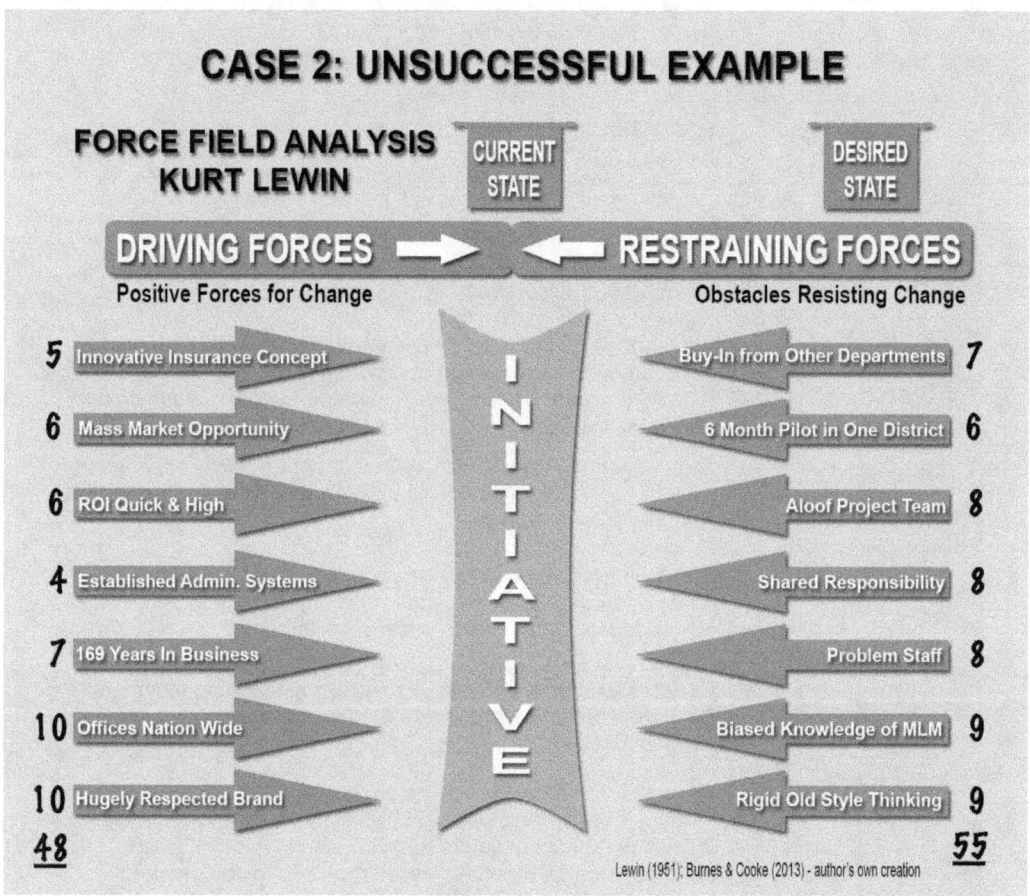

Holbeche's (2006) view that leaders must influence others to change old established practices did not occur, as his direct superiors had too many other departments and responsibilities to deal with. It did not help that they viewed this as a pilot project either; knowing that there were no penalties associated with a missed opportunity *(Goffin*

2007). As head of the department Subject B was a change leader, but without a buy-in from the senior executives, resulting in lack of backing from supporting departments, the project was doomed. In other words, stakeholder engagement from senior management never occurred, which was critical for the success of the project *(Mayfield 2014).*

Kotter (2002) acknowledged that modifying individual's behaviour is a core challenge in each of his eight stages. These steps must be seen as a continuous process rather than individual stages, thereby lessening the disadvantages of skipping a step and failing the change.

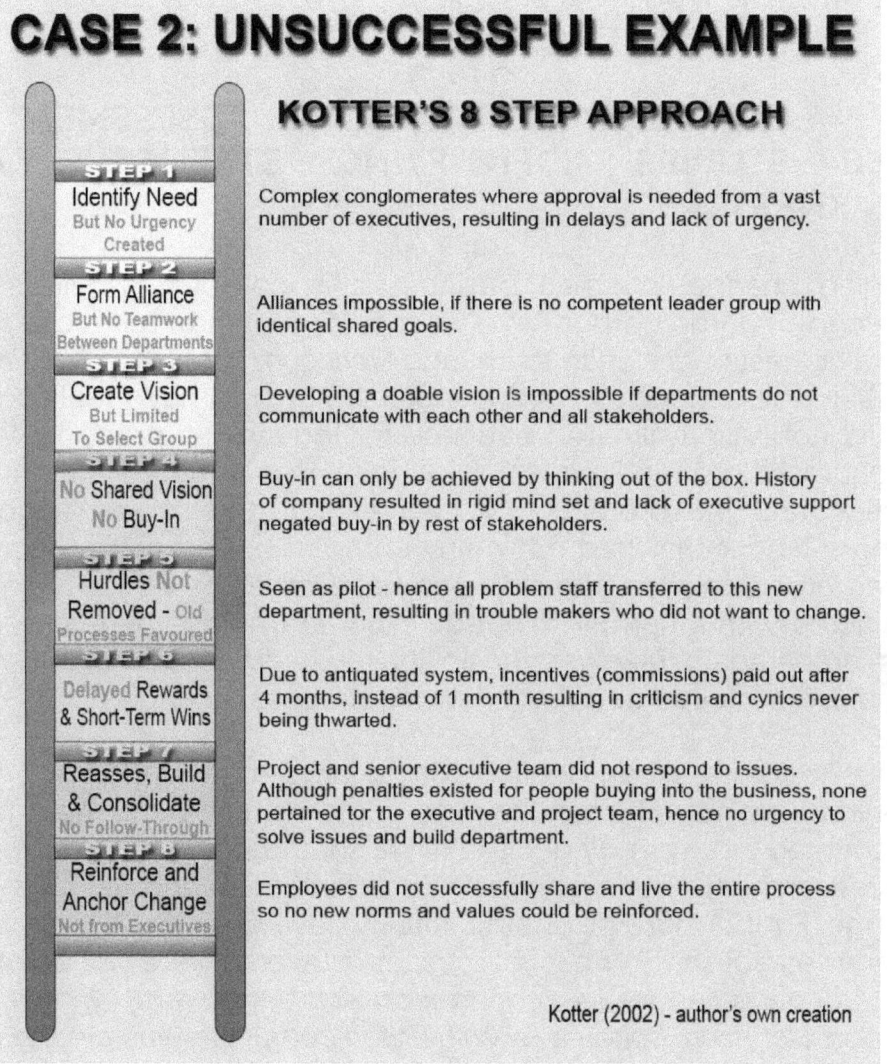

CASE 2: UNSUCCESSFUL EXAMPLE

KOTTER'S 8 STEP APPROACH

STEP 1
Identify Need
But No Urgency
Created

Complex conglomerates where approval is needed from a vast number of executives, resulting in delays and lack of urgency.

STEP 2
Form Alliance
But No Teamwork
Between Departments

Alliances impossible, if there is no competent leader group with identical shared goals.

STEP 3
Create Vision
But Limited
To Select Group

Developing a doable vision is impossible if departments do not communicate with each other and all stakeholders.

STEP 4
No Shared Vision
No Buy-In

Buy-in can only be achieved by thinking out of the box. History of company resulted in rigid mind set and lack of executive support negated buy-in by rest of stakeholders.

STEP 5
Hurdles Not
Removed - Old
Processes Favoured

Seen as pilot - hence all problem staff transferred to this new department, resulting in trouble makers who did not want to change.

STEP 6
Delayed Rewards
& Short-Term Wins

Due to antiquated system, incentives (commissions) paid out after 4 months, instead of 1 month resulting in criticism and cynics never being thwarted.

STEP 7
Reasses, Build
& Consolidate
No Follow-Through

Project and senior executive team did not respond to issues. Although penalties existed for people buying into the business, none pertained tor the executive and project team, hence no urgency to solve issues and build department.

STEP 8
Reinforce and
Anchor Change
Not from Executives

Employees did not successfully share and live the entire process so no new norms and values could be reinforced.

Kotter (2002) - author's own creation

In summary, a major re-evaluation of the department's core focus *(Flamholz & Randle 1998)* never occurred. Vision was not shared from the top down with all stakeholders. The founding group and acting head was left to re-assess constantly, plus communicate with stakeholders outside the company. The senior executive team did not respond to issues. Although penalties existed for people buying into the business, none existed for the executives of the said company, hence they showed no urgency to solve these *(Goffin 2009?)*. Swings in demand & supply should have pushed change *(Senior & Flemming 2006)* but the established 'old ways' where still making huge profits, leaving the executive team un-phased. Therefore a great example and confirmation of *Holbeche's (2006)* views that the biggest challenge is the willingness of staff to take part in the innovative change.

4.   LEADERSHIP PERFORMANCE ASSESSMENT OF CASE STUDIES, IDENTIFYING STRENGTHS AND WEAKNESSES

Leading change in small businesses is completely different to dealing with large corporations as their formal structures can result in the highest impedance to change *(Johnson, Scholes & Whittington 2005)*. In the second example, subject B should have realised that he did not have unlimited patience for loquacious procedures and bureaucratic red tape, especially when it was coupled with internal politics, and the protection of self established power kingdoms. Being a leader that had run many companies and made decisions based on experience and research believed to be ethically correct, conflicted with a narrow-minded corporate mindset where nobody was prepared to take responsibility for their decisions with thirty signatures required to adopt an order/process/change.

Hence in future, when dealing with a large organisation Subject B should allow himself more time to implement the change and not be coerced into speedy decisions. He should place more emphasis on researching the organisation's willingness and readiness to change. Furthermore he should initially have queried, identified and clearly established what his exact powers were in terms of implementing innovative change on his terms, and with whose support *(Johnson, Scholes & Whittington 2005)*. He was clearly not a transactional   leader,   and   favoured   a democratic/collaborative/paternal style leadership which did not fit the current mindset of the company. His hard lesson was to learn and accept the disparity in political, religious, equality and racial issues (especially in the South African context) and that as a leader you will never please everyone. Thus ultimately realising that a leader may need to include a degree of autocratic leadership to keep people in check and the ultimate interests of the organisation at heart. That said, he should have learnt that it is imperative to have the right quality managers **(Kotter 2001)** in his team and in future should place much more focus on screening such posts. Sadly it was only learnt later on that certain problem employees had been passed onto him as well, which didn't help foster the right work environment either.

Newton N. Minow, former Federal Communications Commission Chairman from 1961 - 1963 *(Graham et al 2012)* summarised these issues concisely, "*We've gotten to the point where everybody's got a right and nobody's got a responsibility.*" Therefore leadership needs to focus on prioritising buy-in and personal responsibility from all stakeholders if they ever want to institute successful innovative change.

5. CONCLUSION

The theories on innovation and change are plentiful. All have merit. Applying only one model is limiting as today a plethora of factors influence change, which in turn influence the employee perception of that change (positive or negative). Hence the focus needs to be on managing change effectively in order to negate fears associated with it and promote excitement for change within the people concerned, *(Dawson, 2013)* and by addressing the worker's concerns as *Kuriger (2006, p. 38)* states, "*… make sure the lines of communication run both ways.*"

"The past has taught me to proactively plan for the future while striving to make the most of now."

(Wolfgang Riebe)

CHAPTER 3
STRATEGIC THINKING &
STRATEGIC LEADERSHIP

INTRODUCTION

"However beautiful the strategy, you should occasionally look at the results."

(Winston Churchill, 1874 - 1965)

The main focus of this chapter will be to discuss a literature review of key theories of how strategy is developed and implemented, including the relationship between strategy, innovation and change. This research will then be applied to a critical analysis of selected strategic processes within an organisation, related to the relevant theories, followed by an assessment of the extent to which people within the organisation are engaged with, and contribute to a selected strategy.

Finally recommendations about how strategic processes within the organisation could be improved will be suggested.

1.   A LITERATURE REVIEW OF KEY THEORIES, PLUS THE RELATIONSHIP BETWEEN STRATEGY, INNOVATION & CHANGE

1.1 INTRODUCTION

Historically, strategic thinking can be traced back to the military, the lessons of *Sun-Tzu (500 BC)* to *Napoleon* to current day leaders such as *Colin Powell*. Today strategy is part of everyday corporate thinking; how do I attain a stronger foothold in cross border markets? With whom do I need to partner in order to grow market share by 12%?

However, strategy is not always identified as deliberate, planned and formal (explicit), but can also be practiced without realising that one is strategising intuitively and informally (implicit) *(Markides 2012)*. There are two schools of thought; the first based on Porter's views and positioning the organisation advantageously within a sector, while the other focuses on the new by highlighting the importance of outsmarting and conquering the competition *(Markides 2012)*.

Not only are various types of mental skills, techniques, habits and attitudes required for strategic thinking, but these all need to be integrated within the context of identifying the problem from a plethora of unconnected data and then solving it *(Loehle 1996)*. Therefore, clear strategic thinking and formulation, coupled with insightful strategic leadership is paramount in order to achieve specific successes that are in alignment with the organisations vision and mission statements.

2. STRATEGIC LEADERSHIP AND STRATEGIC THINKING

2.1   STRATEGY DEFINED

A fair definition of strategy can include, *Markides (2012, p. 82)* where he stated, *"Strategy should be a mixture of rational thinking and creativity, of analysis and experimentation, of planning and learning."* Although relevant, this is too broad a definition in the context of today's business world. *Ansoff (1988)* in his book Strategic Planning, postulated that strategy developed as a broad future objective did not suffice for organisations that sought systematic profitable growth - hence additional well-defined guidelines were needed to achieve this.

Even in 1954 when Peter Drucker wrote his book, The Practice of Management, he understood that companies could not afford to be complacent with future plans when nobody knew what the future holds. A workable plan (strategy) is needed to be prepared for all possible probabilities *(Drucker 2006)*.

Since *Ansoff (1988)* first published his book in 1970, times have drastically changed! This 3rd industrial revolution, or 'knowledge revolution' of the 21st century dot.com economy has prompted a new way of thinking in terms of corporate obligation, environmental responsibilities, management execution and leadership strategies. *Mintzberg (2003, p. 142)* summed it up concisely by saying, *"Strategies are both plans for the future and patterns from the past."*

Today countless companies are experiencing new unparalleled growth, while a myriad are being obliterated at an even faster rate. *Grant (2008)* sees this new era with its impact of digital technology, and move from hardware to software, as a completely new challenge in strategic leadership and thinking.

2.2 STRATEGIC LEADERSHIP

Strategic leadership is so much more than simply influencing everyone within an organisation to see the light and work together to achieve envisaged strategic goals *(Johnson 2011)*. It includes; pinpointing environmental impacts, fully comprehending the strategic capacity as well as the needs, plus the influence of all stakeholders *(Johnson, Scholes & Whittington 2008)*. Various authors *(Cable 2008; Hughes & Beatty 2005; Johnson, Scholes & Whittington 2008; Liedka 1998)* concluded that strategic leadership is not only reserved to one person at the top of a company, but also evident in all levels of an organisation, from individuals to teams, and where these strategic leaders encourage strategic leadership in others. They never saw it as a one-person singular event, but rather an emergent process encompassing various strategic management layers from all over the company, including outside consultants.

Additionally, *Jacques (1978)* believed 'considerable ambiguities and complexities' exist in large organisations that need to be prioritised. From executive team requirements to limited resources (internal constraints) and market factors (external constraints) many limiting factors, complicate the strategic change. An interesting view is *Hitt, Keats & DeMarie (1998)* who focused on Adaptive Capacity, postulating that new leaders manage change easier than an old employee who has been promoted. *Hooiberg, Hunt & Dodge (1997)* built on this when they stated that the application of interpersonal skills and endless patience, coupled with understanding the social setting was the real issue.

Today's workforce is understandably completely different to the past *(Cable 2012)*. People are more enlightened, informed and aware. They have been through all the change initiatives. *Cable (2012, p. 46)* felt that *"Leaders must provide their employees with hope, purpose and encouragement to try new things. They must prepare them to adhere to a new method or a new strategy even if, at first, it seems like the new direction will be a failure."* Interestingly, *Adair (2003)* offered an action-centered leadership theory where he described the functions of strategic leadership as three interlocking circles; developing individuals, building and maintaining teams and achieving the joint aims of the company.

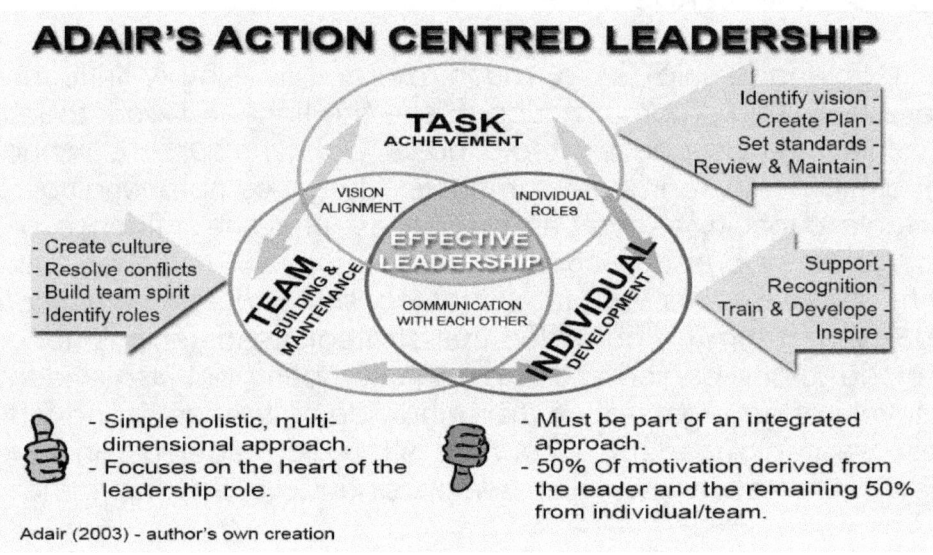

In his 5 P's strategy model (Discussed later) *Mintzberg (1987)* viewed strategic leadership as a ploy to 'get the better' of competitors. *Raynor (2007)* added that it was the ability of a company to conceive and commandeer superior standards within a distinct market segment, plus focus on increasing competition within internal operating units, that improve overall organisational competitiveness.

A good summation was made by *Thompson & Martin (2005)* who stated that various strategies (thinking & planning) continually need to be adapted to a changing environment. Using various resources and expertise at their disposal, leaders bring out the best in employees. Without threats or bullying, measurable goals are willingly achieved through inspiration and guidance. Personal accountability promotes the achievement of the long-term vision that gives the organisation a competitive advantage that makes it stronger, which in turn increases bottom line profits as required by the stakeholders.

2.3 STRATEGIC THINKING

De Wit & Meyer (2005) questioned what occurred in the mind of the strategist and how he thinks. Their theory states that strategists deal with challenging strategic issues that are problematic, i.e. circumstances that need to be resolved, or new problems that have arisen. The resultant action can either be to profit from an opportunity, or react to a perceived threat.

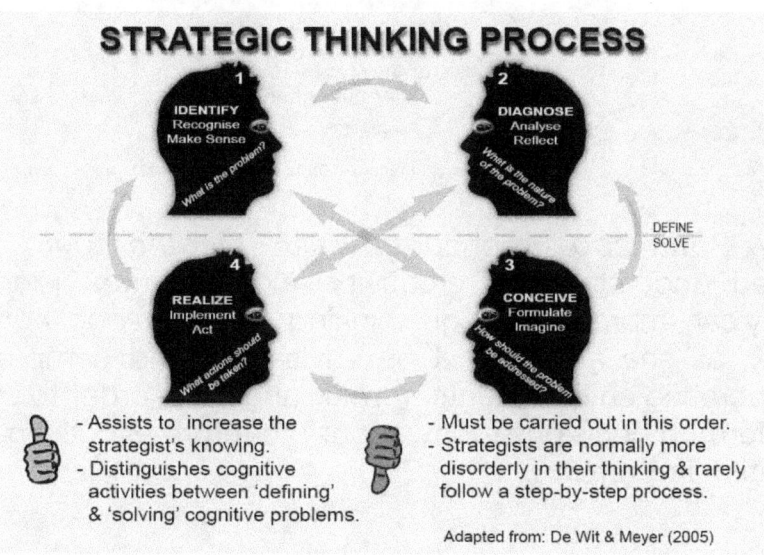

STRATEGIC THINKING PROCESS

Adapted from: De Wit & Meyer (2005)

Simply thinking is not enough, managers need to go through a strategic reasoning process in order to define and ultimately conquer the challenge. Problems can arise when there is no creative activity associated with strategic thinking, or the resultant administrative activity is lacking by the strategic leader. They see this reasoning process as composed of 4 strategic thinking elements.

This falls in line with *Liedtka (1998)* who identified 5 specific elements in her model below, as she believed that strategic thinking could be indicative of a particular 'way' of thinking.

LIEDTKA
THE ELEMENTS OF STRATEGIC THINKING

SYSTEMS PERSEPCTIVE
A complete picture from beginning to end. From external eco-system to all internal inter-relationships

INTENT FOCUSED
Creates sense of direction, discovery & destiny. Repel distraction & productively fixate on achieving the end goal.

STRATEGIC THINKING

INTELLIGENT OPPORTUNISM
Openess to new experiences & all levels of employees in order to learn, adapt & adopt new strategies.

THINKING IN TIME
Correlate the past with the present & link with the future. Learn, from history, create now and plan to realize dream.

HYPOTHESIS DRIVEN
Creative & critical in that new ideas are developed & analytical by testing them in action.

Liedtka (1998); Lawrence (1999) - author's own creation

Similarly *Bonn (2001)* concurred with *Liedtka (1998)* that an integrated understanding, creativity and a future vision of the company can improve strategic thinking. *Conway (2009)* agreed with this view, as she also saw it as envisaging and comprehending future operating environments from all angles, in order to ultimately make informed decisions today about the future effectiveness of an organisation tomorrow.

An abundance of contrasting views exist between strategic thinking and strategic leadership. *Heracleous (1998)* argued that even though they may be distinct, these two approaches are very much complimentary and interconnected. *Mintzberg (1994)* added that strategic planning usually fails due to rigid, analytical and formal procedures that predict a predetermined goal outcome. Whereas strategic thinking corresponds more with a 'thinking out of the box' (innovative) ideology, that involves an amalgamation of intuition and creativity. It is an integrated viewpoint not always precisely expressed, which allows it to surface at unplanned times and places within an organisation.

De Bono (1990) saw lateral thinking as an objective creative process that has a predetermined end goal in mind, while creative thinking is more chaotic and directed at securing new ideas only, no matter how subjective. Interestingly, *Rawlingon (2007)* the CEO of the De Bono Foundation highlighted that logical thinking was left to the clergy back in the Renaissance period as they were always in the search of truth to disprove heretics. Hence creative thinking was left to individuals and as a result the evolution of abstract 'innovative & creative' thinking has been slow. One can only shift perceptions by moving out of a 'comfort zone' of thinking.

2.4 THE PRACTICE OF STRATEGY

Johnson, Scholes & Whittington (2011) promoted a 'Pyramid of Practice' where three questions need to be asked when formulating a strategic plan;

a.   Who are the strategy makers?

Here the executive team's focus needs to be on long-term goals and looking after the interests of the company as a whole, hence strategy planning is ideally left to specifically qualified and formally appointed strategy planners and/or external strategy consultants, i.e. Boston Consulting Group, whose sole focus is the planning of the specific strategy. The problem in this phase is that many companies mismanage the 'productive inclusion' of the correct people in the strategic team with direct access to senior decision makers within an organisation *(Johnson, Scholes & Whittington 2011)*.

Collins (2001) built on this theory, saying that good-to-great leaders understand three basic rules;

1. It's easier to change the world if you start with 'who' rather than 'what.'
2. You need the 'right people on the bus.' Only then will it becomes easier to manage and motivate everyone.
3. Even if you do move in the right direction, you will never have a great company if your people are wrong.

His simple views make sense, especially his emphasis on creating a top team first, and only then determining what to do. *Hamel (1998, p. 10)* expanded on this by stating, *"We all recognize a great strategy after the fact."* Hence he also advocated bringing in *'new voices'* (new people) resulting in this new and different knowledge being brought together in different ways to create a 'Cambrian explosion.'

b.   What are they going to do?

Johnson, Scholes & Whittington (2011) were justly concerned that strategic decisions may not always be objectively analytical and impartial. Therefore they focussed on various factors with regard to strategic analysis; decision-making, issue-selling and communication. With his view of 'confronting the brutal facts' *Collins (2001)* refined *Johnson, Scholes & Whittington's (2011, p. 510)* *"Paralysis by Analysis"* statement by popularising his Hedgehog Concept in order to deflate all problems and challenges into simple ideas. Abbot laboratories, Nucor and Kimberly-Clark are amongst the companies that have successfully understood and applied Collins' 'good-to-great' ideology.

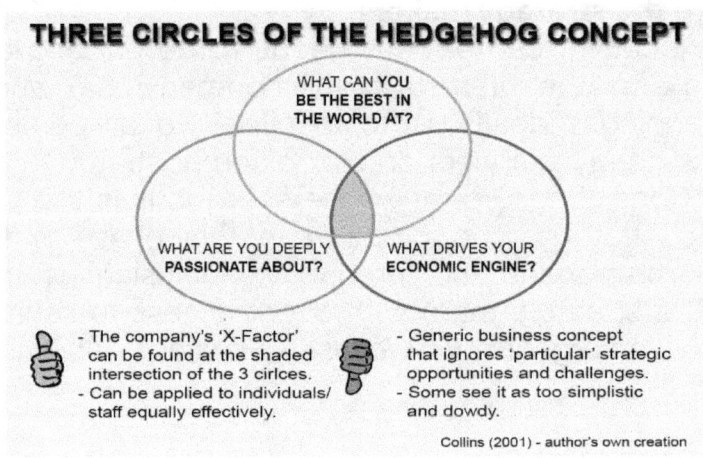

THREE CIRCLES OF THE HEDGEHOG CONCEPT

WHAT CAN **YOU** BE THE BEST IN THE WORLD AT?

WHAT ARE YOU DEEPLY PASSIONATE ABOUT?

WHAT DRIVES YOUR ECONOMIC ENGINE?

- The company's 'X-Factor' can be found at the shaded intersection of the 3 cirlces.
- Can be applied to individuals/ staff equally effectively.

- Generic business concept that ignores 'particular' strategic opportunities and challenges.
- Some see it as too simplistic and dowdy.

Collins (2001) - author's own creation

Idhammer (2014) concurred with *Collins (2001)*, stating that it is imperative to adhere to one holistic system and avoid constantly experimenting with new tricks like the fox. *Grey & Stechly (2010)* in their book 'Leading Good Schools to Greatness' advocated that highly successful 'superstar' school principals follow the hedgehog concept.

In fairness, Eric Isaacs' address to the Alumni at the University of Chicago on 25 January 2013 made a good point when he reflected on a quotation from the poet, Berlin from his 1953 seminal essay that hedgehogs *(Isaacs 2013)*, *"relate everything into a single central vision... a single universal organizing principal."* However, on the other hand, foxes with their interest in various disciplines see themselves as, "... *creative, nimble and dynamic... who see the bigger picture."*

Although Isaacs made a solid point with his description of the fox, I feel that from a purely business perspective, where profit is the end goal, laser focus is imperative and hence favour Collins' approach.

Similarly, *Rosenzweig (2007)* saw the hedgehog strategy as 'high risk' if leaders pick the wrong priorities. However, if strategists adhere to *Collins' (2001)* brutal facts and strict compliance to passion, disciple and embracing technology accelerators – then I believe the odds are in favour of the Hedgehog Concept. *Collins (2001)* summarised the 'What' phase succinctly with his 'Flywheel' example. Initially it takes time and effort to start this massive wheel rotating, eventually becoming easier until it's an unstoppable force (similar to a snowball rolling down a hill, collecting more snow and building speed as it rolls). The 'Doom Loop' (stopping and starting the Flywheel and constantly attempting to push it in different directions) inevitably always leads to failure.

c.   Which methodologies will they use? (Managing the strategy process)

Johnson, Scholes & Whittington (2011) questioned why strategy workshops, projects, hypothesis testing and business cases fail. Each have their merits, but are reliant on a multitude of factors such as commitment from ALL involved, clear mandate, and concise data and resources.

Mintzberg (1998, p. 4) mentioned psychologist *George Miller (1956)* who postulated that as humans we comfortably only retain information in chunks of seven. In the professional speaking and training industry, this is a 'universal given' rule - never more than 7 bits of take home information *(Riebe 2013)*. Could facilitators at these strategy events be sharing too much information? Or as *Mintzberg (1998)* stated, there is a bias in modern management literature towards 'current trends' and the flavour of the day that can result in a trivialised new approach, rather than a tried and tested established strategy.

In alignment with *Johnson, Scholes & Whittington's (2011)* views, *Mintzberg (1998)* emphasised the importance of not only leadership, but of staff also understanding the mission and vision statement regarding current and future strategies. My hypothesis is that these statements are created by company founders using complex terminology that is 'foreign' to the blue-collar worker – hence their lack of insight into the greater picture that leadership has in mind. In contrast, an efficacious example was a printing company in South Africa where the entire staff was asked to define their interpretation of said company's mission and vision, and write it in their own words. All contributions were condensed into a simple purpose with the handprint of every member framed around the company vision. A working example of *Mintzberg's (1998)* strategy as a pattern where consistency in behaviour and thinking remains constant over time due to astute strategy planning by the leadership team.

Hansen & Birkenshaw (2007) built on this by using an innovation value chain, where instead of focusing only on one issue, leaders should look at a complete end-to-end process in order to identify both the weakest and strongest links.

A concluding consideration is that political, social, legal, technical, environmental and economic changes may require strategic responses too. This includes changes to suppliers, customers and competitors. Whether these future changes are slow and progressive, or breakthrough events, this is a further attestation that strategy is jointly linked to innovation and change *(Hamel 1998; Senior & Flemming 2006; Johnson, Scholes & Whittington 2011)*.

2.5 STRATEGIC OPTIONS & SELECTION OF STRATEGIES

Mintzberg's (1987) 5 P's of strategy allows organisations to consider 'everything relevant' in order to develop a successful strategy. Leaders need to flush out all disparity and focus on organisational strengths to prevent flawed plans from being implemented. Strategy as a *plan* is not enough. Combine a plan with a *ploy*, and the organisation can apply for sole distribution rights within an area, or country so as to get the upper hand over competitors. At times, past company behaviour defined strategy, i.e. instead of a deliberate innovative change, an old consistent way of doing business could develop into a strategy. Company X currently has an efficient 'rewards' system in place as a strategy to keep on 'top of mind' with past customers. The current head of department decides to add a 'personalised' hand crafted gift, personally delivered, based on customer spend – thereby enhancing an already successful *pattern*. To achieve a superior *position* in the marketplace, correct planning and use of the right ploy can add huge value. Exploring *strategy* as a perspective, consider the cultural mindset – a global approach to business dealings opens doors in other countries, whereas a local/area bound mindset limits international growth.

Mintzberg (1998) argued that the importance of developing a solid strategy encompasses the following elements;

a. **Strategic direction**
A future direction is planned, however one must remain vigilant of potential dangers, allowing for unplanned changes and strategic flexibility.

b. **Strategy focuses effort**
Although this advocates group movement in the same direction, one must not hinder future growth through a 'groupthink' ethos.

c. **Strategy defines the organisation**
Staff needs to identify with and embrace a clearer understanding of the purpose of the business. Critics claim this leads to stereotyping and oversimplification. Steve Jobs purist, simple perfection counteracts these views when one considers the position of Apple today.

d. **Strategy provides consistency**

Clarity of vision and order become ingrained, resulting in consistent behaviour forward. Steve Jobs' focus on 'simple clarity of vision' lead to the most creative 'out of the box' thinking ever in the computer industry, e.g. the iPad.

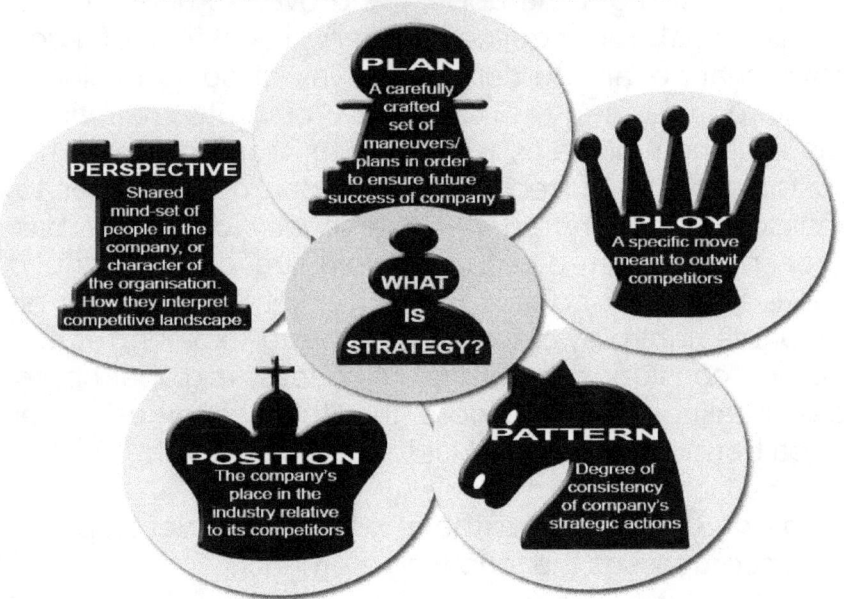

 - A way to ensure you have considered all relevant issues.
- Realistic, practical & solid way of testing initial ideas.
- Ideal to flush out paradoxes and issues not fully invenstigated.

 - Overlap between Strategy as Position can occur & other elements, i.e. you can achieve an intended Position through Planning.

Mintzberg (1997) - author's own creation

When considering how strategy is developed and implemented, and the relationship between strategy, innovation and change, there are a multitude of frameworks used by leaders. These include the, Boston Matrix (*Morrison & Wensley 1991; Henderson 1979*) and Ansoff Matrix (*Richardson & Evans 2007*), GE/McKinsey (*Kar 2007; McKinsey 2008; Johnson, Scholes & Whittington 2011*), Porter's 5 Forces Model (*Porter 1980 & 2008*), SWOT (*McDonald & Payne 1996*) and PESTEL analysis (*Yüksel 2012*) to the more recent Core Competency Model of *Hamel & Prahalad (1994)*.

When reviewing these frameworks, one needs to consider which one is suited to a particular organisation. Some focus on factors that are external, while others focus in a mix of external (macro-environment) views as well as the internal strengths and weaknesses (industry structure) within the company. The 'industrial structure view' focuses predominantly on the macro-industry, whereas the 'resource based view' focuses on the availability of a unique package of prized resources an organisation can use to gain competitive advantage. In contrast the 'relational view' postulates that distinctive inter-organisational connections/relationships in daily transactions add to the competitive superiority *(Kar 2012)*.

According to *Johnson, Scholes & Whittington (2011)*, of the strategy tools available, leaders tend to use a 'strategy toolkit' that comprises of between one and nine different tools.

Common tools include:

2.5.1 SWOT ANALYSIS

The traditional layout is a 2 X 2 matrix focusing on strengths & weaknesses (internal, e.g. finance & operations that are within the control of the organisation) and opportunities and threats (external – such as political factors & competitors), see diagram on the next page. Besides offering a tool for the evaluation of strengths and weakness compared with competitors, research done by *De Witt & Meyer (2005)* indicated that identifying strategic problems tends to be a subjective process as individuals identify with certain issues based on intuitive considerations/own opinions instead of objective factual information only.

Although time consuming, analysis can be explored at different levels, i.e. market sectors, products, services and competitors. It may be effective in lessening substantial situational factors into more manageable elements. However, this oversimplification of a situation, may thus define some factors as arbitrary, e.g. an organisations culture can be seen as a strength, or a weakness. This is confirmed by *Dharmaraj, Sivasubramanian & Sudhahar (2010)* as well as *Johnson, Scholes & Whittington (2011)* who also stated that the SWOT analysis influences organisations to focus on creating 'uncritical' lists without specific levels of priority, rather than the clear-cut issues focused on achieving objectives. *Mintzberg (1994)* even suggested that the SWOT matrix causes an exaggerated formalisation of the strategic process.

SWOT ANALYSIS
ALBERT HUMPHREY

	POSITIVE	NEGATIVE
INTERNAL	**S** STRENGTHS	**W** WEAKNESSES
EXTRENAL	**O** OPPORTUNITIES	**T** THREATS

 - Can be used in any decision-making situation where a final goal has been defined.
- A simple, practical framework helping companies to quickly gather meaningful info in order to maximise their potential.

 - Can create unverified inconsistent and vague long lists of irrelevant information.
- There is a danger of overgenerelaisation.

McDonald & Payne (1996); Johnson, Scholes & Whittington (2011) - author's own creation

SWOT analysis is widely known, easy and quick to use and a fairly efficient starting point to collect numerous key issues. Due to the possible subjective date collection, lack of issue priority and masses of data collected, it would be far more effective to use SWOT in conjunction with another framework such as the PESTEL analysis or the Boston Matrix for more concise results *Johnson, Scholes & Whittington (2011)*.

2.5.2 PESTEL ANALYSIS

According to *Johnson, Scholes & Whittington (2011)* when looking at the macro-environment, the PESTEL framework provides an extensive list of influences, still very much relevant in the 21st century, on probable successes or failures of individual strategies. The acronym stands for Political, Economic, Social, Technological, Environmental and Legal that are intrinsically linked together. Hence analysis of these correlations can lead to protracted and elaborate lists of research material, i.e. Social (increased popularity in air travel) and Environmental (reduction of air pollution).

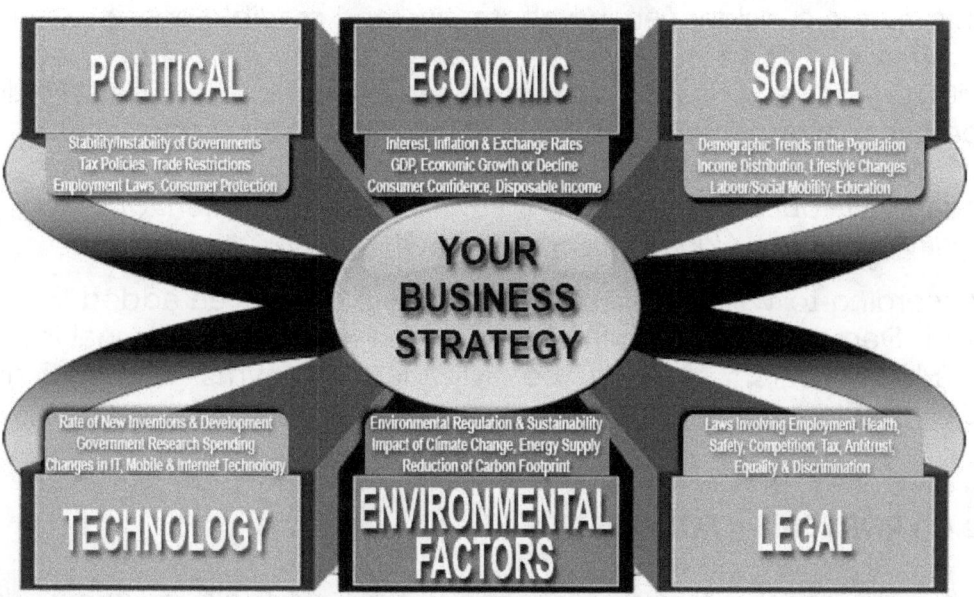

- Simple & based on familiar patterns..
- Good for understanding the 'big picture' of sector in which company is operating.
- Provides a tool that allows the company to explore & identify possible threats, as well as new oppotunities.
- Promotes strategic thinking within the organisation.
- Includes cross-functional skills and know-how.

- Only provides a general view of the macro-environmental conditions.
- Quality & especially massive amount of data collected can lead to problems.
- Data must be evaluated critically and in an unbiased way to avoid wrong strategic decisions.
- Analysed external factors can change at a fast pace, hence future predictions become difficult.

Yüksel (2012); Senior & Flemming (2006); Johnson, Scholes & Whittington (2011) - author's own creation

Therefore it is imperative to focus on high priority 'key drivers for change.' These high-impact elements can have momentous differing effects on the success or failure of a strategy within a specific sector, i.e. IT companies would focus on technology and developments in processor speeds. Failure by leadership to identify these key drivers can hinder effective response and growth. However one also needs to be cognisant of the unprecedented rapid and complex economic, political and environmental changes that have forever changed today's business environment *(Senior & Flemming 2006)*.

Focusing on any one incorrect factor could spell disaster. Therefore it is vital to consider varying alternative and credible possible future scenarios, as part of an organisation's strategy. This should not be viewed as 'soothsaying' the unpredictable, but as deliberating practical alternative scenarios, which have an added value of *"improving organizational learning by making managers more perceptive about the forces in the business environment and what is really important" (Johnson, Scholes & Wittington 2011, p. 57)*.

According to *Wikipedia (2006)*, strategists have even added 'Ethics' and 'Demographics' when doing an external strategic analysis or market research, creating the extended acronyms, STEEPLE and STEEPLED.

2.5.3 PORTER'S 5 FORCES MODEL

Many companies focus on assessing their strategic position within their industry or sector, in terms of strengths and weaknesses, i.e. their competitive advantage. When Porter launched his model in the 1970's, it was seen as revolutionary advancement in strategy formulation. He focused on competitive strategy and building a competitive supremacy by identifying five crucial structural aspects that identify the strength of competitive forces in the macro-environment; buyer power, supplier power, threat of entrants, threat of substitutes and competitive rivalry *(Porter 1980 & 2008)*.

Porter's developed his 5 Forces model as a reaction to the SWOT analysis model which he found unrigorous and ad hoc. However, he still favoured a more 'deliberate' 2 – 5 year approach, even though it was not conducive to today's turbulent business arena *(Porter, Argyres & McGahan 2002)*. In an article on the Forbes website, *Mintzberg's Better Way to Do Corporate Strategy,* Mintzberg with his emergent strategy predicted these changes by stating that, *"The real challenge in crafting strategy lies in detecting the subtle discontinuities that may undermine a business in the future. And for that, there is no technique, no program, just a sharp mind in touch with the situation" (Moore & Lenir 2011)*.

In contrast, research done by *Koo, Koh & Nam (2004)* of 123 firms in Korea found that Porter's competitive strategies were indeed pertinent in current on-line electronic markets. In addition, Porter's model is also useful as a starting point to opening a business, where strategic analysis investigates the attractiveness of a certain sector. Hence if his five forces are high, extensive competition makes the sector less attractive *(Porter 2008)*.

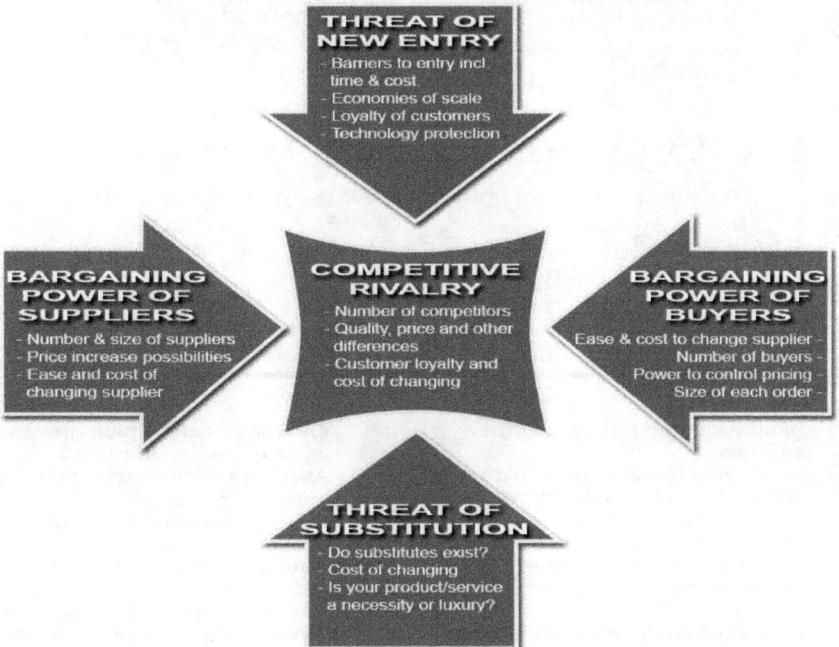

PORTER'S 5 FORCES MODEL

THREAT OF NEW ENTRY
- Barriers to entry incl. time & cost
- Economies of scale
- Loyalty of customers
- Technology protection

BARGAINING POWER OF SUPPLIERS
- Number & size of suppliers
- Price increase possibilities
- Ease and cost of changing supplier

COMPETITIVE RIVALRY
- Number of competitors
- Quality, price and other differences
- Customer loyalty and cost of changing

BARGAINING POWER OF BUYERS
- Ease & cost to change supplier
- Number of buyers
- Power to control pricing
- Size of each order

THREAT OF SUBSTITUTION
- Do substitutes exist?
- Cost of changing
- Is your product/service a necessity or luxury?

- Assesses the balance of power of an organisation compared to their competitors.
- Provides a good base for further research to formulate your company strategy.

Porter (1980 & 2008) - author's own creation

- Model developed in a different environment than exists in today's faster pace of change.
- Non-market forces not examined.
- Provides a snapshot only.
- Based on idea of competition only.
- Difficulty in defining an industry.

2.5.4 BCG MATRIX

In larger corporations, leaders have various portfolios and need to manage each one differently. Thus they need to analyse the synergies, links, strengths and weakness between business units, whether in relation to each other, competitors, or the market in general. A more balanced approach was needed resulting in the development of the BCG Growth-Share Matrix by Bruce Henderson of the Boston Consulting Group. Here market share and growth (industry attractiveness) are crucial variables for analysing competitive advantage *(Henderson 1973; Jurevicius 2013).*

GROWTH SHARE MATRIX
BOSTON CONSULTING GROUP

	HIGH ← MARKET GROWTH RATE → LOW	**STARS**	**QUESTION MARK**

STARS
- High growth and high market share.
- Profit potential.
- Ensure that cashflow exceeds investment for growth.

QUESTION MARK
- High growth, low share.
- Early development phase requiring large investment to grow.
- Needs research and evaluation.

CASH COW
- High market share, but low investment.
- Stable and established.
- Generates cash and funds 'stars' & research.

DOG
- Low growth, low market share.
- Draining company of cash.
- Eliminate as usuall at end of life cycle.

HIGH   MARKET SHARE   LOW

- Simple starting point for further analysis.
- Provides a framework for alloting resources amoung divergent business units.
- Good for comparing various business units at a glance.
- Good reminder that 'Stars' can decline.
- Highlights financial demands in in high growth business units.

- Overemphasises high growth and ignores waning markets.
- Assumes all business units are independent of others.
- Dismisses possibility of synergy between business units.
- Wrongly assumes that high market share always equals high growth.
- Market growth rate seen as a given - better to use GE/McKinsey matrix for this.

Henderson (1979); Johnson, Scholes & Whittington (2011); Jurevicius (2013); Morrison & Wensley (1991) - author's own creation

Exploring the diagram above, dogs have low market share and growth, take time and cost money and produce the least. Ideal candidates to de-invest and close. Question marks have a low market share and require large sums of cash investment to grown into stars and cash cows. However, they can degenerate into a dog if not properly managed. Stars are self-sufficient high cash generators, but also require heavy investment to maintain this high market share. Cash cows are mature business units, generating a high stable cash flow that can also be used to fund question marks (*Henderson 1973; Johnson, Scholes & Wittington 2011; Morrison & Wensley 1991*).

According to *Jurevicius (2013)*, the BCG Matrix has lost popularity, yet still considers it a pragmatic tool if tackled in the following steps;

1.   Identify the business unit by analysing the various brands and products.

2.   Examine the market and define it clearly.

3.   Identify the relative market share by dividing this with that of the   largest competitor.

4.   Appraise the industry growth rate which can often be found in   industry reports online.

5.   Map the various brands/products on the matrix as circles – the   size corresponding to the representative proportion of revenue   generated.

Note the similarity of *Jurevicius (2013)* steps to the GE/McKinsey Matrix discussed next.

2.3.5 GE MCKINSEY MATRIX

Due to the limitations of the BCG matrix, the nine-box GE McKinsey matrix was developed, providing a more systematic approach for multi-business organisations in order to decide where to invest their money. Two factors are employed to determine the future growth of a business unit; the competitive strength and the attractiveness within the industry. The business units are then plotted onto the matrix, the size of the circle representing the market size, and the market share displayed as a pie chart within the circle. Finally an arrow indicates the expected future position of the business unit (*Johnson, Scholes & Whittington 2011; Kar 2007; McKinsey 2008*).

In the diagram on the next page, 'A' is the ideal position for a business unit to be in. B & D Have good growth potential, while positions C, E & G need more analysis and a decision as to try grow, or divest in them. Anything in quadrants F, H & I should be harvested *(Kasi 2010)*. Although an improvement on the BCG matrix, failure to address core competencies and interaction between business units, ideally favours this tool more for use as a quick heads up on which business units display greater potential of return *(Kar 2007; Kasi 2010; McKinsey 2008)*.

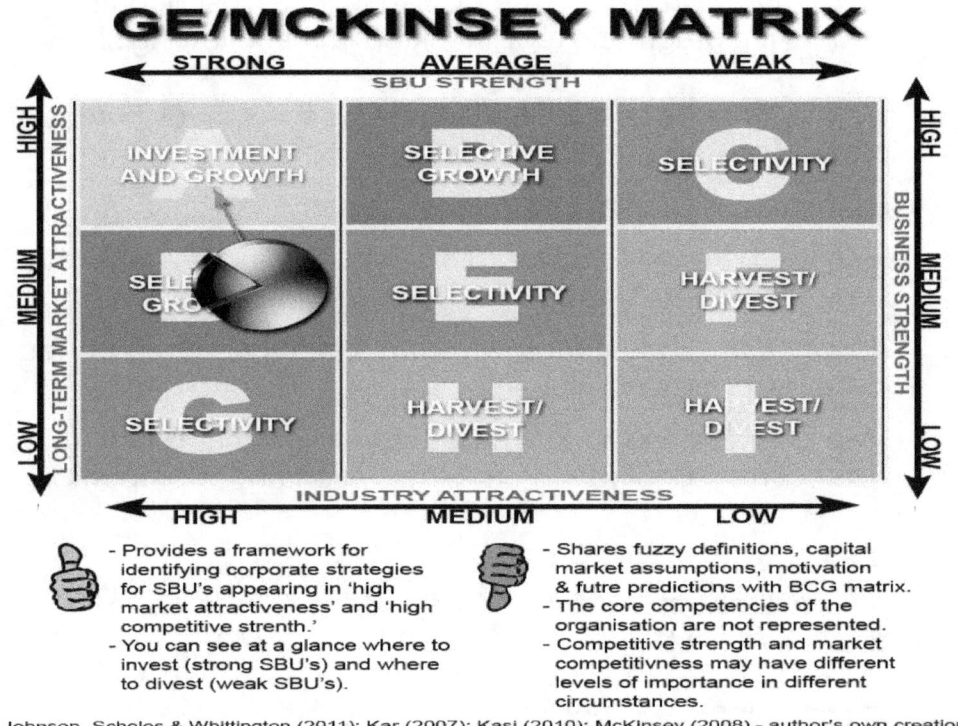

GE/MCKINSEY MATRIX

👍 - Provides a framework for identifying corporate strategies for SBU's appearing in 'high market attractiveness' and 'high competitive strenth.'
- You can see at a glance where to invest (strong SBU's) and where to divest (weak SBU's).

👎 - Shares fuzzy definitions, capital market assumptions, motivation & futre predictions with BCG matrix.
- The core competencies of the organisation are not represented.
- Competitive strength and market competitivness may have different levels of importance in different circumstances.

Johnson, Scholes & Whittington (2011); Kar (2007); Kasi (2010); McKinsey (2008) - author's own creation

2.6 STRATEGIC LEADERSHIP STRUCTURES

Although executive teams and boards of directors are an integral part of large organisations, their mere existence alone does not guarantee the strategic success or stability of the company. *Moore (2008)* cited that only one in ten large corporate leaders reach their growth targets. He shares four reasons;

1. Autocratic leadership style and ignoring the fact that the final outcome is reliant on the slowest member of the team.

2.   Focusing on input rather than "*Throughput.*" It is futile if the leadership create a complex aggressive strategy when those tasked to interpret and implement it, roll their eyes at it!

3.   Operating in 'crises management' mode, rather than communicating and creating a sustainable plan at an individual level. Interestingly he makes mention that in leadership, failure is not an option, and that this philosophy needs to be changed to, "*Not knowing where you are willing to fail means not being serious about success*" (Moore (2008, p. 4).

4.   Not defining success specifically and in a manner that it can be understood and carried out at every level within the company.

Collins' (2001) example of Abbot Laboratories where the CEO rebuilt the entire board, plus executive teams due to nepotism is a perfect example of Newton Minow's quotation, "*We've gotten to the point where everybody's got a right and nobody's got a responsibility*" *(Graham et al 2012).* The previous leadership team believed the prevailing sentiment that big ego, high profile, celebrity leaders, even if they were mediocre, had a right to be in that position. In fact Collins' research stunned the industry when he discovered that it was utmost humility, professional will and a desire to build the organisation that defined great leaders! His conjecture of, "*First who... then what*" makes perfect sense, as it is only when the leadership team consists of

5 QUALITY LEVELS OF LEADERSHIP

LEVEL 5 EXECUTIVE
Builds lasting greatness through an intricate blend of personal humility and professional will

LEVEL 4 EFFECTIVE LEADER
Active committment, high performance standards and a dedicated pursuit of a clear vision

LEVEL 3 COMPETENT MANAGER
Effective coordination of people and resources to efficiently achieve planned objectives

LEVEL 2 CONTRIBUTING TEAM MEMBER
Contributes individual talents towards group objectives and works well with others

LEVEL 1 HIGHLY CAPABLE INDIVIDUAL
Adds beneficial contributions through skills, knowledge, talent and great work habits

Collins (2001) - author's own creation

the 'right people' with self-discipline that responsibility will prevail. His 5 quality levels of a leadership team encapsulate these findings in the diagram on the left *(Collins 2001).*

Successful leaders accept overall responsibility of an organisation and focus on the leadership "of" rather than "in" organisations, where the mission is the 'evolution' of the company in its entirety *(Selznick 1984)*. A decade after *Collins & Porras (2004)* wrote 'Built to Last,' in 1994, R*eingold & Underwood (2005)* reviewed these visionary companies and found that all 18 companies were still household names today. They confirmed that the '*clock building*' as apposed to '*time telling*' philosophy had indeed worked where the focus had been on the '*inner*' rather than '*external*' workings that went beyond the sole quest for profit, but also encapsulated an internal lasting culture of pride in building the organisation.

2.7 STRATEGIC IMPLEMENTATION

The Balanced Scorecard and the European Foundation for Quality Management (EFQM) Model share similarities in that they *"attempt to tie performance metrics to a firm's strategy and long term vision" (Wongrassamee, Gardiner & Simmons 2003, p. 15).* In answer to the question of whether the implementation of either (or both) models is a guarantee of success, *Kaplan & Norton (2001)* highlighted that the quality of the strategy is often mistakenly considered more important than the implementation thereof. Their research indicated that the problem lies with the quality of the leadership and the lack of effective execution of a strategy.

Their solution is the performance based management tool, the Balanced Scorecard that *(Kaplan & Norton 2001, p. 8)*, "*... enabled the early-adopting companies to focus and align executive teams, business unit, human resources, information technology and financial resources to their organisation's strategy.*" In addition, *Johnson, Scholes & Whittington (2011, p. 451)* elaborated on this view with their definition; "*Balanced scorecards combine both qualitative and quantitative measures, acknowledge the expectations of different stakeholders and relate an assessment of performance to choice of strategy.*"

In comparison, the EQFM model assists companies to become more competitive by measuring their current position within the industry, and guides them, in which areas to enhance their efforts. The focus is on striving towards excellence and the model is regularly amended, the last being in 2013 (EFQM 2013).

Both models are similar (measurement based, promote discourse about performance improvement, drive change and action, promote on-going review *(Lamotte & Carter 2000)*. *Shulver & Lawrie (2007)* agreed that each model shares plausible similarities. However, the essential approaches on improving company performance, differs between the models. The Balanced Scorecard supports a distinct focus on concrete strategies and the combined application of said activities by the company on which further leadership operations can be developed. The EFQM Model uses a common set of (conjectured to be real) strategic objectives, across all companies implementing this model within the same sector, based on 'plausible logic.' It is simpler and allows organisations to identify a benchmark comparison of themselves within their industry *(Shulver & Lawrie 2007)*.

Wongrassamee, *Gardiner & Simmons (2003, p. 24)* gave a succinct comparison in the diagram below. Interestingly, research by *Lamotte & Carter (2000)* suggested that both models can be used alongside each other. However, companies must be clear as to why and how they implement these models, coupled with a substantial and disciplined commitment by the leadership team.

COMPARISON BETWEEN THE BALANCED SCORECARD AND THE EFQM EXCELLENCE MODEL USING OTLEY'S FIVE QUESTIONS OF MANAGEMENT CONTROL SYSTEMS (Otley 1999)		
QUESTION	EFQM MODEL	BALANCED SCORECARD
Objectives	Multiple - based on TQM priciples. Emphasises 9 areas: - Leadership; - People Management; - Policy and strategy implementation; - Pesource management; - Process management; - People satisfaction; - Customer satisfaction; - Impact on society; - Business results.	Multiple - based on strategy. Emphasises 4 generic areas: - Financial; - Customer; - Internal business processes; - Innovation & learning.
Strategies & Plans	Not especially addressed, but all weighted criteria and sub-criteria can be used as guidance.	Strategic measures assigned. Uses 'strategy map' to connect each measure to strategy.
Targets	None specifc. Management can set their expected performance levels.	Not addressed. Due to non-prescriptive template, managers are required to assign target performance levels.
Rewards	Requires an appropriate reward and recognition system, but no explicit guidance given.	Suggests that individual compensation system should be linked to strategic measures.
Feedback	Not mentioned. However, the model itself provides feedback information as a default of the assessment method.	Requires double-loop learning which is more complicated than single-loop feedback.

Wongrassamee, Gardiner & Simmons (2003, p. 24)

3. ANALYSIS OF A PERSONAL STRATEGIC PROCESSES WITHIN AN ORGANISATION

3.1 OVERVIEW

I was appointed as brand ambassador to a new channel in one of Africa's largest financial companies who wanted to expand their footprint in the mass market sector in Southern Africa. The aim was to use alternative means of attracting customers that could not be reached via the traditional adviser route. I was asked to consult in validating past ad hoc research, and assist in identifying and setting up a pilot project to run for 6 months, with the potential of becoming a permanent new channel in Group Schemes.

I was led to believe that a proficient project team had initiated a basic SWOT and PESTEL analysis, appointed a team leader who in turn appointed me to be part of the trial phase and assist in marketing the concept.

However, a further detailed PESTEL analysis *(Senior & Flemming 2006)* by myself revealed contemplative political, economic, social and legal issues. South Africa has not only undergone major changes since apartheid, but government has imposed strict 'Black Economic Empowerment' policies to redress the wrongs of the past.

Companies were (are) thus required to employ people who were previously disadvantaged, with the focus on uplifting the majority black population. National government is the anchor client of this particular financial powerhouse, thus strategically, political, legal and economic alignment was a vital driving force for their future growth.

Additionally, government policies resulted in an influx of potential financial advisors applying for posts. Due to lack of education and past social and economic conditions, they did not pass the qualifying exams enabling them to become legitimately compliant as a financial planner/advisor. Legally the company was required to afford them opportunities, but also maintain a high industry standard. At this point PESTEL factors had been identified, all of which affected the company and could be seen as driving forces to implement this new alternative approach and increase short-term insurance market share.

PESTEL ANALYSIS

Yüksel (2012); Senior & Flemming (2006); Johnson, Scholes & Whittington (2011) - author's own creation

3.2 STRATEGY

In planning the strategic direction I assumed that the current leadership had considered Mintzberg's 5 P's of strategy. In order to gain 'perspective' they ascertained that a smaller financial house had found a solution to the above by creating a Multi-Level Marketing (MLM) division, offering short-term insurance products to the mass market. With this current organisation's mega brand and decades old history with nationwide offices, they had a superior 'position' to any competitors, hence a powerful 'market leader mind set' was ingrained in all.

MINTZBERG
THE 5 P'S OF STRATEGY

PLAN
Use Porter's 5 Forces model to identify superior competitive strategy.

PERSPECTIVE
No large financial brand had attempted the MLM approach of increasing market share.

PLOY
Be the first powerhouse brand to infiltrate this market.

MY STRATEGIC PLAN

POSITION
169 Year market leader with offices throughout Africa, Asia, UK & South America.

PATTERN
Trusted brand with consistent earnings for clients. Proven track record.

Mintzberg (1997) - author's own creation

Network marketing was a complex process with much negative press associated around it, thus not aligning to the 'pattern' of financial solutions which formed part of this organisation's brand. However, as a 'ploy' and if structured properly, in accordance with the Financial Services Act, Consumer Protection Act and all laws of the country, we could possible have been the first powerhouse brand to take over this market, plus afford the lower income group a business opportunity.

This led to an additional strategic 'ploy' of offering our 'failing' financial advisors a new 'angle' of earning commissions on short term insurance. When it came to supplier power and market share nobody had our brand and presence and trust in the market *(Mintzberg 1997)*. This was a huge plus factor and a massive inspiration to take this plan forward.

In accordance with *Mintzberg (1997)* the project team formulated a plan for building a superior competitive strategy and supremacy by identifying the five crucial aspects of Porter's 5 Forces Model as in the diagram below;

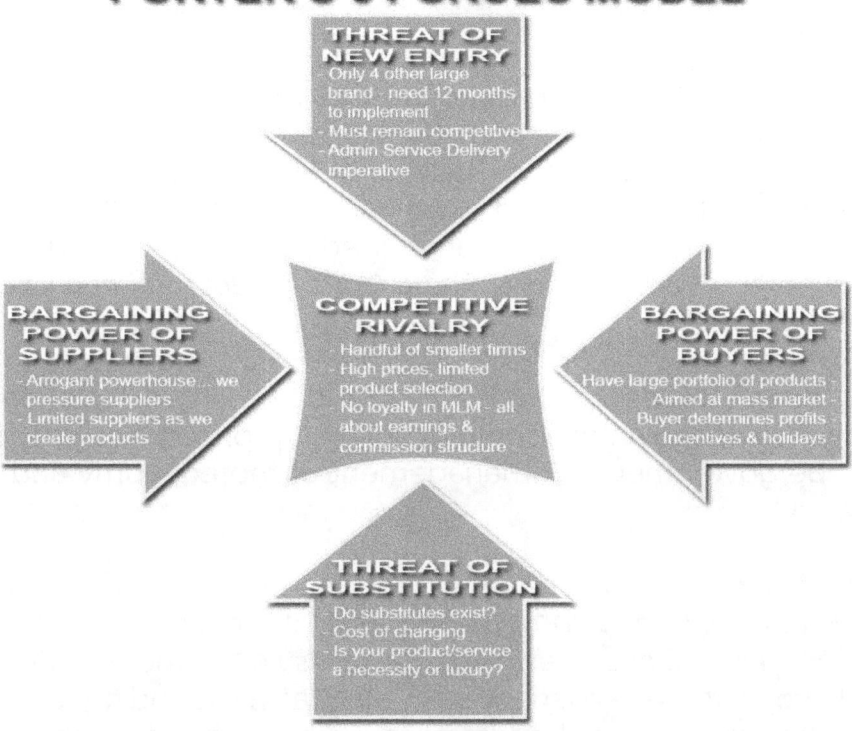

PORTER'S 5 FORCES MODEL

- Trusted brand.
- Offices world-wide.
- First to attempt MLM.
- All admin systems established.
- Brand will add authenticity and
  sell the product.
- Product aimed at mass market.

- Rigid brand 'mind-set'.
- Challenge of achieving central
  vision for all departments.
- Entering market within 6 months.

Porter (1980 & 2008) - author's own creation

a.   Rivalry was minimal - a handful of smaller players.

b.   Threat of new entry presented a possible risk. However, industry research clearly revealed that we were the only mega brand investigating the MLM option. Strategically, this product needed to flood the market within 6 months. Any competitors would take at least 12 months to bring a similar product to the market.

c.   As the largest and most established financial powerhouse in Africa, we had experience and an established range of products to enter this market at rock bottom prices, plus offer higher commissions than the current competitors. Buyers therefore had no need to drive down prices, plus they were earning money off their policies.

d.   Substitutes existed! Even within this company other departments had similar products. However, ours were aimed at a different market segment and thus were complimentary to these existing departments. Nevertheless, the leadership skills where challenged as the appointed head had to influence all these other channels to comprehend the envisaged larger strategic goals and capacity of the company as a whole *(Johnson 2011; Johnson, Scholes & Whittington 2011)*.

e.   As the established powerhouse brand and originator of policies, there was no anguish of suppliers driving up prices. The only factor would be government mismanagement of the economy and a rise in inflation.

As leadership is not only reserved for one person at the top *(Cable 2008; Hughes & Beatty 2005; Liedka 1998)* the channel head tried to focus on, "First Who... then What" *(Collins 2001)* and identified five outside consultants, experienced in MLM as his founding leadership team who would drive the business, and also function as advisors between the outside business partners, himself and the internal project team. I believed this would help us outsmart and conquer any future competition *(Markides 2012)*. Through creative thinking *(De Wit 2005)* I believed the channel head had found a harmonious, innovative and engaging strategy to lead this new channel to success, or so I thought – as discussed below.

4.   EXTENT TO WHICH PEOPLE WITHIN THE ORGANISATION WERE ENGAGED IN THE STRATEGY

The terms 'ambiguities and complexities' *(Jacques 1978)* existing in large organisations rings true. Unbeknown to me, the executive leadership up-line viewed this channel as '*too alternative*', and with little chance of success. They divided the responsibility of the project between the channel head and the project team, resulting in a negative groupthink ethos *(Mintzberg 1998)* amongst the executive/project team compared to the channel head and the external consultants. This corporation consisted of numerous supporting business units (legal & compliance, marketing, IT, HR amongst others). None wanted to take a risk, or responsibility to implement these innovative new ideas. In short, this new channel threatened their comfort zones and demanded responsibility decision making. The six month establishment plaon of this channel was challenged by the rigid 169-year deep routed inflexible financial mind-set, that flew in the face of *Hitt, Keats & DeMarie (1998)* who postulated that new leaders manage easier than old promoted employees. If anything, a 'new face' requires substantial more talents, especially people skills and endless patience *(Hooiberg, Hunt & Dodge 1997)*.

Newton Minow's quotation pops up again *(Graham et al 2012)* and succinctly summarises the eventual failure of the project as everyone felt they had a right to delay and question the innovative strategic decisions of the channel head and founding team. Why? No-one was prepared to take the responsibility of trying something new or believe in a single central vision *(Isaacs 2013)*. Instead, in the words of *Johnson, Scholes & Whittington's (2011: 510)* they killed they project through *"Paralysis by Analysis."*

5. RECOMMENDATIONS HOW STRATEGIC PROCESSES WITHIN THE ORGANISATION COULD BE IMPROVED

If, as a leader, the channel head had had full control to chose his own leadership team, then he would have unequivocally followed *Collins' (2001)* advice of *"First Who... Then What."* Today it makes complete sense that research and the thorough understanding of the social setting plus context of a company is required *(Hooiberg Hunt & Dodge 1997)*. My personal experience, rapid changes in technology, coupled with 'political correctness' issues and lack of responsibility leads me to hypothesise that today it is naïve and inexcusable not to focus on aligning employee attitude to those of the strategic leader and central vision.

Therefore I believe that the current training of leadership in interpersonal skills, empathy, conflict management and cultural diversity acceptance, should also be offered to employees at ground level.

Failure to educate the employees/teams results in the need for autocratic, uniformed and unfair leadership, which is a valid reason for creating '*them*' and '*us*' camps that destroy *"... the psychological architecture necessary for influence and leadership" (Alexander, Reicher & Platow 2011, p. 11).* Only once a central vision has been forged can employees learn to more readily accept, absorb and practice the required strategic processes/changes suggested by the leadership team.

6. CONCLUSION

Strategic leadership is so much more than identifying weaknesses and formulating practical plans for the future growth of a company. It encompasses a plethora of extra factors, including social issues, politics, economics, personal skills and cultural mindset – all of which affect future strategy. Couple this with a rapid changing world and you have an exciting, yet challenging career that requires major passion and constant learning.

"Swimming upstream means you are moving away from the 'masses'. It also means you are entering into unchartered territory where no-one else wants to be... so all the opportunities are yours to take. What's stopping you?"

(Wolfgang Riebe)

CHAPTER 4
CULTURE & INNOVATION IN ORGANISATIONS

INTRODUCTION

"Coming together is a beginning; keeping together is progress; working together is success."

(Henry Ford, 1863 - 1947)

This is without a doubt one of the most important chapters in this book, but also the chapter that took me on an emotional roller coaster in terms of learning to deal with rigid, entitlement riddled and basically outright rude individuals who care about nothing else, except their own agendas.

In this chapter organisational culture, critical theories and the impact of innovation and change by leaders will be critically reviewed. I will also highlight the negative effects of organisational culture within a large South African financial organisation, and share exasperating lessons learnt to hopefully prevent this from happening again in the future.

1. A CRITICAL REVIEW OF THEORIES OF INNOVATION, CHANGE AND ASSOCIATED LEADERSHIP

1.1 ORGANISATIONAL CULTURE (OC) DEFINED

The simplest definition dates back to the sixties when then McKinsey & Co managing director *Marvin Bower (1966)* described it as, *'the way we do things around here'. Hofstede (2001)* appeared to share Bower's simplistic view, as the way people in one company differentiate themselves from those in other companies in terms of their collective thinking as a group.

Schein (2004) similarly compared OC of organisations to the personality of people, stating that we each have unique characteristics, as do groups of people within a company. Even *McNamara (2000)* agreed, referring to it as the *'personality of an organisation'.* However in addition to the above, *Schein (2004)* felt there were many more levels to culture and dug deeper, suggesting a more precise definition as, *"a pattern of basic assumptions that was learned by the group as it solved its problems of external adaptation and internal integration, that has worked well enough to be considered valid and, therefore, to be taught to new members as the way to perceive, think and feel in relation to those problems"* (Schein 2004, p 14).

Schein (1990) further suggested that finding an exact definition of OC is a paradox, as little agreement exists in terms of what it means, how it should be monitored and recorded, or how it can be utilised in assisting companies. His views make sense when one considers the plethora of similar, broad and non-specific definitions. For example, many researchers agree that OC assists us to interpret incongruous and inconceivable behaviour that occurs within companies and groups, and that these collective group learning experiences and beliefs, as a result of the interaction among members, results in 'shared taken-for-granted assumptions, values, beliefs and principles' *(Johnson, Scholes & Whittington 2008; Needle 2004; Ravasi & Schultz 2006 & Schein 2004).*

Figure 1 highlights a few shared characteristics gleaned from the available definitions of OC *(Alvesson & Sveningsson 2008; Hofstede et al 1990).*

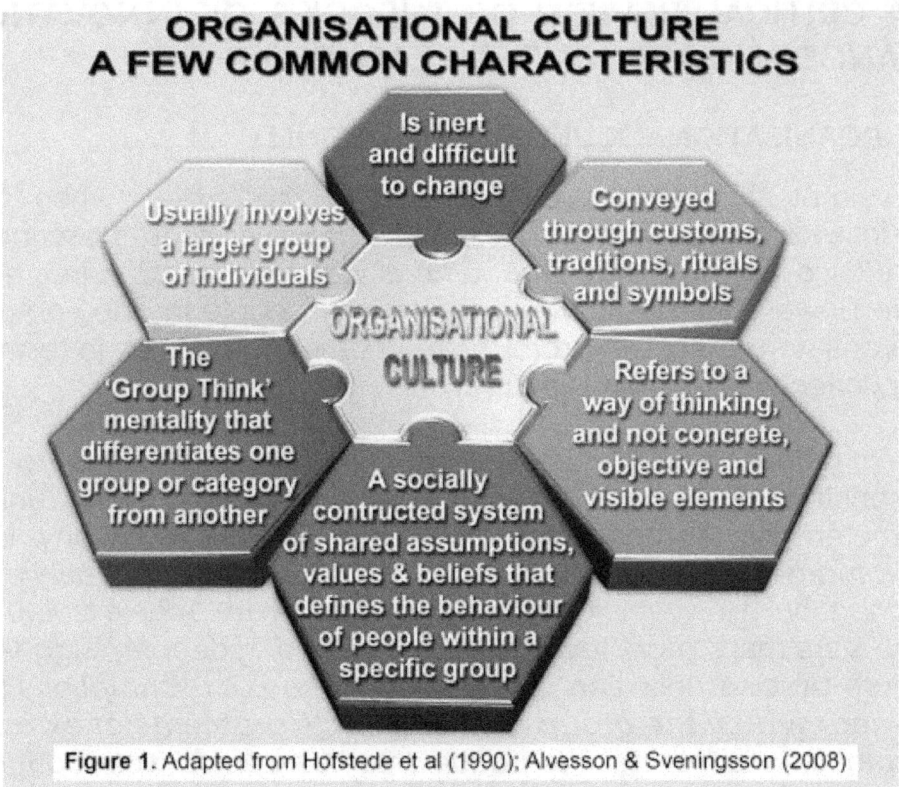

Figure 1. Adapted from Hofstede et al (1990); Alvesson & Sveningsson (2008)

Alvesson & Svengingsson (2008, p. 37) delved deeper when they wrote, *"Culture refers to what stands behind and guides behaviour rather than the behaviour as such". Trompenaars and Woolliams (2003, p. 6)* added an interesting perspective defining OC as, *"the values and norms that people hold to be more effective in surviving in a hostile natural environment."*

Needle (2004) distinguished between organisational and corporate culture, stressing that the latter is purposely established to achieve specific strategic goals by leadership. Whereas OC is more a cumulative assembly of beliefs, principals and values resulting from company history, products, strategy, staff, leadership, amongst others.

Lewis (2006) added a further perspective with his national cultural view, referring to the Big 5 (USA, Japan, Germany, Britain & France) and questioned their complacency and reluctance in handling inter-cultural issues, due to their dominance in world markets, coupled with their isolation and insularity as in the case of the USA & Japan.

Even though *Schein (2004)* argued that the concept of OC was ambiguous, he adds that without a '*stable membership*' coupled with a 'shared history', an organisation has nothing on which to base any culture on. Therefore *Johnson's (2001, p. 314)* view that, *"Culture is often seen as a barrier to change… it is difficult to be clear about what is meant by it or if anything can be done to change it"* makes perfect sense, and offers a refreshing change of perspective to the positive mainstream view that understanding OC is beneficial to innovation and change, rather than detrimental.

In summary one could therefore define OC as the '*group think*' of people within an organisation that hinders, or promotes innovation and change.

1.2 WAYS OF VIEWING ORGANISATIONAL CULTURE

1.2.1 SUB-CULTURES

The military can be viewed as a company having one OC. However, within the military, there are various branches, i.e. navy, air force & army. These usually each have their own sub-cultures (unique characteristics) that are defined by the function of that group. *Schein (2010)* referred to these as micro-cultures. *Alvesson & Sveningsson (2008)* agreed that individuals within a company will have differing views in terms of their unique situation and exposure within that organisation. Gender, occupation, nationality, religion and hierarchical position are only a scattering of complex values that actualise and splinter cultural variety instead of preserving consensus and congruity.

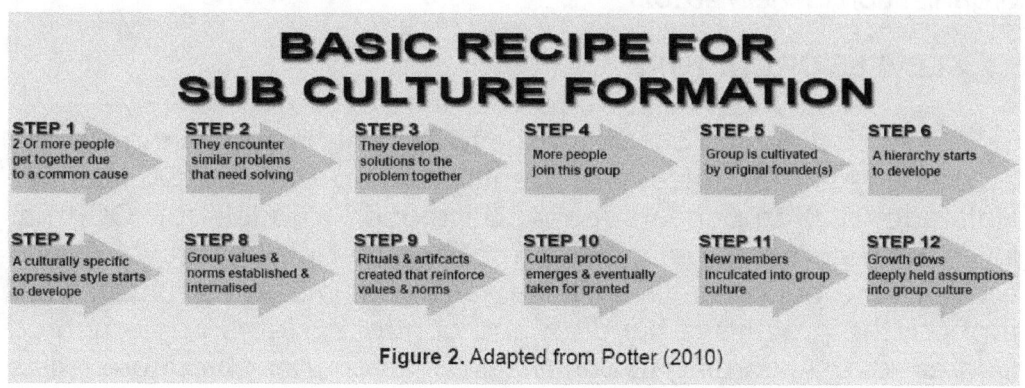

BASIC RECIPE FOR SUB CULTURE FORMATION

STEP 1 2 Or more people get together due to a common cause

STEP 2 They encounter similar problems that need solving

STEP 3 They develop solutions to the problem together

STEP 4 More people join this group

STEP 5 Group is cultivated by original founder(s)

STEP 6 A hierarchy starts to develope

STEP 7 A culturally specific expressive style starts to develope

STEP 8 Group values & norms established & internalised

STEP 9 Rituals & artifcacts created that reinforce values & norms

STEP 10 Cultural protocol emerges & eventually taken for granted

STEP 11 New members inculcated into group culture

STEP 12 Growth gows deeply held assumptions into group culture

Figure 2. Adapted from Potter (2010)

Potter (2010) concurred that sub-cultures occur within a department or team, due to two or more people '*connecting*' due to a common problem that requires solving, as per the 12 steps described in Figure 2 on the previous page.

Schein (2004) expanded on this view, stating that occupations requiring a lengthy education, result in shared values and norms between peers that is reinforced at industry specific networking events, educational gatherings and team collaboration among various members of that specific occupation. Therefore an overall organisational culture remains fragmented, but with a multitude of sub-cultures and shared assumptions within this larger group.

For leadership this can result in problems in terms of organisational task accomplishment, especially if the leader is not cognisant of the cultural diversity present within the department or team. *Schein (2010)* identifies three sub-cultures:

1.   Operator (they focus on service related activities and production),

2.   Engineer (focus mainly on research and design),

3.   Executive (the leaders ultimately in charge of the overall strategic direction).

He believed that most problems accredited to environmental factors, personality conflicts or bureaucracy among leadership is due to the lack of alignment of these subcultures within an organisation *(Schein 2010)*.

1.2.2 LEVELS OF CULTURE

The most challenging characteristic to innovation and change within a company is the intricacy of identifying and defining OC. Schein, Hofstede & Trompenaars each developed models of OC that investigate core values and assumptions that groups develop and adopt over a period of time. They examine how these structures are formed, the processes handled and control systems implemented *(Juarez 2013)*. According to *Schein (2004)*, even though culture exists simultaneously on all three levels of his model, the degree of visibility of the culture to an outsider is where the problem occurs. Figure 3 gives a clear breakdown and explanation of the three levels, including a thumb up and down of the pros and cons.

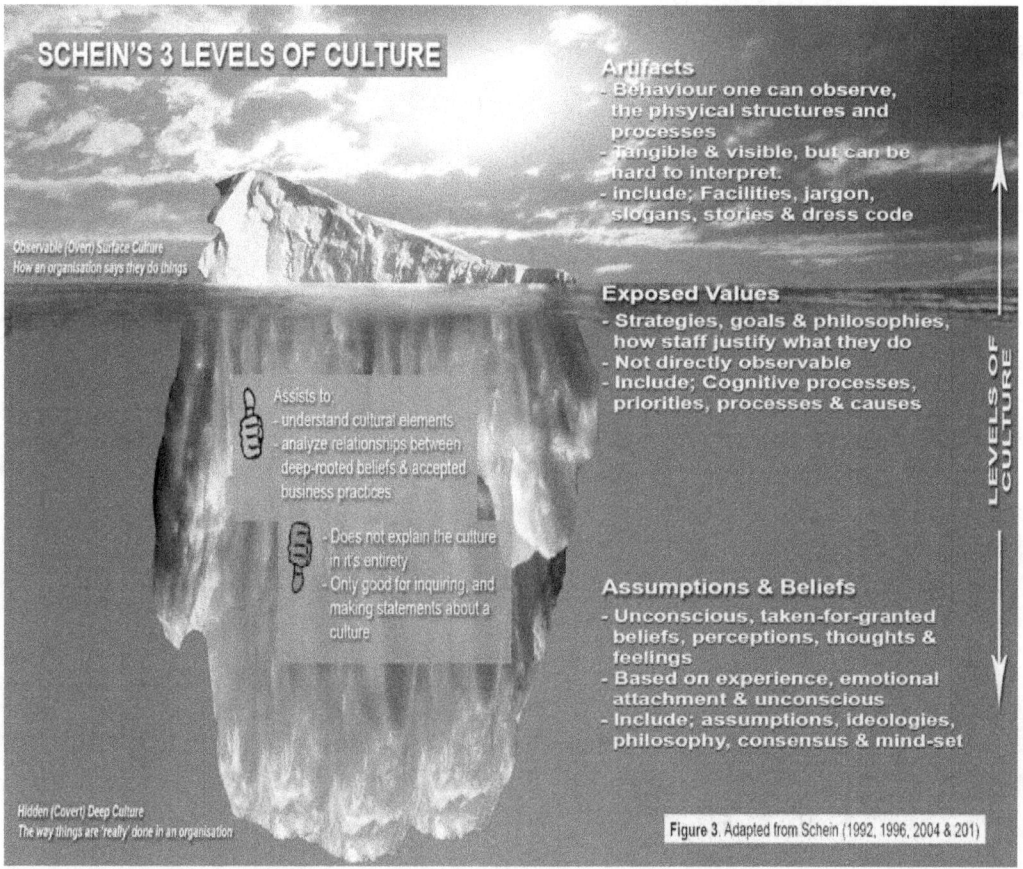

SCHEIN'S 3 LEVELS OF CULTURE

Observable (Overt) Surface Culture
How an organisation says they do things

Artifacts
- Behaviour one can observe, the phsyical structures and processes
- Tangible & visible, but can be hard to interpret.
- include; Facilities, jargon, slogans, stories & dress code

Exposed Values
- Strategies, goals & philosophies, how staff justify what they do
- Not directly observable
- Include; Cognitive processes, priorities, processes & causes

Assists to:
- understand cultural elements
- analyze relationships between deep-rooted beliefs & accepted business practices

- Does not explain the culture in it's entirety
- Only good for inquiring, and making statements about a culture

Assumptions & Beliefs
- Unconscious, taken-for-granted beliefs, perceptions, thoughts & feelings
- Based on experience, emotional attachment & unconscious
- Include; assumptions, ideologies, philosophy, consensus & mind-set

LEVELS OF CULTURE

Hidden (Covert) Deep Culture
The way things are 'really' done in an organisation

Figure 3. Adapted from Schein (1992, 1996, 2004 & 201)

At the first physical visible level (artifacts), *Schein (2004)* referred to all those qualities noticeable to an outsider, i.e. architecture, furnishings, dress code and even company mission and vision statements. The second (exposed values) level consists of shared values such as social principles and standards that are seen to have intrinsic value. A 'hidden reality' is representative of the third (assumptions & beliefs) and deepest level - those aspects that casual observation cannot cognitively identify. These are the implicit, underlying and unspoken elements that can only be identified through in-depth investigation. An example would be staff that professes ethical behaviour on the 2nd level, yet backstab each other on the 3rd level. This can also be construed as one of the reasons change consultants often falter in producing results, as they have failed to identify the deeper issues at hand. The challenge for leaders instituting innovation and change is to fully understand these levels, especially the ingrained, hidden assumptions and the challenges associated with them *(Schein 2004)*.

Although *Mary Hatch (1993)* agreed that Schein's model oversimplified complex phenomena, she acknowledged that in terms of empirical research guidance and theory generation, it remains an important and relevant model. Hatch also criticised the limitations of Schein's model due to the need of having to successfully identify links between artifacts, values and assumptions, that Schein never clearly explained. While Hatch introduces dynamism, she believes Schein's model only has value for non-clinical studies and can be more useful if combined with ideas *"drawn from symbolic-interpretive perspectives" (Hatch 1993, p. 658)*. Hence she reformulated Schein's model, creating her own 'Cultural

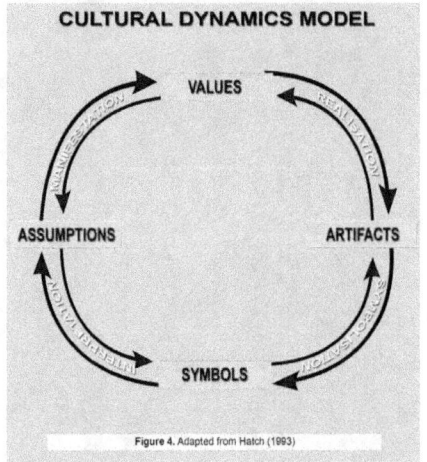

Dynamics Model' (see Figure 4) where 4 processes are examined, namely manifestation, realisation, symbolisation and interpretation that address the gaps in Schein's model. By introducing 'Symbols' Hatch blends Schein's theory with 'symbolic' interpretive perspectives. She shifts the emphasis on the relationships linking the elements of culture (assumptions, values, artifacts and symbols) hence making them less central in her model. Also, as Hatch's model is circular, it can, in principal, be accessed at any point.

Hofstede's (2001) model differs from *Schein (2004)*, in that he added another layer, dividing culture into four layers. The similarity to Schein can be seen in Hofstede's explanation that his lower levels too represent the deeper non-visible layers that are more difficult to change. Additionally, *Hofstede (2001)* talked about 3 levels of uniqueness and states that as humans we are brought up in different circumstances throughout the world, and hence experience life, emotions, thoughts in different ways and at different times throughout our lives. This learned culture (how we think, feel and react - mental programming) is referred to as the 'software of the mind.' However, the 'operating system' of this computer he refers to as our human nature – that which is inherited from our parents, not learnt and not visible to others, but shared by all humans. Personality however, is both partially learned and inherited and specific to an individual, as summarised in Figure 5. Hofstede placed more emphasis on identifying the deeply held values in the centre of the 'onion', as he believed that once set in your ways (culture), it becomes increasingly difficult to unlearn old habits and replace them with new ones.

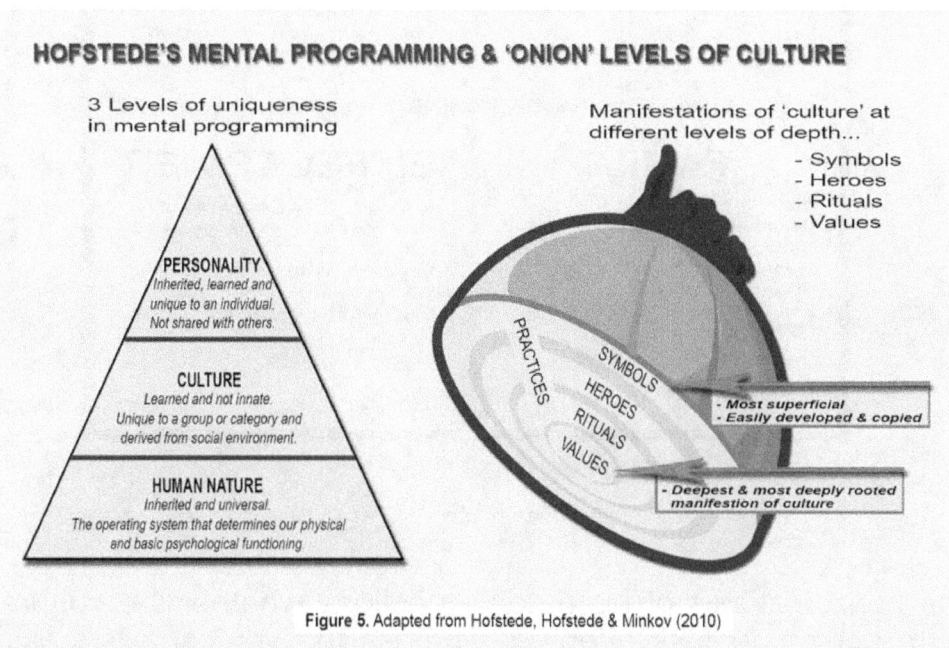

Figure 5. Adapted from Hofstede, Hofstede & Minkov (2010)

Although both Hofstede and Schein researched the values and thinking of employees within a company, *Hofstede (2001)* viewed culture as a system of collectively held values (mental programming) that differentiate groups from each other, whereas *Schein (2004)* saw culture operating at a deeper level of 'basic assumptions' (learned entity) that are unconscious and foster a taken for granted view the company has of itself.

On the other hand, *Trompenaars (2009)* referred to corporate culture, rather than OC and stressed that corporate culture can often override national culture. His model is clearly illustrated above in Figure 6 on the next page.

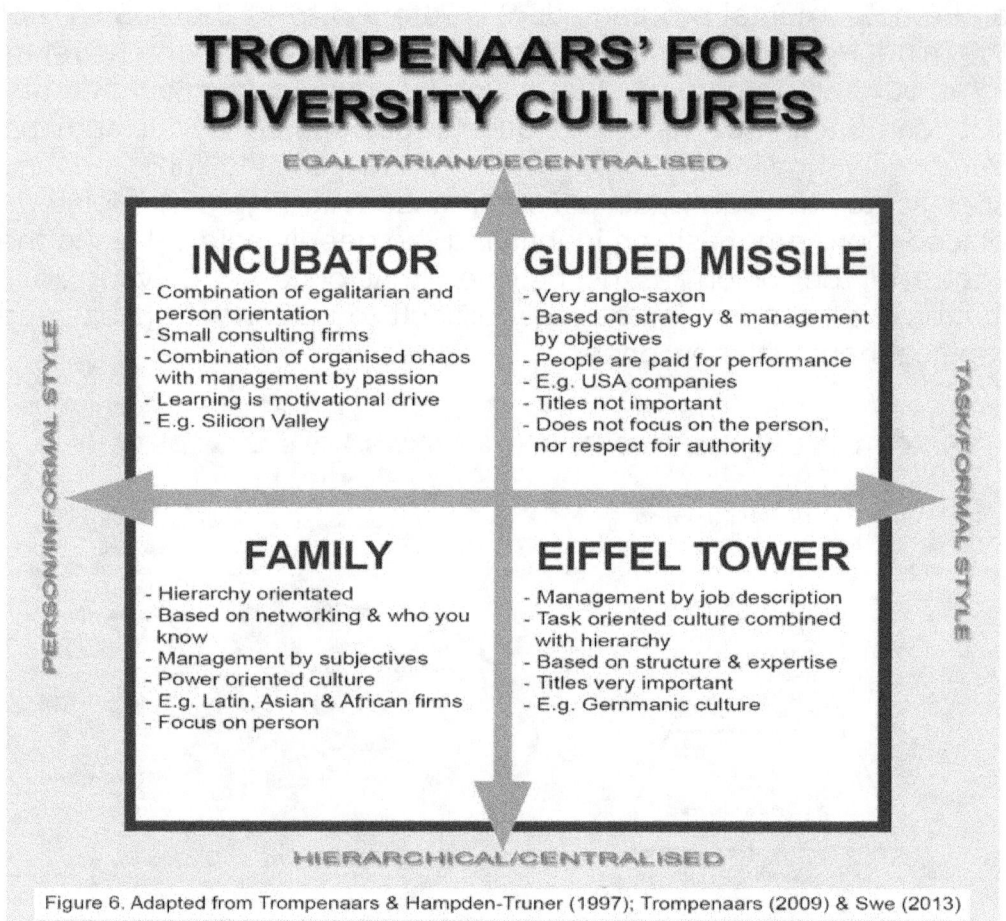

Figure 6. Adapted from Trompenaars & Hampden-Truner (1997); Trompenaars (2009) & Swe (2013)

The horizontal axis of his model questions whether the culture is more person, or task oriented, whereas the vertical axis looks at hierarchical versus egalitarian focus. Rather than just focus on values and thinking, Trompenaars model is used to identify tensions between companies that have different dominant cultures *(Swe 2013)*.

Johnson & Scholes believed that identifying four main elements (Hofstede) was not sufficient to understand, nor measure OC. Hence they developed the Cultural web, analysing 6 connected, deep, broad and stable key elements, as illustrated in Figure 7 on the next page.

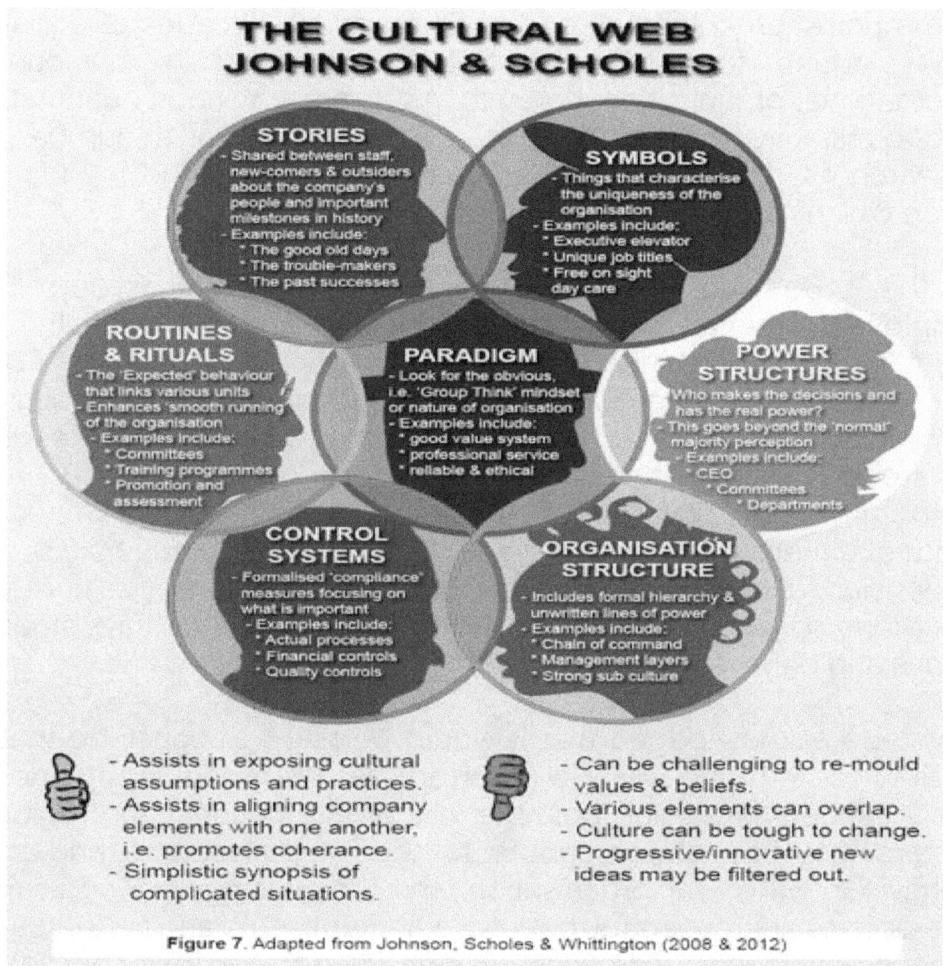

Figure 7. Adapted from Johnson, Scholes & Whittington (2008 & 2012)

They focused on identifying what staff, within a company believe and how it makes them behave, i.e. their current culture *(Johnson, Scholes & Whittington 2008 & 2012)*. Unfortunately, their cultural web ignored internal and external public relations, and focused specifically on what the stakeholders actually do. For leaders that need to identify which aspects of OC need to be changed, removed, introduced of improved, the cultural web has become a practical diagnostic tool that enables paradigm shifts.

2. WAYS OF VIEWING ORGANISATIONAL CULTURE

Although we may believe that the new world 'global village' environment and technology has brought people and nations of different cultures closer together resulting in cross-cultural communication, tolerance and understanding, decades of debates have argued for and against this, especially in relation to international organisational growth. As a result, various quantitative and qualitative models have been developed by a number of researchers. It could be argued that Hofstede set the foundation upon which many models have been built.

In the 1960's he completed a global survey of 117000 IBM employees mental programming in 40 countries. Initially he identified four dimensions, individualism-collectivism (IDV), uncertainty avoidance (UAI) power distance (PDI) and masculinity-femininity (MAS). Over the years 93 countries where studied leading Hofstede to include a fifth (long/short term orientation - LTO) and sixth dimension (indulgence versus restraint - IVR). Hofstede's cultural dimensions scored various countries on a 0 to 120 scale per dimension, allowing leaders to appraise their actions, position and decisions based on insight gained as to how this culture broadly thinks and behaves.

Hofstede acknowledged that it would be naïve to conclude that a society fits into one box. He asserted that his model is a guide to assist leaders in gaining possible insight into national and regional factors that possibly contribute to the internal culture and staff behaviour within an organisation, thus increasing the odds that interactions are respectful, beneficial and amicable and foster future growth *(Hofstede 2001; Hofstede & Minkov 2010; MindTools.com 2014)*.

Figure 8 on the following page highlights pros and cons of Hofstede's Cultural Dimensions. He did however stress that exercised cultures (symbols, heroes & rituals) within companies (sociology) are cosmetic and manageable and can be effortlessly mastered and/or abandoned, compared to deeply rooted beliefs that form the foundation of national cultures (anthropology). Therefore his model is not suitable for comparing companies within one country *(Hofstede & Hofstede 2014)*. However, capturing cross-country differences has received extensive support *(Lyn & Gelb 1996)*. In a nutshell, Hofstede's research suggested that national culture is derived from consistency in values, whereas OC from consistency in practices.

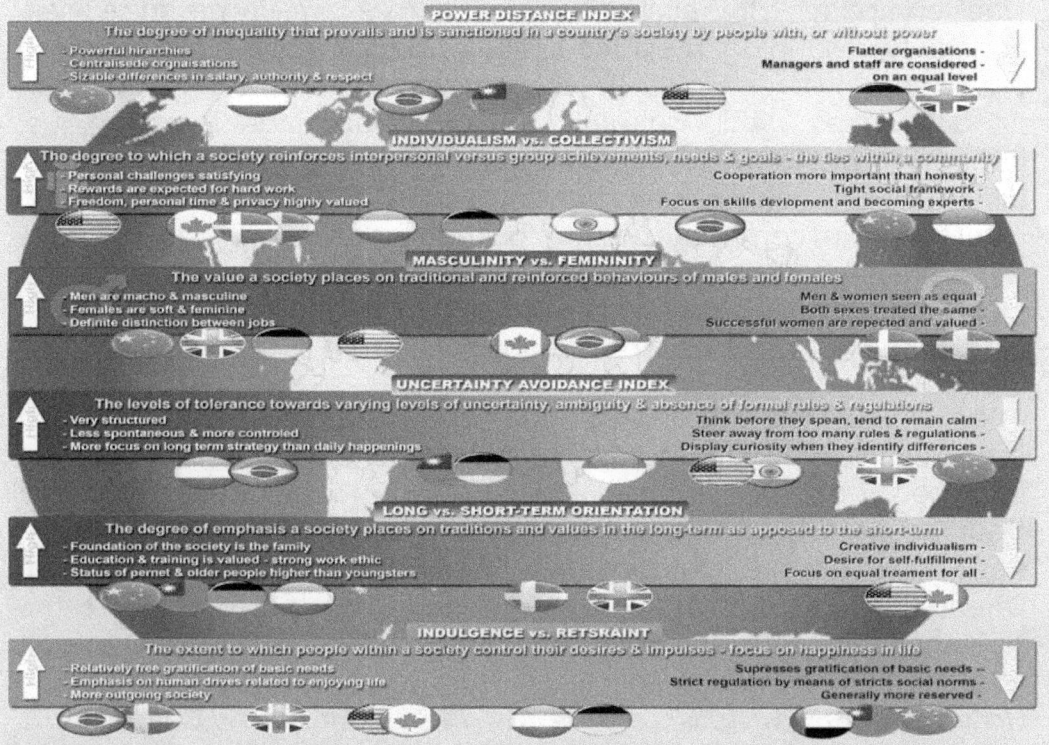

HOFSTEDE'S CULTURAL DIMENSIONS

POWER DISTANCE INDEX
The degree of inequality that prevails and is sanctioned in a country's society by people with, or without power
- Powerful hirarchies
- Centralised orgnaisations
- Sizable differences in salary, authority & respect

Flatter organisations -
Managers and staff are considered -
on an equal level

INDIVIDUALISM vs. COLLECTIVISM
The degree to which a society reinforces interpersonal versus group achievements, needs & goals - the ties within a community
- Personal challenges satisfying
- Rewards are expected for hard work
- Freedom, personal time & privacy highly valued

Cooperation more important than honesty -
Tight social framework -
Focus on skills devlopment and becoming experts -

MASCULINITY vs. FEMININITY
The value a society places on traditional and reinforced behaviours of males and females
- Men are macho & masculine
- Females are soft & feminine
- Definite distinction between jobs

Men & women seen as equal -
Both sexes treated the same -
Successful women are repected and valued -

UNCERTAINTY AVOIDANCE INDEX
The levels of tolerance towards varying levels of uncertainty, ambiguity & absence of formal rules & regulations
- Very structured
- Less spontaneous & more controled
- More focus on long term strategy than daily happenings

Think before they speak, tend to remain calm -
Steer away from too many rules & regulations -
Display curiosity when they identify differences -

LONG vs. SHORT-TERM ORIENTATION
The degree of emphasis a society places on traditions and values in the long-term as opposed to the short-term
- Foundation of the society is the family
- Education & training is valued - strong work ethic
- Status of pernet & older people higher than youngsters

Creative individualism -
Desire for self-fulfilment -
Focus on equal treament for all -

INDULGENCE vs. RETSRAINT
The extent to which people within a society control their desires & impulses - focus on happiness in life
- Relatively free gratification of basic needs
- Emphasis on human drives related to enjoying life
- More outgoing society

Supresses gratification of basic needs --
Strict regulation by means of stricts social norms -
Generally more reserved -

- Hofstede has received over 1000 citations on his study.
- **Pertinence:** Hofstede is considered a pioneer in studying culture, as at the time, companies were only starting to enter the global backdrop.
- **Accuracy:** The framework is based on precise design & systematic data acquisition.
- Many similar studies have questioned/tested (Trompenaars & Hampton Turner (1997) the relevance & accuracy of Hofstede's dimesions and confirmed his result.
- He successfully attribute patterns to national differences in culture as he had eliminated the problems of differences in company culture by only researching staff at IBM.
- In spite of some criticisms to his dimensions, the argument that they capture cross-country differences has received extensive support (Lynn and Gelb, 1996).
- Hofstede remains a pioneer in his field.
- The model should be seen as a 'guide' to assist leaders in gaining possible insight into national and regional factors with a country, as well as internationally for multinationals.

- **Pertinence:** a survey is not always the best instrument to measure cultural variations, especially if the value measured is culturally sensitive & subjecyive.
- **Cultural Homogeneity:** Hofstede assumes anations culture is homogenous when in fact cultures are made up of sub-units/groups.
- **National Divisions:** Cutlures are divided, therefore national identities cannot be limited to within one area/border.
- **Political influences:** Masculinity & Uncertainty avoidance values are questionable, as these were done during the cold war era and political instability. Socialist and third world countries were omitted.
- **One company approach:** Critics argue that data sourced through one company only (IBM) cannot be representative and an entire cultural system.
- **Out dated:** The study was done ages ago and not applicable in todays modern, fast changing climate.
- **Limited dimension:** Too few dimensions used to gain sufficient information.
- **Statistical integrity:** Dorfmann & Howell (1988) discovered a repitiion of an identical questionaire item over more than one scale, possibly resulting in inaccuracy.

Figure 8. Adapted from Dorfman & Howell (1988), Hofstede (2001); Hofstede & Minkov (2010) & Safe (2010)

Dorfman & Howell (1988) specifically questioned the statistical accuracy of his research, yet the most common critique, besides the 'one company' IBM approach, is that we are living in a new constantly changing dynamic global culture, making his research outdated. However, Hofstede acknowledged that he never focused on differences within cultures, but on what made them unique, hence he was able to successfully attribute patterns to national differences in culture as he had eliminated the problems of differences in company culture by only researching staff at IBM. Regardless of what the fault finders claim, Hofstede remains the pioneer in this field. He has been cited over 1000 times and clearly researched the most expansive work on culture to date *(Safi 2010)*.

Augmenting Hofstede's work, *O'Reilly, Chatman & Caldwell (1991)* started investigating cultures within an organisation and developed their self reporting Organisational Cultural Profile (OCP) tool that distinguishes between seven categories; Innovation, Stability, Respect for People, Outcome Orientation, Attention to Detail, Team Orientation, and Aggressiveness. Although created to examine the similarity between individual and organisational values, in 2003 it was seen as one of the top ten culture tools *(Judge & Cable 1997; Howard 1988, Agle & Caldwell 1999)*. *Ashkansay, Wilderom & Peterson (2011)* reviewed 18 culture measures published between 1975 to 1992 and found that the OCP came out tops in terms of supplying details regarding reliability and validity.

HANDY & HARRISON TYPOLOGY

POWER CULTURE	ROLE CULTURE	TASK CULTURE	PEOPLE CULTURE
Power in hands of small minority with special perks. Like centre of spider web - closer you are to centre, the more power you have. Autocratic rule of subordinates & no freedom of expression. Lots of rivalry.	Speciality of individual determines delegated role & responsibilities. Staff decide what they are best at takes full ownership of tasks & challenges. high degree of formalisation, rules & procedures. Staff are role occupants.	Focus on teamwork to solve critical problems. Specialists with similar interests work together. All teams contribute equally & are innovative. Like a net - much of the power located in the interstices of the net. Adapts to market needs.	Employees feel they are more important than the organisation and focus on themsleves to the detriment of the company. No loyalty. Consultants & freelance workers fall into this category. Usually specialists who are needed for their expertise.

Figure 9. Adapted from Handy (1976) & Harrison (1972)

Among the best-known and earliest multidimensional typologies are *Harrison (1972)* and *Handy (1976)* whose concepts where created independently, yet are very similar. They saw individuals and organisations as having 'conflicting' interests and postulated that the solutions companies find to resolve this tension, determined their OC. Hence Handy proposed four types of OC, as illustrated in Figure 9 above.

Peters & Waterman (1982) wanted to prove that people are crucial to business success. They studied 43 Fortune 500 top performing companies that led to the development of the McKinsey 7S framework which highlights 'shared values' when analysing how effectively a company is positioned in order to achieve its long-term goals.

Whereas other approaches considered internal and external factors, a combination of both, or even a harmonisation between various aspects, Peters & Waterman focused on aligning and mutually reinforcing these elements in order to improve performance, as in Figure 10. In the 7S framework, a successful company needs all seven internal aspects aligned, while in Johnson & Scholes' Cultural Web the six alignments assist organisations in assessing what is, and is not working, and what needs to be changed *(Peters & Waterman 1982 & Peters 2011)*.

When considering the relationship between OC and economic performance, *Peters & Waterman (1982)* in their book, *'In Search of Excellence'* cited numerous examples contradicting the use of strict bureaucratic policies, red tape and rules. They disagreed with Handy's Power Culture and the adage of treating staff like children with tons of regulations, and constant supervision. They validated this view, sharing numerous 'excellent companies' examples, e.g. Zumwalt who turned around naval productivity with

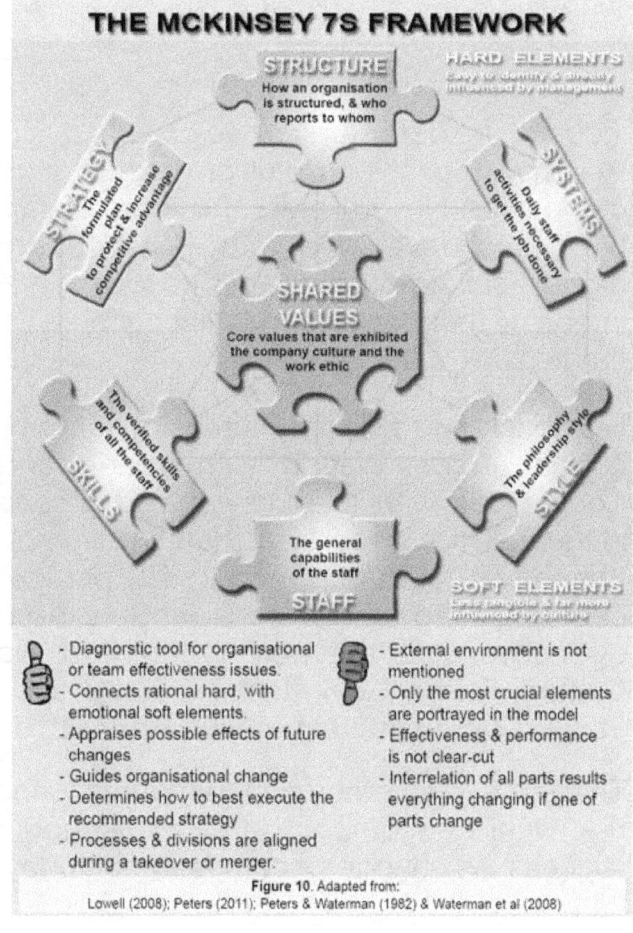

THE MCKINSEY 7S FRAMEWORK

- Diagnorstic tool for organisational or team effectiveness issues.
- Connects rational hard, with emotional soft elements.
- Appraises possible effects of future changes
- Guides organisational change
- Determines how to best execute the recommended strategy
- Processes & divisions are aligned during a takeover or merger.

- External environment is not mentioned
- Only the most crucial elements are portrayed in the model
- Effectiveness & performance is not clear-cut
- Interrelation of all parts results everything changing if one of parts change

Figure 10. Adapted from:
Lowell (2008); Peters (2011); Peters & Waterman (1982) & Waterman et al (2008)

his view that people will resonate well with being treated like adults. They revealed that employees are the primary source of profits ('People-orientated philosophy') and argued that eight common themes define a company's success, Figure 11.

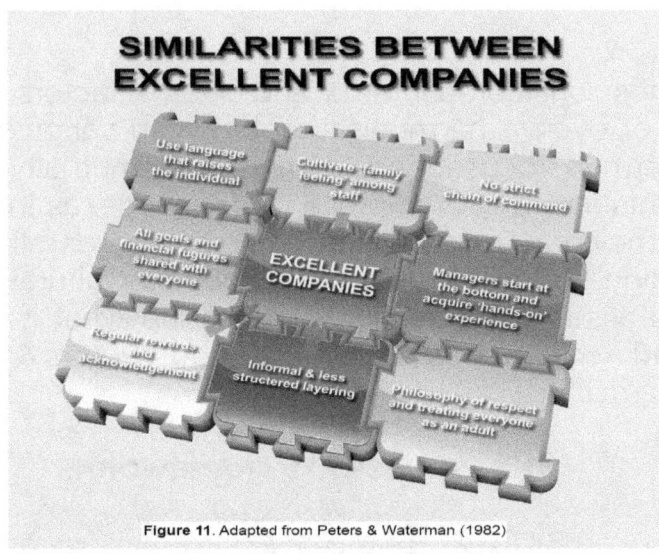

Figure 11. Adapted from Peters & Waterman (1982)

Even though their model was hugely popular in the 1980's, they were severely criticised, as a number of their 'excellent' companies (NCR, Atari & Xerox) did not remain successful. *Chapman (2006)* also complained that most of their excellent companies were established industry leaders. *Rosenzweigh (2007)* similarly criticised Peters & Waterman for their 'delusion' of only studying already 'performing' companies. Nevertheless, for a project that wasn't planned to be a book, and developed with limited budget, it remains one of the biggest selling business books today. In 2001 Peters admitted in an interview that they had mistakenly believed their eight points where timeless.

Feedback and risk are increasingly important when one considers current preoccupation with speed and access to information. Couple this with the view that the social element of work is as influential, if not more so than the financial element, then Deal and Kennedy's cultural model is particularly relevant today in comparison to the previous models discussed. They focus on four distinctive culture types; Work Hard/Play Hard Culture, Process Culture, Tough Guy/Macho Culture and Bet Your Company High Stakes Culture as illustrated in Figure 12 on the following page.

These are affected by two marketplace factors, i. e. the nature of the risk within a company and the speed of feedback in terms of success. As change occurs faster in today's economic environment, their reliance on speedy feedback reinforces the current validity of their model *(Deal & Kennedy 1982 & 2000)*. This is where Handy's model falls short as he make no allowances for this in their four structures. Interestingly, few leaders fall exactly into one of the four culture types that highlight the weakness in using only one of these models *(Bensimon, Neumann & Birnbaum 1989)*.

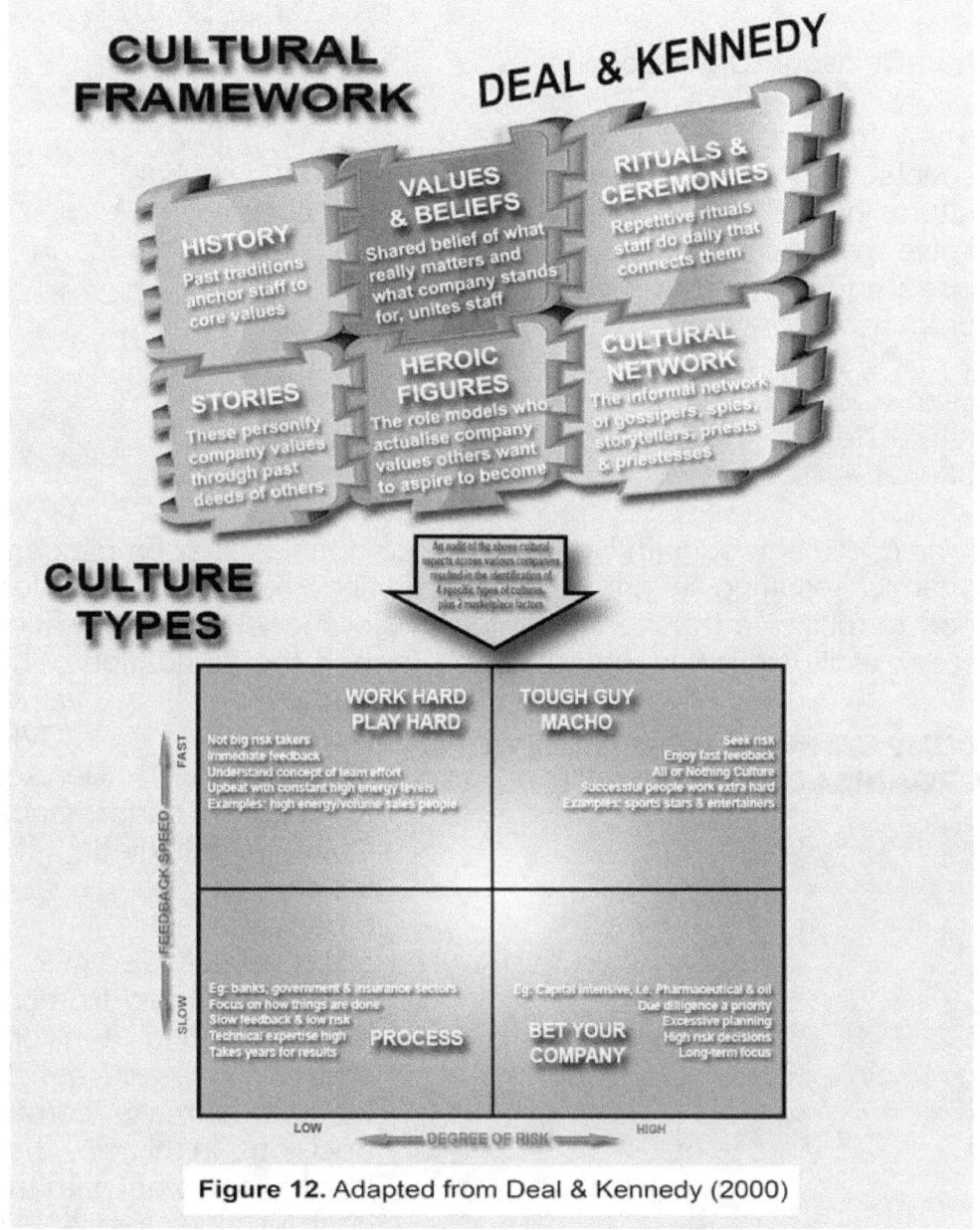

Figure 12. Adapted from Deal & Kennedy (2000)

Hence *Denison, Hooijberg & Quinn's (1995)* shift to emphasise cultural complexity and recognise that most organisations contain some, if not all aspects of the cultural types as proposed by Handy, Deal and Kennedy. Their view asserted that leaders needed to manage and balance this mix in order to assess a company's strengths and weaknesses with regard to performance.

The Denison Organizational Culture Survey (DOCS) has sixty items measuring specific aspects of a company's culture in the four traits and twelve management practices illustrated in Figure 13. In comparison to other models, the DOCS is systematic and acknowledges numerous cultural levers that influence culture *(Denison 2007)*.

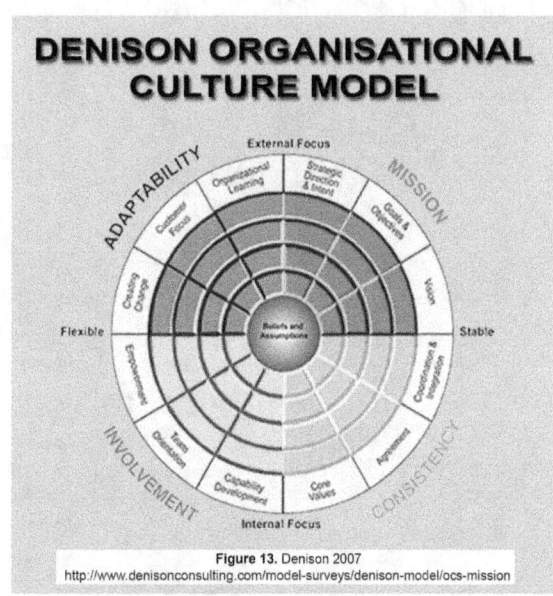

DENISON ORGANISATIONAL CULTURE MODEL

Figure 13. Denison 2007
http://www.denisonconsulting.com/model-surveys/denison-model/ocs-mission

Quinn (1988) agreed with Denison that companies are complex and dynamic, resulting in numerous competing expectations leaders need to fulfil. He thus took the four major models of organisation theory, as illustrated in Figure 14 and formed the foundation of his Competing Values Framework (CVF). Whereas Denison focused on performance, Quinn identified the indicators of organisational effectiveness. Today it is extensively used to focus on competing tensions and conflicts and assists leaders to make correct decisions. In this way they identify and work with the contradictions present in

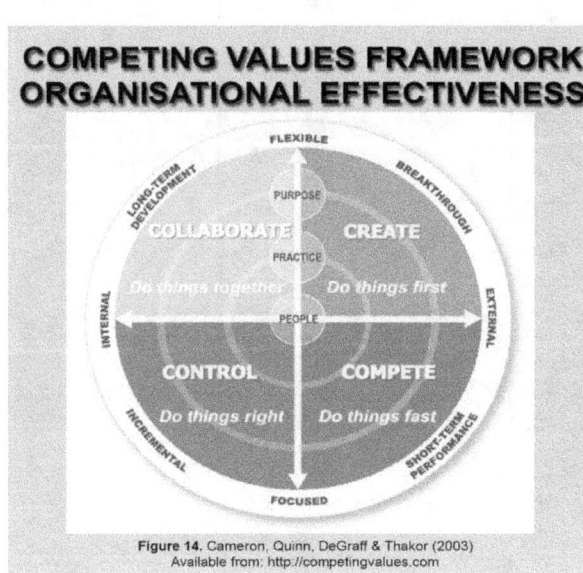

COMPETING VALUES FRAMEWORK ORGANISATIONAL EFFECTIVENESS

Figure 14. Cameron, Quinn, DeGraff & Thakor (2003)
Available from: http://competingvalues.com

a company, thus improving value and effectiveness *(Denison & Spreitzer 1991)*.

Although the CVF assists companies in understanding their culture, and determine effectiveness, it additionally locates their starting point, and predicts possible tensions and trade-offs to be expected when implementing change. This suggests that even the most transformational and innovative organisations have predictable patterns. Interestingly, *Yu & Wu (2009)* argued that although two dimensions may appear to be insufficient to measure OC, the CVF can integrate most OC dimensions suggested by literature, i.e. it sinks everything up.

Besides identifying key values & assumption and allowing leaders to respond to these cues, *Cameron & Quinn (2006)* wanted to further identify an organisation's culture profile. They built on the CVF and developed the Organisational Cultural Assessment Instrument (OCAI). It differs from the CVF in that the OCAI assists companies to identify 'current' and 'preferred future' cultures in order to enable action plans in attaining these changes. Research by Suderman (2012) confirmed where a new leader lacks organisational experience the OCAI provides gainful insights in understanding the past and highlights possible future hurdles.

They advocated a simple six-step process to reach agreement on the current (1) and the desired (2) future culture. From here to identify what these changes will and won't mean (3), followed by reaching an agreement as to defining the current culture (4). Finally a consensus must be reached on the desired future (5) culture and what these changes will and won't mean (6). Figure 15 on the next page clearly illustrates the pros and cons of the four scenarios.

While there are varying schools of thought on changing culture, it is interesting to note that many researchers agree that it is difficult to change, is a long-term project and involves shared responsibility at all levels within the organisation *(Alvesson & Sveningson 2008; Cameron & Quinn 2006; Kotter & Heskett 2011; Pedler, Burgoyne & Boydell 2004)*.

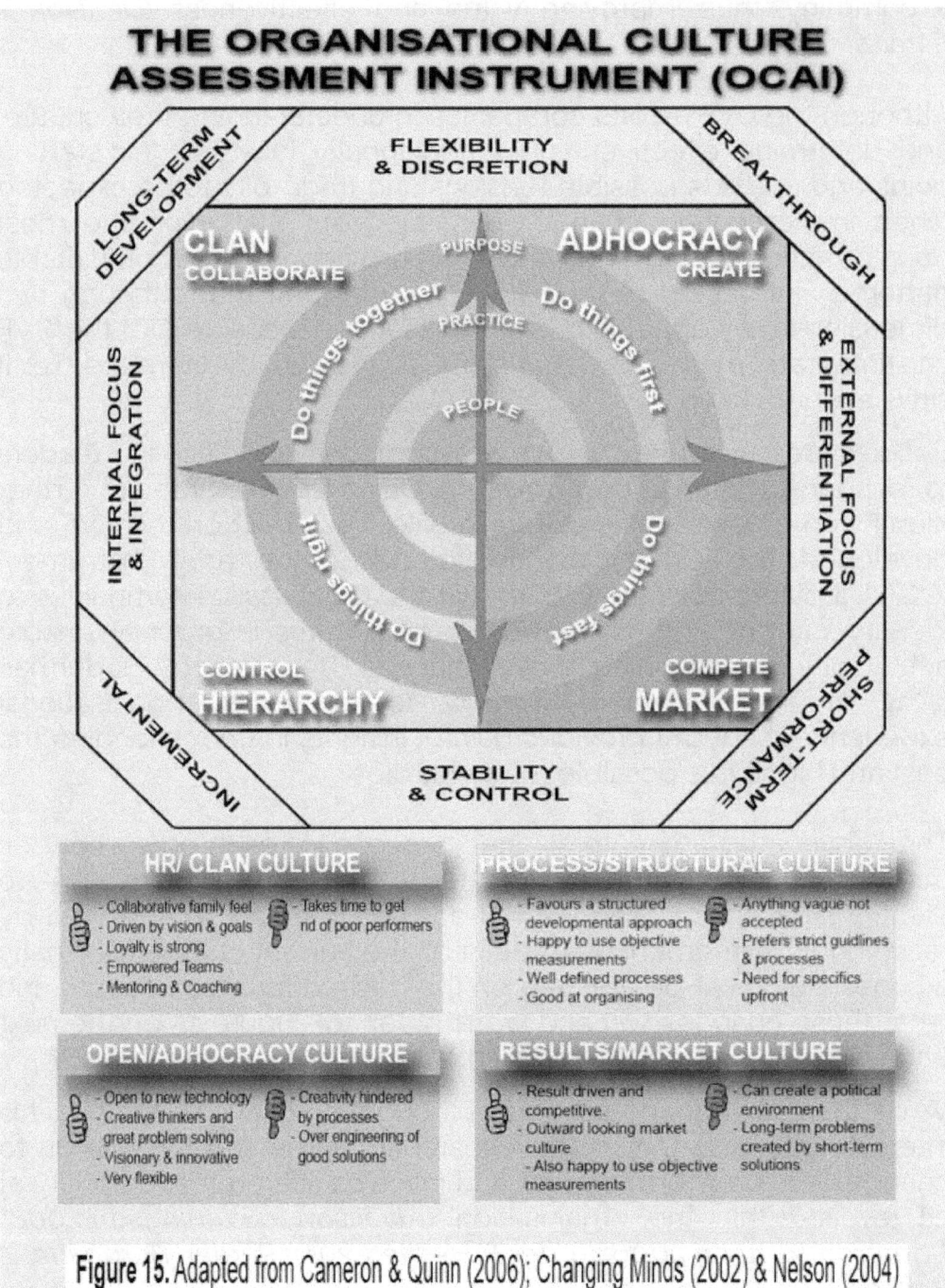

Figure 15. Adapted from Cameron & Quinn (2006); Changing Minds (2002) & Nelson (2004)

Keller & Price (2011) felt that understanding OC leads to the organisation gaining a competitive advantage, whereas *Deal & Kennedy (2000)* together with *Schein (2004)*, suggested that OC enhanced performance and effectiveness of an organisation. However, according to *Kotter & Heskett (2011)* this is very much dependant on the fit between the market characteristics and OC. When it comes to multinational enterprises, the dimensions of Hofstede, Trompenaars & GLOBE have done much in understanding the diversities of cultures and how to better understand the differences in thinking of people in different countries.

3. FORMING & CHANGING CULTURE

3.1 ORGANISATIONAL CULTURE AND LEADERSHIP

Effective communication is imperative in leading organisations today, especially when dealing with international organisations. Language use and non-verbal communication can differ hugely across cultures. Furthermore, praising a leader for sensitivity in one culture preferring a low power difference can be seen as a weakness in another country that prefers a high power difference *(Den Hartog et al 1999)*. Das & *Kumar (2010)* agreed that these 'misunderstandings' can cripple effective collaboration.

This led to *Earley & Ang's (2003)* studies on cultural Intelligence (CQ). Later *Ang & Van Dyne (2008) & Livermore (2009 & 2010)* refined this concept and definition as a leader's capability to operate efficaciously across 'national, ethnic and organisational cultures.' They developed the 4-step cycle of CQ where

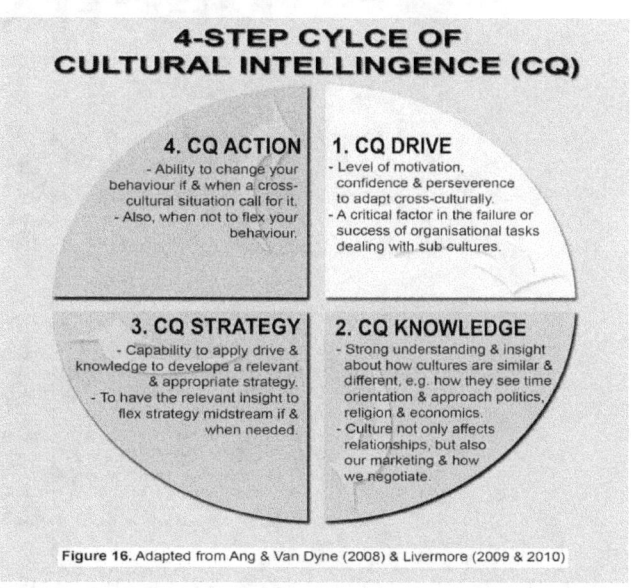

Figure 16. Adapted from Ang & Van Dyne (2008) & Livermore (2009 & 2010)

leaders question CQ; drive, knowledge, strategy & action in order to offer a conduit to effectively navigate the challenges and opportunities awaiting us in culturally diverse organisations today, as illustrated in Figure 16.

Schein (2004) had an alternative view, professing that although culture is a 'shared experience' it results from the leader(s) initially imposing their values & beliefs on an organisation that they start from scratch, Figure 17.

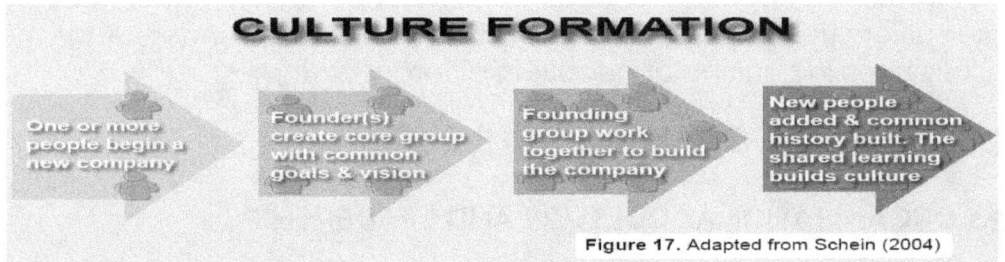

Figure 17. Adapted from Schein (2004)

He further added that a future culture cannot survive if the founder(s) leave and the remaining members are in conflict during this growth period. Hence, *Schein (2004)* emphasised vital primary and secondary-embedding mechanisms to create the future climate as described in Figure 18.

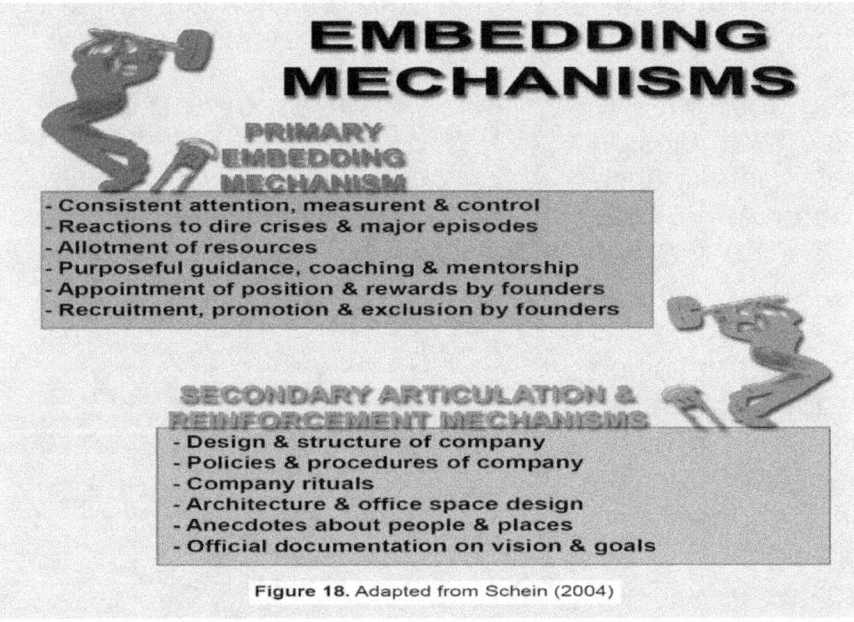

Figure 18. Adapted from Schein (2004)

Similarly, *Kotter & Heskett (2011)* believed that competent leadership was the core factor differentiating success in cultural change from failure. They further differentiated between 'Adaptive (healthy, forward looking and foster positive change) Cultures' and 'Unadaptive (self serving, inward focus and bureaucratic) Culture' that undermines change. They found that a strong organisational

culture leads to increasing long-term economic performance characterised by:
-        Adaptive managers who care about customers, stakeholders and staff;
-        Place high value on people and processes that foster useful change;
-        Accept risks associated with change, while still focusing on customers needs.

        Conversely, a negative culture takes time to develop and is characterised by managers who are:
-        Self-serving and favour risk reduction;
-        Display arrogance, political favouritism and see their traditions   as superior;
-        Prone to find difficulty in taking advantage of changes.

They identified the origins of this unhealthy culture as a lack in outside focus and leadership, while inwardly hiring and promoting managers. This pressure on management is internal and fosters arrogance and a resistance to change.

3.2 ORGANISATIONAL CULTURE AND INNOVATION

Amabile (1998) wrote that creativity could only lead to innovation if it responds to, and solves a customer's needs, i.e. it must be appropriate. According to *Amabile et al (1996, p. 1154)*, *"All innovation begins with creative ideas."* However, they postulate that strict control and productivity regulations in companies discourage a desire for creativity, thus innovation is more often destroyed than encouraged. Interestingly, *Busco et al (2012)* disagreed in principal, suggesting that organisations should have a 'twofold purposeful imbalance at work'; firstly between creativity and control and secondly between the *"various elements of a package of controls where formal (results control) and informal (social control) mechanisms help manage the concurrent and ongoing need for creative design and efficient production processes"* (Busco et al 2012, p. 36).

Gottfredson & Aspinall (2005) offered an interesting argument, adding that complexity destroys innovation and profits, and referred to an 'innovation fulcrum' - the amount of products/services that optimise both income and profits. Therefore overoptimistic sales forecasts, misleading economic date, entrenched leadership assumptions and extensive product choices need to be streamlined.

On analysing the 1356 results of the Innovation Survey conducted by the American Management Association and Human Resources Institute in 2005, *Jamrog, Vickers & Bear (2006)* found that customers and their satisfaction, was the predominating driver of business innovation. However, this alone does not guarantee an innovation; companies also need resources, teamwork, autonomy, risk-tolerance and other qualities as in Figure 19.

EXHIBIT 1		
Factors for Developing an Innovative Culture, by Rank		
Factors	Today	In 10 Years
Customer focus	1	1
Teamwork/collaboration with others	2	2
Appropriate resources (time and money)	3	6
Organizational communication	4	3
Ability to select right ideas for research	5	4
Ability to identify creative people	6	5
Freedom to innovate	7	7
Ability to measure results of innovation	8	8
Encouraging both small ideas and big ideas	9	9
Innovation accountability/goals	10	10
Culture of risk-tolerance	11	12
Organizational structures	12	11
Diversity	13	13
Balancing incremental improvements and breakthrough discoveries	14	14

Figure 19. Jamrog, Vickers & Bear (2006)

It would appear that the CVF is an appropriate model to create positive tension, through diverse groups between all four quadrants by placing the right suitable individuals into appropriate quadrants in order to produce the right type of innovation that the organisation is looking for.

4. ORGANISATIONAL POLITICS

Plato is believed to have said, *"One of the penalties for refusing to participate in politics, is that you end up being governed by your inferiors" (Wikiquote 2014). Peters (1994)* stated that in order to achieve anything in life, you need to learn to 'love' politics. Furthermore he simultaneously suggested that one should never squander time worrying about it, instead one should get in, sell the idea, build support and get on with it. He viewed organisational politics as relationship building coupled with trust. In contrast, *Mintzberg (1985)* negatively described politics as being 'illegitimate' behaviour in contrast to expertise and officially sanctioned formal structures. He further described four possible political arenas:

1.   An all-inclusive political arena defined by rivalry that is all-out and omnipresent.
2.   The showdown where the clash is all-out but contained.
3.   An unstable partnership where the strife is tolerable yet contained.
4.   The politicised company where the strife is tolerable, but omnipresent.

Mintzberg further cited *Allison (1971)* who aptly described political hustle as 'games' and identified thirteen moves as in Figure 20 on the next page.

Figure 20. Adapted from Mintzberg (1985) & Changing Minds (2002)

Buchanan & Badham (2008) were very much in alignment with Mintzberg's views and referred to this political game as 'backstaging', but they also argued that not all politics is underhand. However they did profess that a 'squeaky clean' self-righteous attitude is naïve and that today one has to be prepared and equipped to effectively handle power plays within organisations.

In South Africa, with the implementation of Black Economic Empowerment (BEE) and organisations focusing on employing only previously disadvantage people after 1994, a completely new arena with it's associated complexities emerged *(Albertyn 2001; Griffiths & Prozesky 2010 & Steyn & Foster 2008).*

Baddely & James (1987) developed a two dimensional descriptive model (Figure 21), focusing on 'reading' the politics within a company and identifying the skills people bring into a situation - whether it is behaving with integrity or feigning the psychological game. Although these two dimensions are closely unified they enable us to distinguish four types of behaviour, namely, innocent, inept, clever and wise.

Figure 21. Adapted from Baddeley & James (1987)

Buchanan & Badham (2008) described various mainstream political tactics (i.e. build friendships with power brokers and key players) used to bring about political change, to lesser-known unprincipled tactics lacking integrity (i.e. misinformation and blaming others). *Yukl (2010)* delved further into the subject, questioning whether the tactics are in line with current player's role, position of influence, return on investment, predicted contention and relevance of the change. He explained the use of proactive influence tactics and divides them into two groups (Figure 22), namely core tactics (Rational persuasion, inspirational appeals, consultation & collaboration) and supplementary tactics (Apprising, exchange, integration, legitimating, personal appeal, pressure and coalition) and further states, *"Whether a combination of two or more tactics is better than a single tactic depends on what tactics are combined. The effectiveness of a combination seems to depend in part on the potency of the individual tactics and how compatible they are with each other" (Yukl 2010, p. 230).*

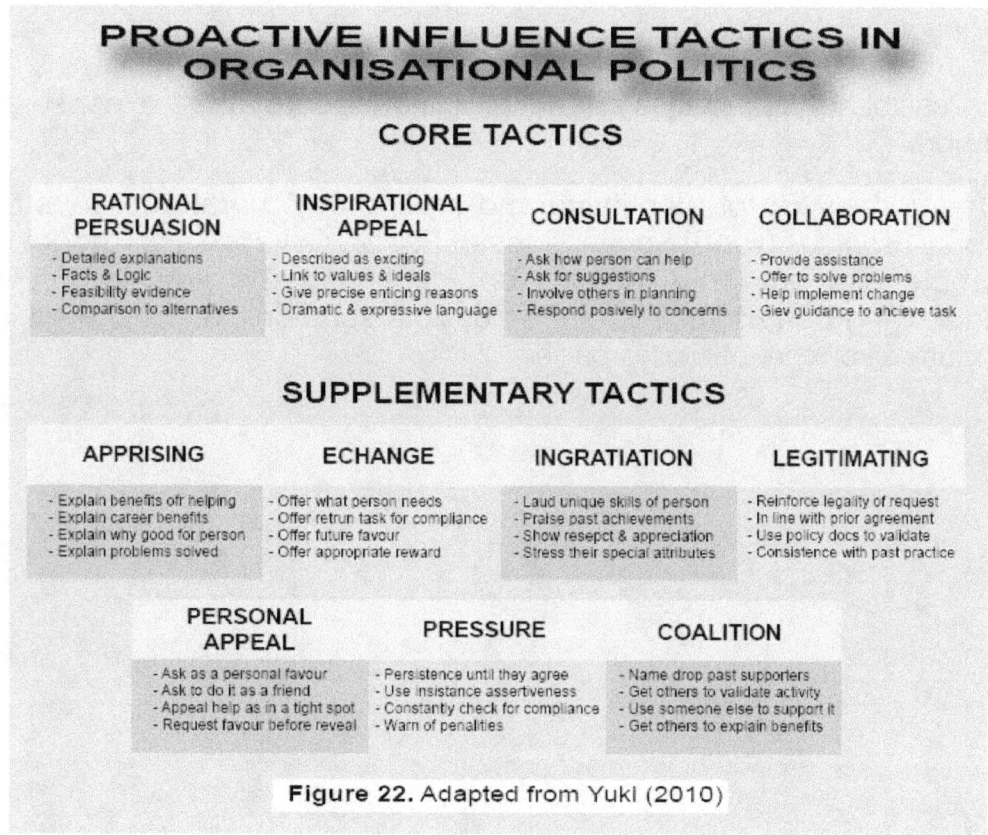

Figure 22. Adapted from Yukl (2010)

5. ETHICS

Wikipedia (2014) simplistically defined ethical leadership as knowing what the right thing to do is. However an immediate question that comes to mind is, "What is right or wrong?" *Yukl (2010)* also viewed identifying what is morally justifiable as a dilemma. When studying individuals, cultures, religions and countries that each have differing views, this task becomes a huge challenge. Additionally, leadership needs to base their "... *decisions in a way that satisfies not only their own consciences but also the objections of other people affected by a given decision*" (Stansbury 2009, p. 33).

Yukl (2010) further explained that leadership is about influencing others to change their behaviour, and questions whether this behaviour is always ethical. His reasoning being that the interests of the leader and company may:

a. Not be in alignment with the values and beliefs of the followers.

b. Involve risky actions.

c. Possibly benefit only a certain group of people at the expense of others.

One framework for identifying and solving any moral decline is to apply *Jennings (2006)* Seven Signs of Ethical Collapse. Her model is simple and not only focuses on identifying the source of the underlying behaviour, but offers possible solutions, as illustrated in Figure 23 on the following page.

JENNINGS' 7 SIGNS OF ETHICAL COLLAPSE

	PRESSURE TO MAINTAIN THE NUMBERS	FEAR & SILENCE	YOUNG 'UNS & BIGGER THAN LIFE CEO	WEAK BOARDS
PRESSURES	- The pressure to attain targets coupled with poor ethics.	- Employees can see the problem, but are afraid to lose their job so they remain silent.	- 'Yes men' and staff that 'suck-up' to leaders, plus very charismatic strong CEO's.	- Could be a friendship clique, lacking in experience, or conflicts of interest and age.
SOLUTIONS	- Get rid (fire) unethical staff. - Watch for verbal & non verbal signs and rectify. - When staff in difficut situations, allow time out to rectify this.	- Encourage openess and provide a hotline to report fraud. - Never fire staff for identifying unethical behaviour. - Rewards discovery of illegal activities.	- Keep an eye on charismatic leaders. - Monitor hiring & firing as well as replacements. - Have ethical mentorship for young 'uns.	- Challenge decisions & results. - Insist on a 'strong' board. - Investigates perks of board members. - Investigate dicrepencies among board members.

	CONFLICTS	INNOVATION LIKE NO OTHER COMPANY	GOODNESS IN SOME AREAS ATONES FOR EVIL IN OTHERS
PRESSURES	- Conflicts resulting from favouritism & nepotism.	- The belief that you are simply the best and normal rules don't apply to you.	- The consistent belief that you are good due to constant recognition of good deeds.
SOLUTIONS	- Have conflict policies in place and enforce them. - Always stick to the rules. - Keep an eye on ownership and interrelationships. - Choose to either manage or not manage the conflict.	- Recognise limitations. - Never forget the basics of economics. - Stay clear of Group Think. - Focus on candor & honesty.	- Start thinking differently about social responsibility. - Explore current community involvement. - Practice skepticism of social responsibility & philanthropy

- Identifies 7 issues to be aware of in detecting ethical contraventions.
- Supplies possible solutions to resolve ethical issues.
- Directed at identifying the source of the underlying behaviour.
- Simple and clear model to apply.

- Doesn't identify the 'grey' areas.
- Culture still dependant on individual character of leaders.
- May have to change the macro-ethical culture in the financial reporting.
- Don't be naive to think that this is an easy task - very difficult to do!

Figure 23. Adapted from Jennings (2006)

6. PRACTICAL EXAMPLE

6.1 INTRODUCTION

Johnson (2001, p. 314) highlighted that *"Culture is often seen as a barrier to change."* Hofstede *(2014)* stated, *"Culture is more often a source of conflict than of synergy. Cultural differences are a nuisance at best and often a disaster."* The Globe project's Anglo Culture distinctive separate cluster for white South Africans and the Sub-Saharan Africa cluster for black South Africans could well support this view. Eleven official languages and turmoil rich political past and present - cultural and political issues are the norm in business for anyone living in South Africa. Although a controversial topic, even 21 years after apartheid, I would like to say that I have broadened my understanding, impacted my leadership skills, and learnt to positively influence my circumstances, regardless of the history and political influences within a company and country. Sadly, my personal experience has shown me that even if the leader is open to change, it is of no avail if the staff are not of the same mindset.

6.2 BACKGROUND

A large financial services provider in the country, and government's main policy provider, had religiously implemented and also been severely impacted by the Black Economic Empowerment (BEE) regulations in South Africa, as discussed in the previous chapter. As brand ambassador and part of the start-up team of their new multi-level marketing project in the mass market segment, unbeknown to me, the 'Assumptions and Beliefs' *(Schein 2004)* were severely deeply ingrained and our new MLM was in complete contradiction to the stifled stiff trusted reputation of established powerhouse organisation as highlighted in Figure 24.

Additio*nally this company displayed a classic Power Culture* (Handy 1976) in that a small group of executives controlled everything. They had their own 'executive floor' and were always too busy to listen to concerns of their teams, resulting in extreme rivalry and backstabbing within the managerial ranks.

SCHEIN'S 3 LEVELS OF CULTURE

ARTIFACTS	EXPOSED VALUES	ASSUMPTIONS & BELIEFS
Observable behaviour... - Powerful company - Trusted brand - Interntaional footprint - Massive buildings - National offices - Market leader - 169 Year history - Part of SA culture - The top brand - Slogans everywhere - Recognisable colours	- We do things our way - Not really into change - We are the best, hence we don't negotiate. - You do business on our terms - We look after our staff from internal shopping malls, sports clubs to training - Very focused on BEE & meeting government's tranformational targets	- Head office moved to London to escape political pressure & instability of SA market - Hence two differing national cultures - Built up on old apartheid beliefs - attempts to create 180 degree turnaround resulting in unrealistic and biased behaviour towards the 'new' - Unchanging, rigid, infelxible hierarchical structures

Figure 24. Adapted from Schein (1990 & 2004)

6.3 MY NEGATIVE EXAMPLE OF ORGANISATIONAL CULTURE

If one looks at *Schein's (2004)* six steps to cultural change, a sense of urgency (step 1) had been reached as the short-term insurance market sector was taking strain. Sadly, the covert culture (Assumptions & Beliefs) was further influenced by *Kotter & Hesket's (2011)* Unadaptive (self serving, inward focus and bureaucratic) Culture' that undermined change. Managers displayed arrogance, political favouritism and saw their traditions as superior. If anything, Marvin Bower's phrase of *'the way we do things around here'* was arrogantly, shockingly and successfully ingrained into the internal mindset at all levels of staff.

They believed their traditions were superior and their managers were put into a project team to assist in developing this channel. Additionally, they insisted that during the pilot phase all decisions where 'shared' between the new department head and this internal project team. Even though the channel head had requested his own founding team with experience in MLM, this internal project team looked down on the advice shared by the outsiders, with typical unadaptive remarks such as, *"This is company A and we do things our way!"* A perfect example of being self serving and avoiding any risk *(Kotter & Heskett 2011)*.

Amongst the lower economic sector in South Africa (the target market of this channel) funeral policies had always been the money-spinner, due to the high incidence of HIV & AIDS. By linking the most trusted brand in the country with the MLM concept and offering these individuals an opportunity to earn money from their policies, this was a 'no-brainer' in terms of becoming hugely successful. I was positive and believed that 'Rational Persuasion' *(Yukl 2010)* would work to turn the project team and executive leadership team. Not once did I ever imagine that ingrained beliefs and forced autocratic leadership compelled the project team to do it the 'old' way.

My first warning came when the proposed payment gateway was adapted to their old 'established' system, rather than the suggestions of the new external founding team. In MLM one debit order incorporates a policy and business support fee. The internal/IT processes then filters the correct amounts to the relevant departments. This organisation was not prepared to adapt their payment system. Members with limited incomes suddenly received two separate deductions within a month! Numerous meetings with the IT and project teams were fruitless. *Kotter & Heskett's (2011)* self serving explanation stood strong.

An analysis of this organisation on *Deal & Kennedy's (1982)* model typically fitted into the 'Process' culture where the focus is on slow feedback and implementation of systems. Being accustomed to working independently, or with privately owned companies where decisions were made then and there, this became hugely challenging. Promises made to launch on a specific date where continually delayed and systems were never put in place.

Peters & Waterman's (1982) research clearly indicated that excellent companies focus on appointing proper qualified people who are up to the job. Sadly, on top of deeply ingrained traditions, excessive BEE pressures from government made this virtually impossible. Very much in contradiction to *Collins' (2001)* 'First Who, The What' philosophy!

Couple this with huge barriers (bureaucratic policies and red tape) around every corner, characterised by a predominant all inclusive political arena defined by rivalry that was all-out and omnipresent *(Mintzberg 1985)*, the channel head and his original founding members still managed to surpass all predicted sales figures by attaining the annual target within three months, further reinforcing the potential of channel. Shockingly, the project was closed down a year later with senior executives officially stating that this channel did not align with the organisations broader business approach.

6.4 LESSONS LEARNT

Having personally experienced that changing a culture is definitely not an easy task *(Schein 2004)* I now will never accept an offer before doing thorough research into the OC of a company. In order to fully comprehend S*chein's (2004)* third level of Beliefs and Assumptions, plus *Hofstede's (2010)* 'Values' I would start by using *Johnson, Scholes & Whittington's (2008)* cultural web. Had I just answered one question under each element, it would have immediately brought up red flags with Company A.

Pedler, Burgoyne & Boydell's (2004) views that change only occurs when many people change their behaviour rings very true. Additionally, understanding that it takes a lot of time *(Holbeche 2006) now* makes perfect sense. However, the pinnacle issue here is that one person may find it virtually impossible to create change. *Alvesson & Sveningsson (2008)* most insightfully highlight that top management has to start the process and that 'shared values' *(Peters & Waterman, 1982)* need to be fostered in order to create forward movement.

Suderman's (2012) research indicated that for new leaders lacking research, the OCAI provides much needed insights. Analysing *Cameron & Quinn's (2006)* OCAI instrument online, it became clearly evident that Hierarchy Control and a Collaborative Clan culture predominated within Company A, as in Figure 25 on the following page.

Additionally in South Africa, the current political, racial and economic turmoil has created an inept *(Baddeley & James, 1987)* donkey culture within most large organisations, particularly government departments, adding a dimension not experienced in other countries. This augments *Jennings (2006)* first two of his seven signs of ethical collapse in that there is a pressure to maintain numbers based on racial quotas. Additionally white South Africans are afraid to lose their jobs – therefore remain fearful and silent, thus condoning the reverse racist behaviour *(Albertyn 2011; Griffiths & Prozesky 2010 & Steyn & Foster 2008).*

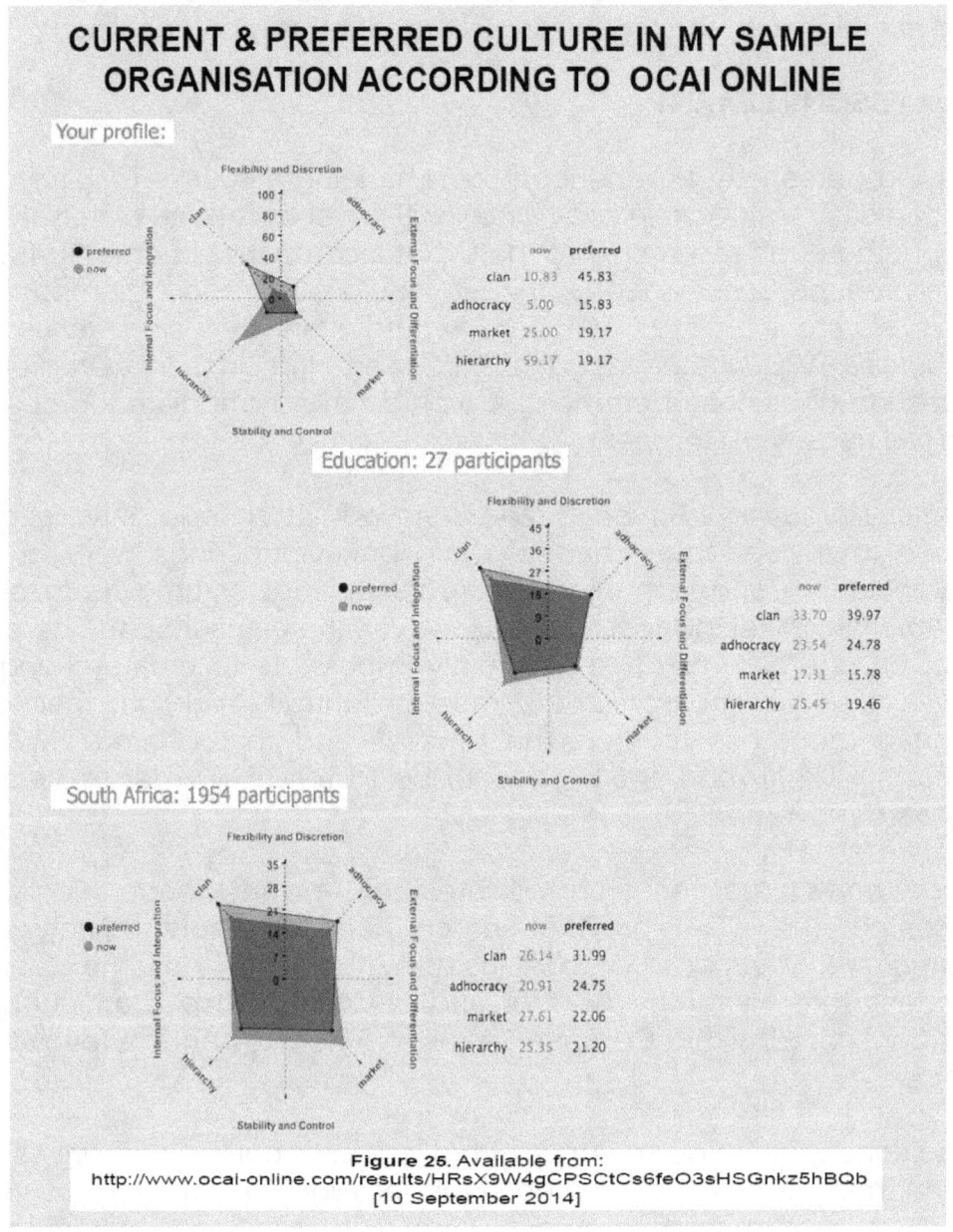

Figure 25. Available from:
http://www.ocai-online.com/results/HRsX9W4gCPSCtCs6feO3sHSGnkz5hBQb
[10 September 2014]

6.5 RECOMMENDATIONS

Today my focus would be on organisational effectiveness by beginning with using the Competing Values Framework to identify the tensions and conflicts, as a starting point for implementing the change. Working as a unified team with shared interests was the leading overall problematic issue in my example. Hence my focus would shift on moving away from the control and competing dimensions with the intention of bringing about collaboration. Politically I would strive to be the owl *(Baddely & James, 1987)* and focus on win-win situations to gain support. Figure 25 displays the OCAI results for company A and clearly illustrates that change is needed to occur from a hierarchy structure to a clan structure.

I am in total agreement with *Schein (2004)* and *Cameron & Quinn (2006)* that culture is a group activity and can only be changed within the context of a particular organisational strategy. Hence it concludes me to believe that in future, my first plan of action when I join a company would be to; Firstly negotiate the terms of my contract and retain full control over my staff so that executives do not move known trouble-makers into my team. Secondly, to develop new training and social programs to align my team with the preferred values and beliefs of my department, and finally to promote employees on all levels who walk the talk and live the desired culture n order to generate support from the rest of the team *(Alvesson & Sveningsson, 2008)*.

7. CONCLUSION

Changing organisational culture is a massively difficult process and affected by many factors. If you are considering an innovation or new job - first ask three questions relating to culture:

1.   What is currently going on 'inside' this organisation?
2.   What are the past experiences of the culture?
3.   What do I need to change?

Only at this point can the leader assess what needs to be done, plan realistic and often, long-term goals with the aim of changing the thinking of the people within that organisation to align with future plans *(Alvesson & Sveningsson, 2008; Cameron & Quinn (2006)*.

"If you immediately judge people according to their religion, race or culture, then the only problem lies with you."

(Wolfgang Riebe)

CHAPTER 5
THE ESSENCE OF LEADERSHIP

INTRODUCTION

"The biggest risk is not taking any risk... In a world that changing really quickly, the only strategy that is guaranteed to fail is not taking risks."

(Mark Zuckerberg)

This chapter covers a critical evaluation of the role leaders play in influencing innovation and change within an organisation, as well as critically evaluates various leadership theories and models, including theories of motivation, team roles and group behaviour.

To summarise, a case study of a senior executive is explored within a large multi-national company and critically assessed in relation to the various theories and models analysed within this chapter. In conclusion and overview of the learning is discussed in terms of analysing and improving the particular leadership style of the case study.

1. A CRITICAL EVALUATION OF THE ROLE OF LEADERS IN INFLUENCING INNOVATION AND CHANGE IN ORGANISATIONS

1.1 INTRODUCTION

Leadership has been studied since Egyptian times and the concept of charismatic leadership has evolved since '0' BC to the organisational leadership approaches of the modern world today as in Figure 1 *(Paul et al 2002)*.

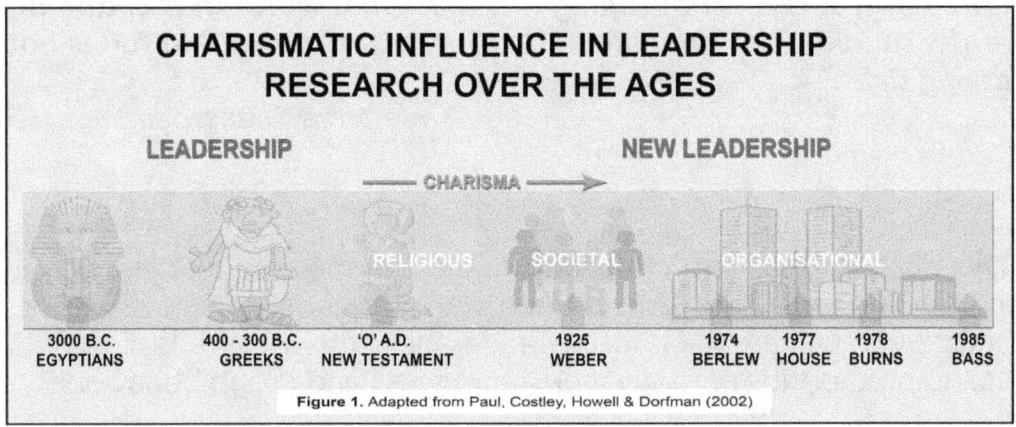

Figure 1. Adapted from Paul, Costley, Howell & Dorfman (2002)

1.2 WHAT IS LEADERSHIP?

There are many schools of thought; one views leadership as individuals who hold senior posts within large organisations, from churches, governments, blue chip companies to the military. Another defines it as a 'certain quality' select individuals posses that differentiates them from others *(Silva 2014)*. However, senior positions in large organisations can also be managerial posts, and this lead to the controversial debate of how management & leadership differ. Both Kotter (1990) and Zaleznik (1977, 1992 & 2004) acknowledged many similarities and describe leaders as individuals who harvest organisational change, whereas managers actualise predictability and alignment. Figure 2 illustrates comparative views of leadership versus management. In later years, *Kotter (1999)* even described most companies in the United States as over-managed and under-led.

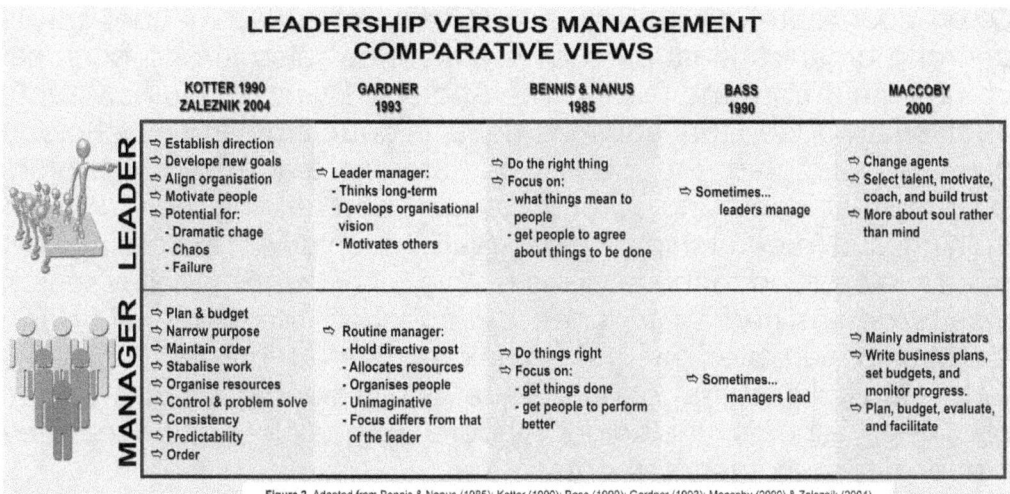

Figure 2. Adapted from Bennis & Nanus (1985); Kotter (1990); Bass (1990); Gardner (1993); Maccoby (2000) & Zaleznik (2004)

According to *Yukl (2010)* individuals cannot be placed in a 'one size fits all' paradigm, there are too many complexities and over-lapping characteristics. Therefore in the context of this chapter, *House et al (1999, p. 184)* fittingly defined leadership as, *"the ability of an individual to influence, motivate, and enable others to contribute toward the effectiveness and success of the organisation..."* Bennis & Nanus (1997, p. 31) summed it up masterfully when they wrote, *"The management of meaning, mastery of communication, is inseparable from effective leadership."*

1.3 ARE LEADERS MADE OR BORN?

Debate on this topic has been immense! Although *Ruvolo, Petersen & LeBoeuf (2004)* believed that leaders are born, they still believed that companies must foster an organisational culture of leadership development and activities cemented in a structured plan of developmental theories and doctrines. *Avolio (2006)* concurred, additionally believing leadership qualities to be genetic and impossible to learn. *Teng Kok (2013)* further added that born leaders display that extra 'will' to lead. Research done by *Brotherton (2013)* of more than 300 C-level executives found that 52% of subjects believed that leaders are made through experience and developmental opportunities. Interestingly the 48% 'borns' in this research believed that companies should target those people whom current leaders believe will benefit from the development.

Olson (2009) agreed with *Brotherton (2013)*, yet added that not only is a strong organisational process required, but also strong personal commitment from the leader. The *Strategic Direction Journal* (2008) additionally added that advancements in education and psychology have disentangled the guesswork around leadership, therefore realising that identifying potential leaders and guiding them through training and mentorship is what really counts. An absorbing, yet plausible addition to these views is *Arvey et al (2006)* - their research results determined that genetics influenced the personality and leadership variables by 30%. Their expanded model (Figure 3) further postulated that genetic variations in people affect a variety of career aspects, including leadership qualities influenced by personality and other elements.

EXPANDED MODEL OF GENETIC INFLUENCES ON WORK RELATED VARIABLES

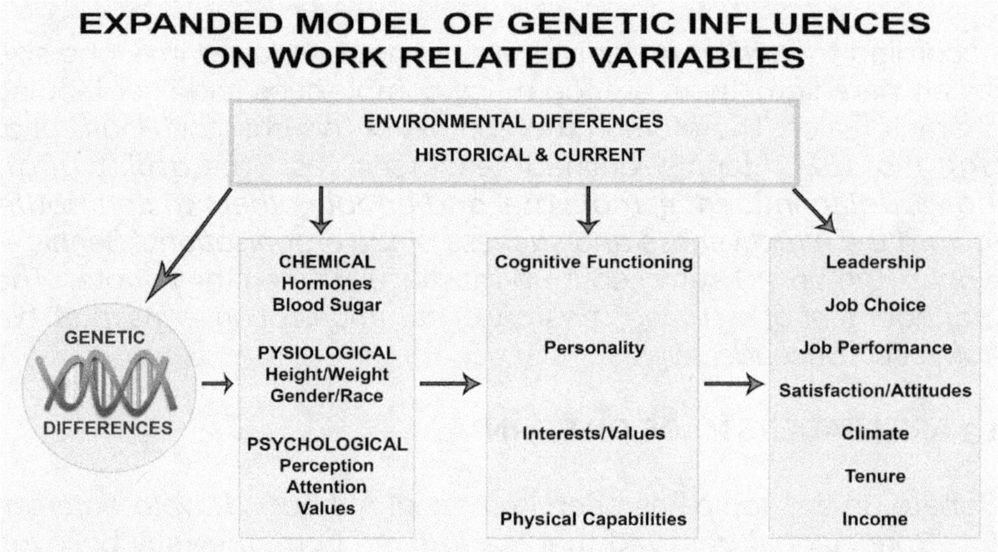

Figure 3. Adapted from Arvey, Rotundo, Johnson, Zhang & McGue (2006)

Whether you believe leadership qualities to be genetic and impossible to learn, or influenced by personality and other elements *(Arvey et al 2006; Avolio 2006; Brotherton 2013; Olson 2009 & Ruvolo, Petersen & LeBoeuf 2004 & Teng Kok 2013)*, *Gladwell (2008)* in his book, 'Outliers' investigated the reason for high levels of success amongst leaders and proposed two additional variables; namely the '10 000-hour rule' - where successful leaders have spent at least 10 000 hours on a specific task, hence they are champions at it. He specifically mentioned Bill Gates who as a child at the age of 13 had access to his High School computer and spent years, plus at least

10 000 hours programming on it. Besides the hours, computers were not commonplace at the time; hence he questioned whether Bill Gates would have achieved the same success, had this not occurred in his youth. The second variable is timing, and Gladwell shared an observation that Canadian hockey players born in the first few months of a year had a physical advantage of those born in the later months, hence their predominance as elite players. He further discussed the timing of Bill Gates and Steve Jobs (and others) births as falling into an 'advantageous' period. He objectively questioned whether they would have reached the same success, had they been born in a different period and leaves the reader contemplating that besides genetics, work influence/experience, advantageous upbringing and inheritance, maybe just plain luck could also play a role.

1.4 MUST LEADERS BE MORALLY DECENT?

Jim Collins (2005, p. 137) according to his 5 levels of leadership asserted that, *"Good-to-great transformations don't happen without level five leaders at the helm."* His example of Darwin Smith's, stunning turnaround of Kimberly-Clark is a classic 'good to great' example. Coleman Mockler (past CEO of Gillette), Abraham Lincoln and George Cain (past CEO of Abbot Laboratories are spot on examples. As a change management keynoter and someone that has trained and spoken for hundreds of blue chip companies, personally I am smitten by Collins' direct, simplistic and yet insightful research findings. I conquer fully with his views and over

5 QUALITY LEVELS OF LEADERSHIP

LEVEL 5 EXECUTIVE
Builds lasting greatness through an intricate blend of personal humility and professional will

LEVEL 4 EFFECTIVE LEADER
Active committment, high performance standards and a dedicated pursuit of a clear vision

LEVEL 3 COMPETENT MANAGER
Effective coordination of people and resources to efficiently achieve planned objectives

LEVEL 2 CONTRIBUTING TEAM MEMBER
Contributes individual talents towards group objectives and works well with others

LEVEL 1 HIGHLY CAPABLE INDIVIDUAL
Adds beneficial contributions through skills, knowledge, talent and great work habits

Figure 4. Adapted from Collins (2001)

28 years have personally experienced the powerful effect of humble, inspired and ethical leaders, compared to power hungry junkies. His conclusion that placing people who lack level 5 qualities in leadership positions is the leading reason so few companies move from good to great, makes perfect sense, especially if you follow his conjecture of, "*First who... then what*".

It is only when the leader has 'the right seed' (qualities) that greatness will prevail. Sadly, the ego driven, attention seeking CEO's have, and may always be those in the limelight and on the cover of Forbes because of their strong personalities. Yet I agree with Collins that his level five qualities of a leader will always be the key component that grows an organisation from good to great *(Collins 2001)*.

George (2005) also concurred with Collins, stating that the mainstream media lauds ego driven leaders that others try to mimic, rather than focus on the most important character of a leader, namely authenticity. Similarly *Higgs (2003)* and *Alimo-Metcalfe & Alban-Metcalfe (2006)* advocated five personal qualities of successful leaders, and both agreed that integrity, honesty and consistency are paramount. *Avolio & Luthans (2006)* added that the current ever changing, complex and turbulent world has shifted leadership relevance to that of authenticity in order to achieve meritorious results, and promote their authentic leadership development (ALD) framework to expedite authenticity in leaders. They believed that unnecessary attention is wasted on negative issues, which overshadows potential positive moments - in a sense similar and parallel to Collins' "F*irst who... then what*" approach.

Authenticity in itself is no new concept with its origins in Greek mythology. Even humanist psychologist, *Abraham Maslow (1908 - 1970)* defined it as '*being aware of the inner self*' and understood that such individuals tend to make objective self-actualising choices rather than 'following' the masses in opinion *(Maslow 1993)*. *Longenecker (2014)* asserted that administrators and managers have taken a back seat, while the focus has shifted to effective leaders that can transform the organisation and its people. After studying 100 focus groups researchers complied the 12 best practices of a leader as briefly summarised in Figure 4 below (*Longenecker, 2014*).

12 BEST PRACTICES OF GREAT LEADERS

- is driven by the mission and results
- makes people their priority
- has a great game
- is prepared for battle
- clarifies efficiency expectations and empowers people
- is trustworthy and transparent
- builds teams and fosters cooperation
- A GREAT LEADER
- is a great coach who celebrates successes
- is a time and resource steward
- creates & maintains a work-life balance
- brings the passion and 'mojo'
- makes it easier to get work done

Figure 5. Adapted from Longenecker (2014)

Goleman (1996) added another dimension to leadership, as emphasised by Collins & Longenecker, postulating that leaders need to prioritise focusing their attention on the task at hand, without being distracted. Research revealed that we use various neural pathways simultaneously while executing diverse tasks, hence successful leaders need to develop a trilogy of cognition that include a focus on the inner self, on others and a broader outward focus.

2. A CRITICAL REVIEW OF LEADERSHIP THEORIES & MODELS

Initially the 1840's 'Great Man Theory' popularised by *Carlyle (1888)* professed that people were born with ingrained characteristics that made them natural leaders, and as the title suggests, were fundamentally male and military focused. However, in 1860 Herbert Spencer *(Carneiro 1981)* argued that these 'great men' were products of their societies whose actions were not possible without the social conditions created before their existence.

LEADERSHIP TRAITS & SKILLS
(Stodgill 1974)

TRAITS

- Adaptable to situations
- Alert to social environment
- Ambitious and achievement-orientated
- Assertive
- Cooperative
- Decisive
- Dependable
- Dominant (desire to influence others)
- Energetic (high activity level)
- Persistent
- Self-confident
- Tolerant of stress
- Willing to assume responsibility

SKILLS

- Clever (intelligent)
- Conceptually skilled
- Creative
- Diplomatic and tactful
- Fluent in speaking
- Knowledgeable about group task
- Organised (administrative ability)
- Persuasive
- Socially skilled

- Numerous traits were identified and it was found that there were no specific traits that occured consistently.
- Repitition of traits occured, but results are ultimarely inconclusive.
- During 1930's & 40's hundreds of studies took place, but failed to find any traits that guaranteed success.

- Common approach used in the military for identiying commissioned officers, and still used today.
- A number of traits did appear frequently, 'charisma' having been explored the most.
- Recent research focuses on traits (values) that characterise ethical leadership.

Figure 6. Adapted from Bolden et al (2003); Stogdill (1974) & Yukl (2010)

This was followed by the Trait Theory, *(Stogdill 1974)* who identified a plethora of skills and traits that he believed to be critical for successful leadership, as clearly illustrated by Figure 6 with pros and cons on the page that follows.

Traits such as integrity and diligence were difficult to measure, hence in the 1950's the Behavioural School became popular focusing on what managers 'actually do.' *Douglas McGregor's (2006)* view that assumptions about human nature affect leadership strategy, led to his Theory X (Autocratic) and Theory Y (Participative) of management suppositions in Figure 7.

THEORY X & THEORY Y OF HUMAN MOTIVATION & MANAGEMENT

THEORY X (0%)   **THEORY Y (100%)**

ATTITUDE

- inherently hate work and avoid it where possible.	- have a naturall affinity for work and enjoy it.

RESPONSIBILITY

- are rather lead than take responsibility on theri own.	- enjoy and seek responsibility and self control.

LEADERSHIP

- must be threatened to take action & work.	- exercise self discretion and enjoy setting personal targets.

CREATIVITY

- are only driven by financial reward & job security.	- are creative and imaginative when given the opportunity.

MOTIVATION

- are generlly dull and lack creative in the workplace.	- have the desire to improve and seek self-fulfillment.

- Management authoritarian with strong control. - Results in depressed workforce an no development.	- Empowering & liberating management style. - Promoting responsibility and workforce is enabled and growing.

Figure 7. Adapted from Bolden et al (2003); Huether (2011); McGregor (2006) & Yukl (2010)

While this school of thought continued and believed that initiative, insight and intelligence enabled leaders to make decisions and motivate staff, gradually group dynamics with it's focus on staff broke down the stereotypical view and lead to the popular, yet different Contingency Theory and Situational Leadership approach. Both are an addendum to the Behavioural Theory and concur that differing situations within the same organisation require different leadership styles that can be internally and externally affected by various factors and result in success or failure *(Peretomode 2012)*.

Situational leadership adapts to the current situation and combines transactional as well as transformational behaviour and is relatively flexible and while moving along a continuum *(Bertocci 2009; Peretmode 2012 & Yukl 2010)*.

Examples include Tannenbaum & Schmidt who developed their continuum consisting of seven leadership styles in 1958, as illustrated in Figure 8 below. Although the styles vary from strictly autocratic to democratic, in their model the final accountability always remains with the leader *(Tannenbaum & Schmidt 1958/73/86)*.

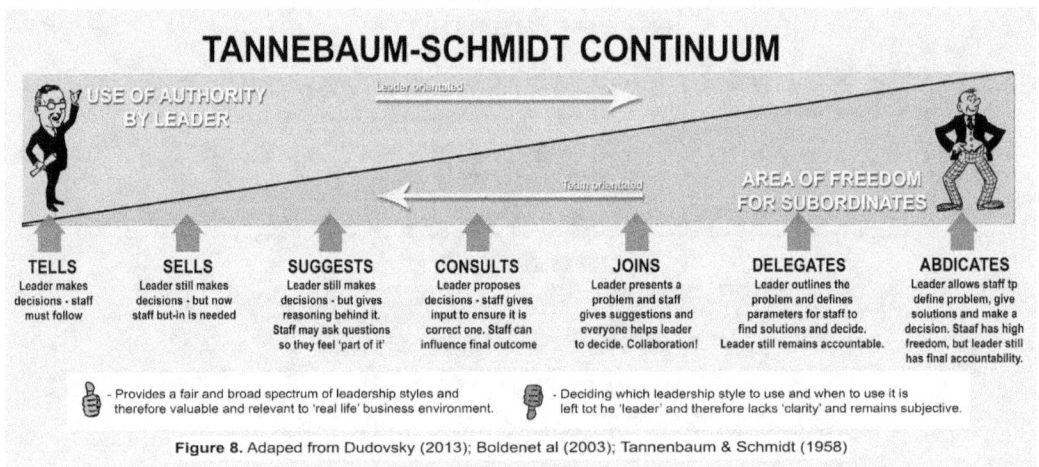

Figure 8. Adaped from Dudovsky (2013); Boldenet al (2003); Tannenbaum & Schmidt (1958)

Similarly *Hersey & Blanchard (2001)* contended that an effective leader must match his or her leadership style to the maturity level of the staff member and the specifics of the task at hand. Successful task accomplishment is dependent on the right mix, of more or less attention, to the job or relationship with the team being led. Their model in Figure 9 on the next page clearly indicates that as task confidence increases as they move from top right to the bottom left, as in the 2 x 2 matrix.

Situational leadership theories advocate that a task driven autocratic leader can therefore become a people driven democratic leader, by successfully identifying where the team is on the development continuum and modify the leadership style suitably.

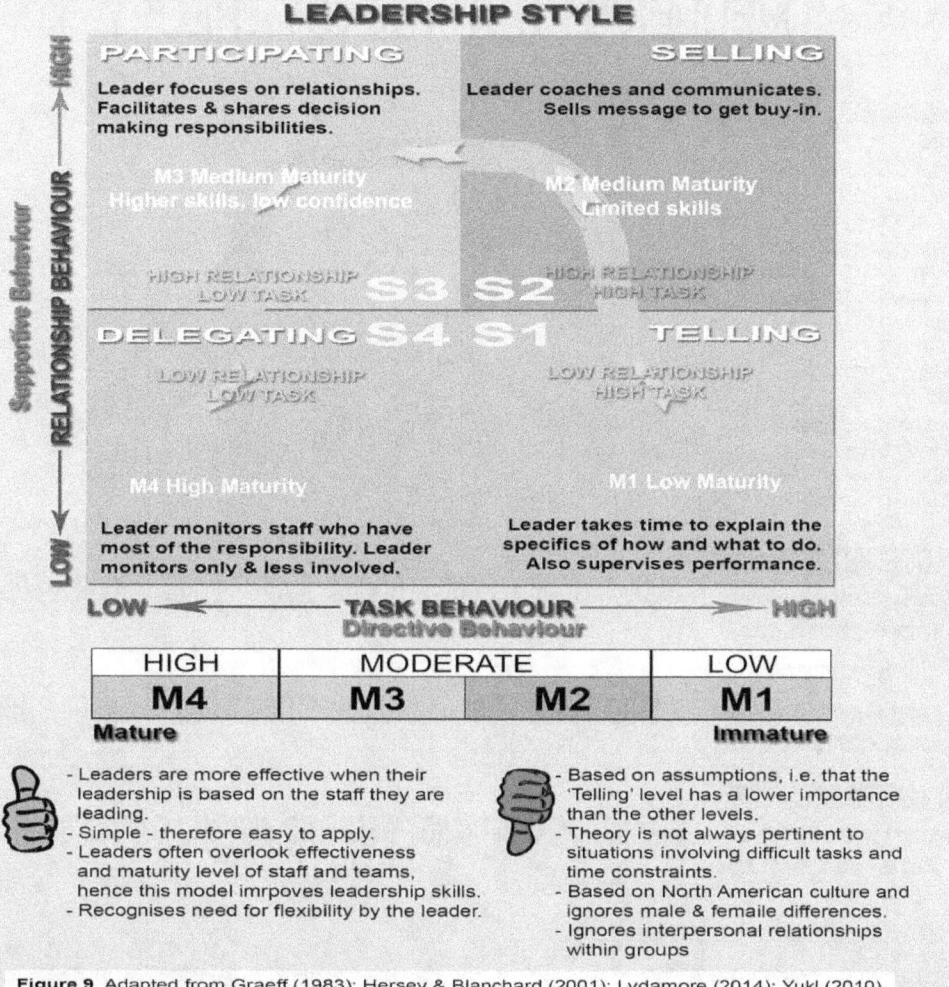

Figure 9. Adapted from Graeff (1983); Hersey & Blanchard (2001); Lydamore (2014); Yukl (2010)

Yukl (2010, p. 191) said that, "... *most of the contingency theories are stated so ambiguously that it is difficult to derive specific, testable propositions."* On the other hand, *Fiedler (1972, p. 453)* stated that, *"The contingency model postulates that group performance depends on the match between situational favourableness, that is, the leader's control and influence, and leadership motivation (as measured by the Least Preferred Coworker scale).* Fiedler believed that a leadership style is fixed and falls into either task, or relationship orientated leadership. His two-step model, in Figure 10 began with identifying the Least-Preferred Co-Worker (LPC) on a scale of 1 – 8 scored against various factors.

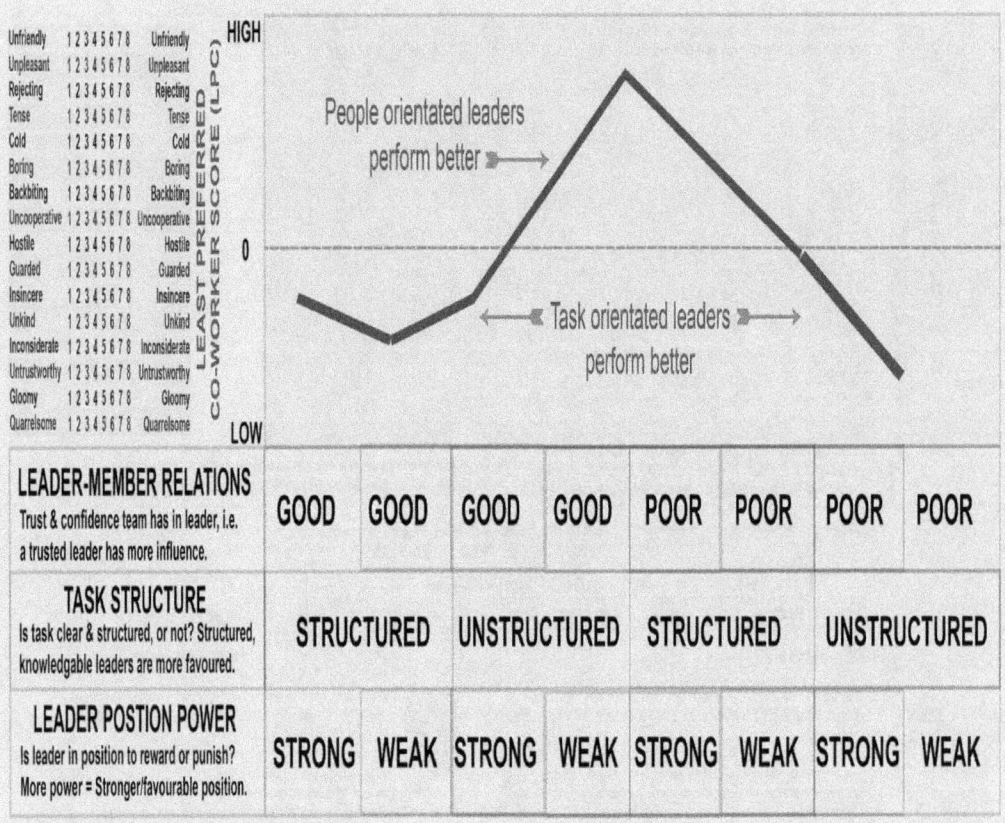

FIEDLER'S CONTINGENCY THEORY

Unfriendly	1 2 3 4 5 6 7 8	Unfriendly
Unpleasant	1 2 3 4 5 6 7 8	Unpleasant
Rejecting	1 2 3 4 5 6 7 8	Rejecting
Tense	1 2 3 4 5 6 7 8	Tense
Cold	1 2 3 4 5 6 7 8	Cold
Boring	1 2 3 4 5 6 7 8	Boring
Backbiting	1 2 3 4 5 6 7 8	Backbiting
Uncooperative	1 2 3 4 5 6 7 8	Uncooperative
Hostile	1 2 3 4 5 6 7 8	Hostile
Guarded	1 2 3 4 5 6 7 8	Guarded
Insincere	1 2 3 4 5 6 7 8	Insincere
Unkind	1 2 3 4 5 6 7 8	Unkind
Inconsiderate	1 2 3 4 5 6 7 8	Inconsiderate
Untrustworthy	1 2 3 4 5 6 7 8	Untrustworthy
Gloomy	1 2 3 4 5 6 7 8	Gloomy
Quarrelsome	1 2 3 4 5 6 7 8	Quarrelsome

People orientated leaders perform better →

← Task orientated leaders → perform better

LEADER-MEMBER RELATIONS Trust & confidence team has in leader, i.e. a trusted leader has more influence.	GOOD	GOOD	GOOD	GOOD	POOR	POOR	POOR	POOR
TASK STRUCTURE Is task clear & structured, or not? Structured, knowledgable leaders are more favoured.	STRUCTURED		UNSTRUCTURED		STRUCTURED		UNSTRUCTURED	
LEADER POSTION POWER Is leader in position to reward or punish? More power = Stronger/favourable position.	STRONG	WEAK	STRONG	WEAK	STRONG	WEAK	STRONG	WEAK

- Research was initially done on a broad sampling of situations and settings, indicating a good extrenal validity.
- Based on voluminous research supporting the hypothesis that 'situational favourableness', i.e. proper match between leader and group is important.
- The model predicts the relative ease of educating leaders on how to change their situational control, also known as 'job restructuring.'
- It gives companies a quick way to pair the right leader with the right team.
- As it does not identify all possible situations and only professes to give general guidance, the model is felxible enough to apply to a varied selection of teams, leaders and group-leader relationshps.

- Lack of flexibility. Fiedle saw leadership style as ridgid and if problems occured, believed that the leader, rather than the staff need to change.
- The Least preferred Co-Worker score (LPC) fails to be clear as to what style of leader is required when the scores are in the middle/
- Leader position of power is subjective. What one leader considers to be a high position of power in one situation, could be seen as low by a different leader in the same situation in a different organisation.
- Leader-member relations also subjective based on leader's perception of his/her acceptance by the group.
- LPC score only valid for closely supervised groups.
- LPC scale said to be vague & context free.

Figure 10. Adapted from Fiedler (1972); Lester, Borden & Fiedler (1977); Miner (2005) & Mitchell et al (1970)

A high score indicates a relationship-orientated leader (good at conflict management and decision making), whereas a low score favours a task-orientated leader (efficient in task completion and group organisation). The second-step involves identifying the 'situational favourableness' by determining Leader-Member Relations (Team's level of trust in leader), Task Structure (Leader's knowledge) and Position of Power (leader's power position to reward or punish). As a general guidance framework to quickly identify the suitability of a leader in a particular group, this model can still be an important tool today, especially considering the pros & cons (thumb up and down) summarised in Figure 10 on the next page *(Fiedler 1972; Lester, Borden & Fiedler 1977; Miner 2005 & Mitchell et al 1970)*.

2.1 TRANSFORMATIONAL VS. TRANSACTIONAL LEADERSHIP

Burnes (1978) described transactional leadership as focusing on clear structures, tight supervision and keeping things the same. Performance is contingent on punishment and reward mechanisms therefore it is based on contingency. He later described transformational leadership as a process whereby leaders and followers mutually transform one another, in order to arrive at a higher moral position. Focusing more on social values, it is a process that encourages collaboration and appeals to the higher values and ideals of the followers.

Bernard Bass (1985) added the 'social change' element to Burns' work, developing a full range transformational model where the premise is that an enthusiastic and ethical leader with vision will get people to follow. Although charisma is needed, it is insufficient on it's own, as these leaders lead from the front by example and succeed by believing in the team, rather than themselves. The followers are the product of the transformation *(Stogdill & Bass 1990; Bolden et al 2003; Burns 1978; Covey 2013 & Yukl 2010)*.

Although *Bass & Riggio (2005)* believed that effective leaders are both transformational and transactional, they see transformational leadership as a 'better fit' for today's complex organisations, as employees need someone to guide them through these uncertain times, and simultaneously challenge and empower them. *Bass & Riggio (2005, p. xi - xii)* clearly stated, *"Better leaders are transformational more frequently; less adequate leaders are passive or concentrate more on corrective actions."* Additional they added that transformational and transactional leadership can very much be participative and directive. Figure 11 summarises the clear distinctions between transformational and transactional leadership.

TRANSFORMATIONAL vs. TRANSACTIONAL LEADERSHIP

TRANSFORMATIONAL LEADERSHIP	TRANSACTIONAL LEADERSHIP
- Proactive leadership & focus on values.	- Active leadership, i.e. mangement.
- Promotes the human desire for finding meaning in life	- Promotes the human need of job accomplishment and having to survive.
- Transcends dialy issues.	- Boged down in dialy issues.
- Staff motivated to achieve objectives by striving for high values & standards.	- Goads and objectives achieved through reward & punishment.
- Focuses on purpose, ethics & meaning.	- Focuses on power & position.
- Leaders inspire & stimulate staff.	- Leaders set goals & promise rewards.
- Transforms organisational culture.	- Works within current organisational culture.
- Reinforces principal values by aligning internal structures.	- Efficiency, bottom-line and short-term profit structures are reinforced.
- Focus on long-term goals & keeping values.	- Emphasis on short-term and hard-data.
- Promotes rational thinking and problem solving, gains trust and respect.	- Reliquishes responsibility and steers away from making decisions.
- Focus on team-building & collaboration.	- Leaders handle all the details.
- Opportunity for staff to grow professionally and personally while they are striving to reach higher performance levels.	- Staff focus of organisational goal attainment while keeping employees productive on the front line only.

Figure 11. Adapted from Stogdill & Bass (1990); Bolden et al (2003); Burns (1978); Covey (2013) & Yukl (2010)

3. MOTIVATIONAL THEORIES

The concept of a 'job for life' is an antiquated idea and not valid in the twentieth century *(Steers, Mowbray & Shapiro 2004)*. Today staff needs to be motivated - what has changed? Various researchers and academics provided models that analyse what motivates people. *Carol Reade's (2003)* research concluded that job satisfaction (enjoyment & friendly colleagues) is rated higher than earnings when it comes to motivation. Similarly *Rothlin & Werder (2008)* found that if you answer, "Yes" to more than four of the questions in Figure 12, you suffer from demotivation ('boredout') due to repetitive, un-stimulating and un-challenging work.

'BOREDOUT' QUESTIONAIRE

1. Do you deal with your personal affairs at work?
2. Do you feel understretched or bored?
3. Do you, from time to time, pretend to be working - when you actually have bothing to do?
4. Are you tired and jaded in the evening, although you have been under no stress at all?
5. Are you rather unhappy with your work?
6. Do you lack any sense that your work has real meaning?
7. Could you actually work faster than you do?
8. Would you rather do something else, but are reluctant to change, because you would earn too little in that job?
9. Do you send private e-mails to colleagues during work?
10. Does your work not interest you, or have only a little interest?

Figure 12. Adapted from Rothlin & Werder (2008)

Buchanan & Huczynski (2010) citing *Hewlett & Luce (2006)* found that people in 'extreme jobs' with 60 or more hours working weeks, coupled with performance stresses are more prone to enjoy job satisfaction. This basic premise is almost similar to *Locke's (1984)* views, except that his focus was on 'not too challenging goals'. Couple this with Rothlin & Werder's 'Boreout' approach and an investigation into the theories of motivation is justified. Currently they consist of two broad categories - Content and Process Theories.

That which makes people tick, is seen as Content Theories that consist of desires and needs. Maslow followed a humanist approach and is considered the founding father with his Hierarchy of Needs Theory. He postulated that humans all have five typical basic types of needs that act as likely drivers of behaviour that he ranked hierarchically with the most basic at the bottom of the pyramid *(Buchanan & Huczynski 2010, Maslow 1987)*.

Buchanan & Huczynski (2010, p. 280) made similar assumptions to Maslow and developed their '*two factor theory of motivation*' focusing on factors that affected job satisfaction and dissatisfaction, namely Motivators (job content factors) and Hygiene (organisational context) factors, as described and compared in Figure 13 below.

MASLOW'S HIERARCHY OF NEEDS

SELF ACTUALISATION — *(The need for development/ creativity). These are met through autonomy & achievement*

EGO — *(The need for self-esteem, power, prestige & recognition). These are met through achievement, recognition, promotions and bonuses.*

SOCIAL — *(The need for being loved, belonging & inclusion)*

SECURITY — *(The need for safety, shelter & stability)*

PHYSICAL — *(The need for air, water, food, exercise, rest, freedom from diseases and disabilities)*

DEFICIENCY NEEDS

- Simply step by step process
- Helps in identifying & understanding one's needs.

- Cannot achieve self actualisation before fulfilling physiological needs, esteem love, creativity – some see these as desires rather than needs.
- Gender biased & Culture centred
- No flexibility – have to satisfy first need before moving to the next level
- Vague and does not predict behaviour
- Was based on white middle class values of the 20th century.

HERZBERG'S DUAL FACTOR THEORY (HYGIENE/MAINTENANCE) OF MOTIVATION

FACTORS FOR SATISFACTION	FACTORS FOR DISSATISFACTION
Achievement	Company policies
Recognition	Supervision
The Actual Work	Relationships (peers
Responsibility	and supervisors)
Advancement	Work conditions
Growth	Salary, status & security

- Involves 2 stages - firstly you need to eliminate the dissatisfactions, then only can you help them find the satisfaction.
- It has made a huge contribution is assisting leaders to understand basic human behaviour.
- The theory is easy to grasp and inspired many alternative theories.

- Involves 2 stages - firstly you need to eliminate the dissatisfactions, then only can you help them find the satisfaction.
- The theory assumes a strong connection between productivity and job satisfaction.
- Today satisfaction and dissatisfaction no longer seen as separate scales.
- The theory does not allow for unique individual differences, i.e. personality traits that affect the individual's response to hygiene/motivating factors.
- Herzberg's research methodolgy, empirical validity and assumptions have been questions.
- Many academics and researches crticise the theory for being 'oversimplified'.

MEANING: Based on concept of human needs & their satisfaction.

BASIS OF THEORY: Based on the hierarchy of 5 human needs and their satisfaction in motivating employees.

NATURE OF THEORY: Simple & descriptive based on extensive experience about human needs.

APPLICABILITY: Most popular & widely cited theory and applicable mostly to 3rd-world countries where money is the main motivation.

MOTIVATORS: Any need can be a motivator, unless is is not satisfied.

MEANING: Based on the use of motivators, i.e. opportunity for growth, achievement & recognition.

BASIS OF THEORY: Refers to Hygiene (dissatisfiers) & Motivating factors with no hierarchical arrangement.

NATURE OF THEORY: Prescriptive and based on real research from 200 interviews of engineers & accountants.

APPLICABILITY: An extension of Maslow's theory. Also narrow and applicable mostly to rich countries where money is a lesser motivating factor.

MOTIVATORS: Lower level (Hygiene) factors DO NOT act as motivators. Only higher order needs, i.e. achievement, recognition & challenging work.

Figure 13. Adapted from Gardner (1977); House & Wigdor (1967); Herzberg (1968 & 1983); Buchanan & Huczynski (2010), Maslow (1987); Taormina & Goa (2013)

Both theories compare needs and their role in motivation, couple productivity with employee satisfaction and are based on average assumptions, when in fact individuals can differ vastly in terms of which motivational factors influence them *(Gardner 1977; Herzberg 1968/1983; House & Wigdor 1967 & Buchanan & Huczynski 2010).*

Alderfer built on, and simplified Maslow's Hierarchy by reducing the levels to three needs, Existence, Relatedness and Growth (ERG). Although Alderfer also professed a general order in pursuing these needs, he acknowledged that they are not as fixed as in the case of Maslow's Hierarchy of Needs. He differed from Maslow as he stated that individuals can be motivated by needs from more than one level simultaneously. He included a 'frustration-regression' element, meaning that an unsatisfied higher

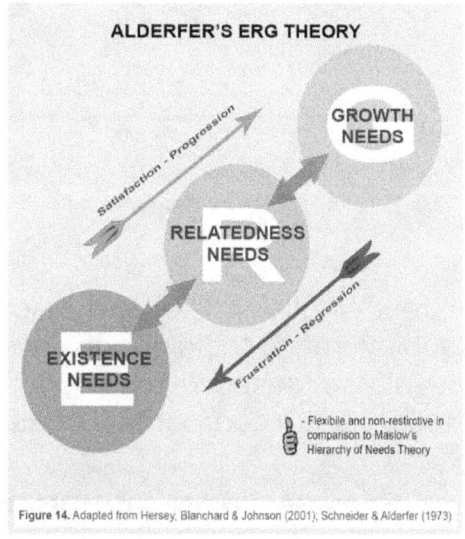

Figure 14. Adapted from Hersey, Blanchard & Johnson (2001); Schneider & Alderfer (1973)

level need, results in the individual pursuing a lower level need again. Finally he acknowledged that need importance varies as circumstances change during various life changes *(Hersey, Blanchard & Johnson 2001; Schneider & Alderfer 1973).*

McClelland (1988) also built on Maslow's Theory of Needs by identifying three learned motivators that affect people in different ways, namely a need for achievement, affiliation and power - hence it has also become known as the Learned Needs Theory. These are all derived from the individual's culture and life experiences. Individuals with high power needs enjoy influence and control, whereas strong affiliation needs are characterised by shy people who don't liked to be singled out. Achievers are motivated by moderately challenging tasks with a 50/50 chance of success or failure as illustrated in Figure 15 that follows on the next page.

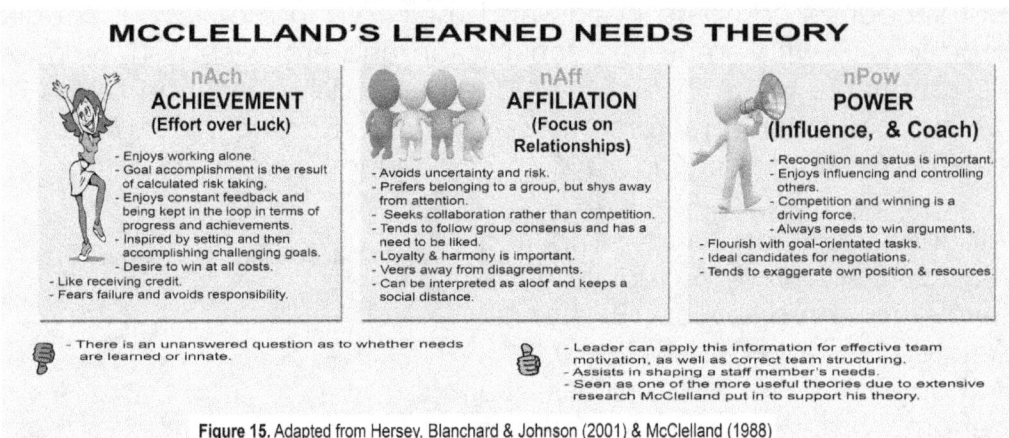

Figure 15. Adapted from Hersey, Blanchard & Johnson (2001) & McClelland (1988)

Interestingly, McClelland discovered that the desire for power and achievement took priority over affiliation as the individual's career levels increased *(Hersey, Blanchard & Johnson 2001 & McClelland 1988)*. See a comparison of all three models in Figure 16.

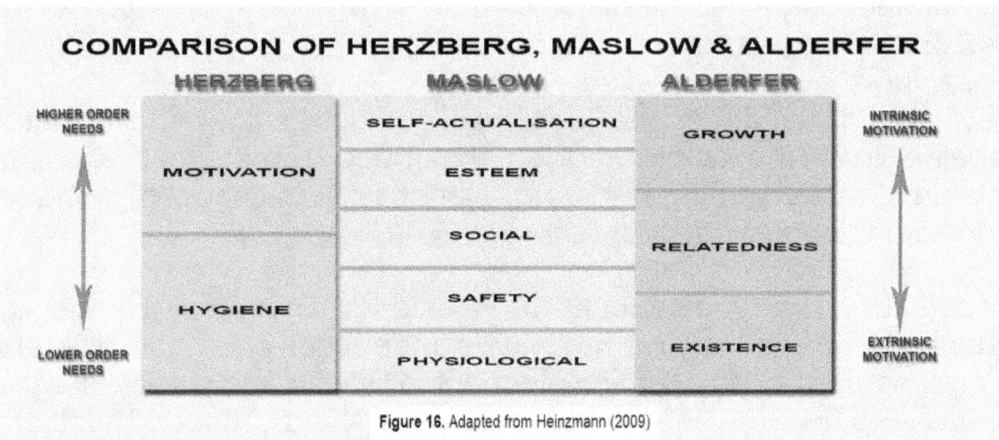

Figure 16. Adapted from Heinzmann (2009)

In the 1970's Schein and De Long initially developed five (later increased to eight) career anchors using a forty-item questionnaire (Career Orientation Inventory - COI) with the aim of identifying an individual's unique career anchor. Although this model is criticised for lacking empirical support, *Steel & Francis-Smythe (2007)* conducted the first independent large research study of 606 people and found support for the model which has made COI a viable measure in career guidance today.

SCHEIN'S CAREER ANCHORS

NEEDS -BASED

AUTONOMY/INDEPENDENCE
- The need to do things in one's own way, within own area of expertise and at own pace.
- Seek freedom to demonstrate one's own abilities and value pay for performance.
- Prefers to go it on own without supervision.

SECURITY/STABILITY
- Seeks predictability, security, benefits and a retirement plan.
- Wants to be rewarded for steady, predictable performance.

LIFESTYLE
- Work/life balance important, i.e. career must integrate with family needs.
- Requires flexibility to change as family needs change.

TALENTS -BASED

GENERAL MANAGERIAL COMPETENCE
- Seeks to rise to top of organisation levels with associated high responsibility.
- Leadership position must contribute to the success of the company
- Pay according to position and merit based.
- Constant striving for higher, rank, title, bigger budgets and more staff.

ENTREPRENEURIAL CREATIVITY
- Thrives on creating new services & products, building new businesses, or even taking over another company.
- Enjoys public recognition and visibility.
- Savours power, freedom & ownership.

VALUES -BASED

SERVICE/DEDICATION TO CAUSE
- The need to do their bit to improve the world.
- Seek 'service' professions such as ministry, teaching and nursing.
- Place value on recognition for service with equivalent pay and the opportunity to reach positions of influence in order to operate autonomously.
- Focus on serving a higher purpose in line with own value system.

PURE CHALLENGE/COMPETITIVENESS
- Enjoys impossible challenges and solving unsolvable problems.
- A variety of situations that challenge the individual self.
- Enjoys winning against tough opponents.
- Highly self-motivated.

- People can have needs in each anchor, but only one prominent anchor.
- Power & creativity, which are broader motivators can be satisfied in various different career options.
- Lacks empiracal support.
- Was devleoped only using a small sample of MIT alumini.

- Thought to share more relevant information about what people want from their careers, compared to other models.
- Allows for broader view of an individual's values.
- Good for providing guidance and direction to individuals.

Figure 17. Adapted from Arnold (2004); Coetzee & Shreuder (2009); Schein (1990); Steele & Francis-Smythe (2007)

3.1 PROCESS THEORIES OF MOTIVATION

Leading innovation and change involves inspiring people to do what is required. Fostering a clear relationship between effort, performance and reward, results in increased work effort by employees as argued by a number of theories. According to *Adams' (1963)* Equity Theory a fair balance is essential between an employee's inputs (recognition & relevance, i.e. skills & qualifications) and their outputs (salary & benefits). As long as their outputs remain greater than their inputs, they should remain content and motivated. Any disruption in this balance can result in de-motivation. Conversely, improving employee performance and job satisfaction can be achieved by promoting higher levels of inputs & outputs.

In 1964 Victor Vroom took this a step further, emphasising that the desire to act (be motivated) rests on the existence of a strong/high link between three variables:

1.   **Effort** - a belief that extra effort improves performance.
2.   **Performance** - High level will trigger good reward.
3.   **Outcomes** - must have value/be attractive *(Hamington 2010; Van Eerde & Thierry 1996).*

In 1968 the Goal Setting Theory postulated that performance improvement occurred when working toward specific challenging (within reason) goals, coupled with leadership feedback and knowledge of past successes *(Locke & Latham 1984)*. The Job Characteristics Model of *Hackman & Oldman (1980)* was inspired by Herzberg's Motivation/Hygiene Theory; adding that work motivation relies on three psychological states (experienced meaningfulness, responsibility for outcomes and knowledge) of the work activities. Five core job dimensions - skill variety, task identity & significance, autonomy and feedback, further influence these.

With the advent of these various theories, much criticism was voiced. *Locke & Latham (2009, p. 22)* condemned these unscholarly attacks on goal setting stating, *"Organizations cannot thrive without being focused on their desired end results any more than an individual can thrive without goals to provide a sense of purpose."*

Understanding how to motivate employees is essential and delegating the task is as important, yet lacking in implementation according to *Hunt (2010)* who noted that only one in ten managers understands how to empower employees. Figure 18 below summarises the delegation process.

DELEGATION GUIDELINES

WHAT TO DELEGATE	WHEN TO DELEGATE	HOW TO DELEGATE
- Tasks that another person is better at. - Releavnt to this person's character. - The appropriate difficulty to suit this person. - Urgent, yet not highly important tasks. - Can be pleasant & unpleasant. - Tasks not central to the leader's role. - Task that help develope the skills of the person you are giving the task to. - Tasks where you are prepared to give credit for a job well-done! - Tasks where the responsibility of completion also rests on this person. - Tasks that will not boomerang back onto your desk.	- If someone else has the expertise to complete the task. - If the leader has limited time, and can identify a suitable person in their team that can do the job as well if not better. - Provides an opportunity for growth development of this individual. - The leader must have enough time to adequately train and check progress with this person. - There are time constraints, or... - Alternatively there is time to redo the task if it is not done properly - therefore situation dependent. - Consider that this other person must have. the time and willingness to do the task effectively, efficiently and timeously.	- Clarify the responsibilities right away and ensure the person accepts these responsibilities. - Be clear about the precise expected outcome. - Delegate proportionate responsibility, including the reporting requirements, including limits of discretion. - Ensure that all appropriate people know of the decision. - Be available for support and assistance. - Make sure all information and tools are available for task to be completed successfully. - Share reasons behind the delegation and make sure the person understands the 'bigger picture', including future opportunities, recognitions, financial rewards and all other consequences pertinant to this task. - Monitor the process regularly.

Figure 18. Adapted from Youngworth (2010); Yukl (2010); Zwilling (2013)

4. TEAMS & GROUPS

In terms of a company, *Katzenbach & Smith (1993, p. 42)* offered a succinct definition of a team as, "...*a small number of people with complementary skills who are committed to a common purpose, performance goals, and approach for which they hold themselves mutually accountable.*" However, teams don't just work, there are a six basic conditions that enhance performance, as in Figure 19.

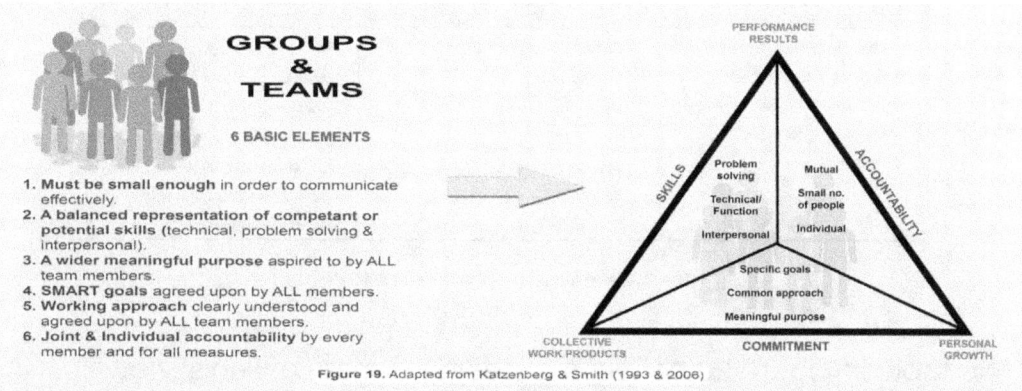

Figure 19. Adapted from Katzenberg & Smith (1993 & 2006)

On the other hand, the man famous for this theory of 'groupthink', *Irving Janis (1982, p. 3)* cited a warning from Nietzsche, "...*madness is the exception in individuals, but the rule in groups.*" This makes complete sense when one considers that huge companies have gone bankrupt, and large government institutions have led countries to the verge of war, due to systematic errors and 'collective miscalculations' while making group decisions *(Janis 1982)*. The space shuttle catastrophe of 2003 is a prime example where engineers where professed to have knowledge of the foam shedding, and collectively decided that the risks were acceptable. Janis questions why teams would arrive at exemplary decisions in one instance, and a calamitous one in the next. Various symptoms are offered, including group cohesion, outside pressure, strong charismatic & persuasive group leader, collective rationalisation, illusions of unanimity and invulnerability and strong outside pressure to reach a decision. These are offered as a probable reason that groupthink could or could not occur *(Janis 1982)*.

However, *Whyte (1989, p. 54)* argued that, "*Reliance upon prospect polarization to understand excessive risk seeking in group decision making implies that egregious errors in group judgment are not solely the product of group dynamics. Rather, they also are the product of the way group members frame decisions and choose between alternatives."*

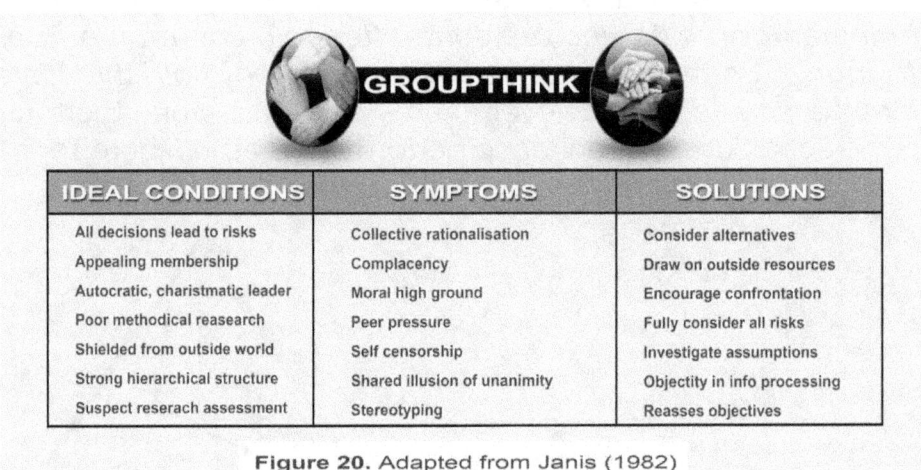

Figure 20. Adapted from Janis (1982)

The table in Figure 20 conveys a clear summary of Janis' views.

4.1 TEAM ROLES

Traditionally team roles were allocated by; seniority, gender, race and hierarchy. Later it was hypothesised that high intellect teams would succeed over lower intellect teams. *Belbin's (2010 & 2012)* research surprisingly revealed the opposite, and concluded that 'balance' and the role compatibility of team members was the essential ingredient.

Hence members with similar strengths tend to compete against each other, rather than focus on overall team goals.

The NINE Belbin Team Roles

Team Role		Contribution	Allowable Weaknesses
Plant		Creative, imaginative, free-thinking. Generates ideas and solves difficult problems.	Ignores incidentals. Too preoccupied to communicate effectively.
Resource Investigator		Outgoing, enthusiastic, communicative. Explores opportunities and develops contacts.	Over-optimistic. Loses interest once initial enthusiasm has passed.
Co-ordinator		Mature, confident, identifies talent. Clarifies goals. Delegates effectively.	Can be seen as manipulative. Offloads own share of the work.
Shaper		Challenging, dynamic, thrives on pressure. Has the drive and courage to overcome obstacles.	Prone to provocation. Offends peoples feelings.
Monitor Evaluator		Sober, strategic and discerning. Sees all options and judges accurately.	Lacks drive and ability to inspire others. Can be overly critical.
Teamworker		Co-operative, perceptive and diplomatic. Listens and averts friction.	Indecisive in crunch situations. Avoids confrontation.
Implementer		Practical, reliable, efficient. Turns ideas into actions and organises work that needs to be done.	Somewhat inflexible. Slow to respond to new possibilities.
Completer Finisher		Painstaking, conscientious, anxious. Searches out errors. Polishes and perfects.	Inclined to worry unduly. Reluctant to delegate.
Specialist		Single-minded, self-starting, dedicated. Provides knowledge and skills in rare supply.	Contributes only on a narrow front. Dwells on technicalities.

Figure 21. Belbin (2012)
Avaliable from: http://www.belbin.com
[22 September 2014]

Similarly, members with matching weaknesses, weaken the entire team.

He highlighted that team members need to understand their role within a team, in order to build on strengths and develop weaknesses. Knowing this, tensions are resolved and members' individual contributions to overall team goals are improved. Therefore, today successful teams consist of a mixture of different people with varying behaviours, as explained by the 9 team roles in the diagram from *Belbin's (2102)* website above.

Margerison & McCann (1995) argued that defining team roles was not enough, but that leaders need to place team members into roles they enjoy. In contrast to Belbin, their Team Management Profile (TMI) is a psychometric tool and consists of 60 questions that investigate how a person makes decisions, relates to those around him/her, organises themselves and goes about gathering information.

4.2 TEAM LEADERSHIP

In the context of this chapter I am exploring vertical team leadership (formal, hierarchical where the team leader is outside of the team's task work and focuses on motivation and supporting their team) rather than shared leadership where various team members have leadership roles *(Hoch & Morgeson 2014)*.

As a leader, it is not enough to identify team members, put together a team charter and allocate tasks. According to *Katzenbach & Smith (2005)* in order to build team performance, a leader additionally needs to ensure that the team:

a. Has urgency and a meaningful purpose.

b. Members are selected because of their skill set and not personality.

c. Has specific rules of conduct.

d. Receives performance orientated tasks and goals that can be achieved fairly early in the project.

e. Spends enough time together in order to 'connect' as a team.

f. Receives positive reinforcement by constantly supplying feedback and recognising achievements.

g. Is assisted and guided to sort out mistakes and shortfalls.

5. LEARNING TO BE A BETTER LEADER

If one researches the writings of popular academics & authors, they identify varying similar qualities such as honesty, ethics, self belief, integrity, self awareness, vision, teamwork and communication skills, to name a few *(Bennis & Nanus 1997; Bass 1985; Collins 2005; Covey 2013; Higgs 2003; Klemp 2001; Rankin 2008; Miller, Rankin & Neathley 2001)*. However, an engaging research by *Yeung & Ready (1995)* questioned core leadership abilities, investigating 1200 managers across eight countries in ten large international companies and found that although the ability to express a definite vision, strategy and values ranked highest. Traits such as leading strategic change, focusing on results and being customer focused received different levels of priority in each country. Additionally *Leslie & Velsor (1998)* cite *Wallace, Sawheny & Gardjito's (1995)* investigation of admired leadership attributes between countries, and further suggested that a mixture of economic variables, religious beliefs and job-related values influence this differing view of admired leadership traits.

Dr. Marques (2007) presented a fascinating objective research of hugely influential and diversely different leaders including the likes of Castro, Christ, Ghandi and Al Capone. Amongst the abundance of similarities (confidence, hard work, courage, empathy for subordinates, strategic insight, appropriate intelligence, determination and resilience) she found that the unifying trait was a heightened passion for their purpose and the desire to develop their own leadership traits - in agreement with *Boyatzis & McKee (2005)* process for developing competency. However, what stands out is her observation that all leaders researched, *".. demonstrated a significant lack of connection with those closest to them"* (Marques 2007, p. 122).

Comparing the varying ideologies above, one could question whether *Boyatzis & McKee (2005)* did not possibly identify that 'extra something' and answered the core question of what makes someone who has all the common competencies rise above the rest? Their five-step self development process of finding your ideal self, your strengths & weaknesses; creating a future learning agenda; not being afraid to experiment and learn plus understanding that you need to involve others around you, would appear to offer a succinct answer to this question.

Additionally, *Alimo-Metcalfe & Alban-Metcalf's (2006)* views on effective leaders caring for staff and assisting in developing them, plus *Bass' (1985)* 'individualised concerns' approach coupled with *Raffert & Griffin's (2004)* 'supportive leadership dimension, further validated *Boyatzis & McKee's (2005)* competency of involving others around you.

However, I am in total agreement with *Bryman (2004)* that one should never disregard the considerable influence of banal leadership traits such as ensuring the availability of sufficient resources in order to complete all tasks at hand.

6. BEHAVIOUR EVALUATION OF SELECTED LEADERS

6.1 BACKGROUND

It may be the norm to propose various leadership styles and theories, but when you have an executive team, and staff that don't 'play the game' it becomes almost impossible to lead. This is the premise of my practical example.

Imagine being a consultant to a major financial company where you assist a new department head with setting up an innovative 'mass market' channel in the short-term insurance sector. Your task is to guide and assist this leader to bring this new department to fruition. To recap; this major financial institution was seeking to expand its footprint into the lower economic sector with a network-marketing concept to sell funeral and life policies via direct marketing by recruiting individuals to start their own businesses and be paid for the people they bring onboard.

6.2   OBSERVATIONS

As this financial giant had limited knowledge of network marketing, they headhunted a highly capable channel head from a competitive company. Unfortunately according to *Collins' (2005)* '5 levels of leadership', he was only a 'level 1' leader with skills, knowledge and great work habits. The executive leadership team (which should have been 'level 5') overseeing the process where not qualified, or even anywhere near 'level 1' capabilities.

How does something like this happen in a multi-national company? For anyone outside South Africa, this may be perplexing. However, a sad reality within the country since the change of government in 1994, and to redress the wrongs of apartheid, many companies (especially those dealing with government contracts) adhere to Black Economic Empowerment *(Albertyn 2001; Griffiths & Prozesky 2010 & Steyn & Foster 2008)*. Positions are filled based purely on race and these individuals given a crash courses in leadership. The '10 000 hour rule' *(Gladwell 2009)* is basically non-existent. This has resulted in experienced managers and staff, carrying lesser-experienced members.

Over and above the allocated staff, the managing director and executive head appointed their own Project Team (with no knowledge of network marketing) to develop the channel in partnership with the channel head while irresponsibly splitting the final responsibility of any decision-making between the project team and this new channel head.

Even though the channel head had been employed to spearhead the process, his hands were tied in terms of any operational decisions. As successful task accomplishment is dependent on the right mix, of more or less attention, to the job or relationship with the team being led *Hersey & Blanchard (2001)*, the split responsibility and shared staff majorly complicated matters.

Additionally, as executives had 'dumped' their problem staff into this team for the channel head to lead, there was no balance, role compatibility and hence no role enjoyment *(Belbin 2010 & Margerson & McCann 1995)*. Members had not been selected because of their skill set and not spent enough time connecting as a team *(Katzenberg & Smith 2005)*, yet the channel managed to survive for an entire year. Why? He created smaller teams, facilitated group discussions that resulted in meaningful goals and introduced not only joint accountability *(Katzenberg & Smith 2005)*, but individual accountability as well. He focused on positive re-enforcement and constantly supplied feedback.

In fact *McGregor's (2006)* Theory X, coupled with an entitlement attitude *(Hoffman 2008)* predominated in the mindset of most of these executives, according to my observations. Additionally there was no balance between the channel head and executive leadership in terms of *Longenecker's (2004)* 12 best practices of leadership, as per the comparison in Figure 22.

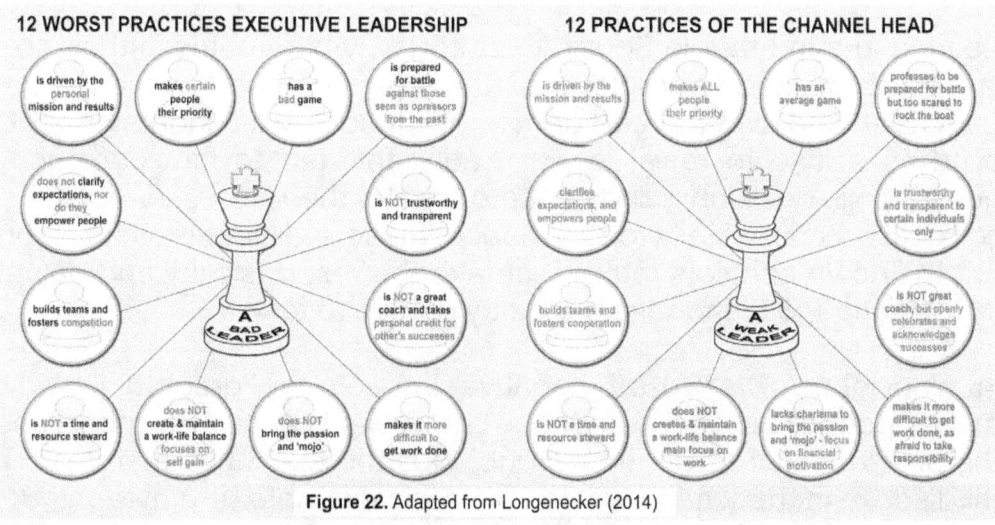

Figure 22. Adapted from Longenecker (2014)

Sadly team leaders, constantly challenged the channel head - possibly due to 'ego deficiency needs' *(Maslow 1987)*. The channel head did his best to eliminate all dissatisfactions *(Herzberg Dual Factor Theory 1968)* by initially and possibly wrongly only focusing on transformational leadership. Furthermore, as the authority on network marketing he attempted to follow the *Hersey-Blanchard (2001)* Situational Leadership model in order to empower the team. Unfortunately the ingrained old 'stiff upper lip' financial mindset, coupled with 'entitlement' issues resulted in a team mindset of not accepting the innovation and change from S2 quadrant of the model onwards.

Furthermore, as the project team reported directly to the executive head, and ignored the channel head, they viewed this innovative channel as 'too alternative', thus lagging on deadlines. This in turn resulted in staff targets not being met and snowballed into administrative problems for the independent outsiders that signed up into the business. *McClelland's Human Motivation theory (1988)* could shed further light on the crises in that 'Achievement' in terms of process and administration of staff, or independent outsiders never occurred. Due to various factions 'Affiliation' (especial racial) were in constant conflict, and within the teams constant friction occurred in terms of training and positions of influence, again race related. Arriving at a higher moral position through members and leaders mutually transforming each other while focusing on social values *(Burnes 1978)* was thus also a disaster.

Bearing in mind that in South Africa today, white males in their 50's are least desirable employees, the channel head, as an older Caucasian and experienced democratic leader, was understandably overly sensitive to racial issues. Sadly, this led to him constantly question his decisions, and hesitate to take the necessary objective corrective action. He wrongly hoped these individuals would sort out their own conflicts rather that take the responsibility and power *(McClelland 1988)* and take the guilty parties to task.

In hindsight, *Janis' (1982)* negative impacts of 'groupthink' now makes perfect sense, as between the project team as a group and the problem staff as another group, plus the executive team as the third spoke in the wheel, we had a classic example of *Whyte's (1989, p. 54)* argument that, *"... egregious errors in group judgment are not solely the product of group dynamics. Rather, they also are the product of the way group members frame decisions and choose between alternatives."*

Risk and compliance abandoned the channel citing internal conflicts and disagreements, when the real problem was misguided & ineffective leadership at the top. Again, in hindsight, *Bennis & Nanus' (1997)* views on visionary leadership where employees who feel they can make a difference and who believe in the task at hand, do so with more energy and passion rings true. Sadly the aligned views of the staff in this instance where negatively influenced and aligned to the wrong and flawed visions of the biased senior executive leadership who were not willing to accept the innovative potential of this new channel. Hence a further confirmation of their views that charismatic leadership may not always be transformational.

6.3 LESSONS LEARNT

I have used the scenario above with good reason, as it has reinforced the power of 'groupthink' and how mismanagement of your leadership role can hugely impact the lives of many people. Furthermore, you need to understand that being appointed in a consultant role is meaningless unless the person you are guiding actually has the executive and personal power, plus level 5 leadership qualities *(Collins 2005)* to implement the advice given. In addition to agreeing with *Collins (2005)* and *Ten Kok's (2013)* belief that leaders require that *'extra will'* to lead, reinforces the reality that this was impossible for the channel head in my example to do so. He simply could not follow Victor Vroom's teachings, even though he had the desire to act and put in the effort, his performance was restricted resulting in poor outcomes *(Hamington 2010; Van Eerde & Thierry 1996)*.

Being a leader at the top of the hierarchy chain may well allow one to apply the theories and models in this chapter with relative freedom. However, when one has an executive leadership structure above you that is inexperienced, and has alternative agenda's, it adds an almost impossible variable. Additionally *Bass & Riggio's (2005)* view of personalised transformational leaders that are pseudo-transformational and self serving, as this was very much the case within the top structure of company A, with everyone protecting their own domain and only showing an interest in themselves, made any leadership style impossible. Therefore in future you should try adopt *Collins' (2005)*, "First Who, Then What" view and first investigate 'who' your executive leadership team is, before you join any organisation. They would need *to convince you that they fully comprehend leadership best practices (Longenecker 2014)* and have transcended *Maslow's (1987)* self-actualisation needs, over and above strict clarification of your exact powers and responsibilities before joining the company.

Now take this one step further and imagine that you have been approached by a competitor (company B) to head up your own similar channel. Your experiences at company A have suddenly been immensely valuable, not only learning from other leader's mistakes and the resultant failure of that channel, but also analysing yourself and questioning what you would have done differently.

Some possible learned experiences could result in you first interviewing 'your bosses to be' and negotiate your own terms of employment. The most important being, that you get to choose your own team members without any 'top down' interference. This would need to be done based on identifying each individual's need for achievement, affiliation and power *(McClelland 1988)* that compliment each other and are all similarly dedicated to the common purpose of this department *(Katzenbach & Smith 1993 & 2005)*. Having experienced the problems between team members in company A, regardless of racial issues & history *(Norton et al 2006)*, you should now be able to appreciate the impact of 'balance' and role compatibility as essential ingredients for success *(Belbin 2010)*, coupled with placement in roles they enjoy *(Margerison & McCann 1995)*. Once this foundation is cast, then only can you apply *Hunt's (2010)* delegation guidelines and ideally follow a transformational leadership style *(Bass 1990, Bolden et al 2003, Burns 1978, Covey 1992 & Yukl 2010)* leading your team through the *Hersey-Blanchard Situational Leadership Model (2001)* from S1 to S4 to ultimately empower them with the responsibility to reach higher performance levels and grow professionally.

Goleman, Boyatzis & McKee (2003) stressed the importance of managing the emotions of groups as a leader. In company A the leadership was dissonant; try becoming a resonant leader in Company B and attuned to your team's emotions. This can only be done by fostering a team spirit from day one, by creating smaller teams, facilitating group discussions that result in meaningful goals and the introduced not only joint accountability (Katzenberg & Smith 2005), but individual accountability as well. You need to grow your interpersonal intelligence *(Gardner 1983)* and learn to understand the feelings, emotions and desires of everyone in your team. Contrary to the leadership in company A, your focus should be on positive re-enforcement and constant feedback, plus of course celebrating all our successes as a team as we head towards the future.

7. CONCLUSION

Understand that innovative leadership is very much a complex intertwining of various models and frameworks, focusing not on 'selling', but very much on transformational principles such as consulting and negotiation with the aim of being people focused, by motivating and changing through collaboration.

*"If you don't hold on to anything,
no one can take anything away from you."*

(Wolfgang Riebe)

CHAPTER 6
COMPLEXITY VERSUS INNOVATION

INTRODUCTION

"But innovation comes from people meeting up in the hallways or calling each other at 10:30 at night with a new idea, or because they realized something that shoots holes in how we've been thinking about a problem."

(Steve Jobs, 1955 - 2011)

Have you ever been irritated by the complex procedure to return an item to a store? What about building frustration and the red tape and bureaucracy involved in dealing with large or government organisations? Consider deciding to buy an item off a website, only to find that the selection is so vast and overpowering, that you become so confused and not buy anything in the end? Alternatively, do you hold a senior leadership post and have limited authority in terms of decision making and implementation of innovative ideas, due to complex policies, procedures and red tape?   The author questions whether this type of thinking, known as complexity thinking, has in fact improved innovation and productivity in organisations or made it worse. This paper investigates, through research and five case studies, complexity thinking in terms of how it originated and is defined, its effects on innovation and leadership and ultimately actions and tools to manage this complexity thinking.

Special thanks needs to go to Dr Perry Haan for supervising my dissertation, as well as Dr Anton Van Wyk, Young Carr, Mike Butner, Andre Du Plooy and Frank van den Brink for being part of my case studies.

1. COMPLEXITY THINKING

1.1 BACKGROUND

For the last 30 years the corporate environment has transformed tremendously. It has become clear that change is unavoidable and innovation is the norm; those who do not embrace it will be left behind. The business world has changed dramatically and companies have endeavoured to be innovative by adjusting operations to stay ahead of the competition. However, a prevailing aftermath of these changes has resulted in excessive complexity and a mediocre, if any profit growth resulting in despondency among leadership *(Gottfredson & Aspinall 2005)*.

A brief overview of past global events validates that the world has been subjected to immense upheaval and revolution: the Chernolbyl disaster in 1986; the fall in the Berlin wall in 1989; the fall of Apartheid in South Africa in 1994; the introduction of the Euro in 1999; the September 11 Al-Quada attacks in the USA; petroleum reached $100 per barrel in 2008 and the Iceland volcanic ash cloud disrupting air traffic across Europe in 2010, to name a few. These were all unexpected, resulting in profound and at times, complex societal change mechanisms that altered the face of how we do business *(Scharmer, 2010; The Telegraph, 2011)*.

Companies need to foster a new understanding of these ever transforming realities, understand how they affect their organisations, employees, customers and internal systems and adapt these to fit these changes *(Schneider & Wishnie 2014)*. This interconnected, interdependent world economy has, and is becoming increasingly complex, placing extreme pressure on leadership to innovate and increase performance while attempting to overcome the challenges of these uncertain times *(Dervitsiotis, 2012)*, such as the global financial crises of 2008 *(Grabel, 2013)*.

However, according to *Sirkin, Keenan and Jackson (2005)*, although change is difficult, coping with and actually doing it is where the problems arise. Leaders tend to have differing views due to their own unique circumstances. The focus has been on soft issues such as culture and motivation, rather than measurable hard issues which include the number of people needed to actualise the change plus the financial implications of that change.

Couple the above with a faster, non-linear corporate environment where forecasted outcomes rarely match the results, leadership experts simply cannot foresee which products or organisations will be successful in the future. *Sherman and Schultz (1998)* concurred that assets can become liabilities overnight and that a competitive advantage today may only be momentary.

Not only has this epoch of colossal dramatic societal, political and corporate change resulted in complex ever-changing business interactions, but the additional increased preoccupation with political correctness has placed an extra burden on leadership as so aptly stated by *Schafer (2014)*. *"Political correctness is now being marketed as 'insta-win.' If you are losing an argument or failing to bend others to your will, pull out a can of 'Insta-win' – accuse them of racism, homophobia, or sexism"* (p. 1).

Hence today, the need for leaders to develop and apply successful, innovative and systematic complexity thinking is more challenging than ever before; from obstacles in teamwork, including personality conflicts, non-performance, differing business styles and stress to effectively managing personnel, grooming talent, resolving conflicts and adjusting to rising conflict and acclimatising to growing trends and technology *(Mason 2011)*.

1.2 HISTORY

During the industrial age the economic environment was relatively stable and fairly straightforward for leaders to forecast future company targets accurately *(Dervitsiotis 2012)*. Differentiation and low cost were pretty much the only company strategies *(Porter 1985)*. Furthermore, conventional leadership models therefore only concentrated on maximising production *(Bass 2008)*.

The 1970's saw a change in thinking when organisations began a move their organisational cultures and activities towards a quality discipline, known as the Total Quality Management (TQM) principal. Japan was the initiator, originally dominating the global market. Soon other economies realised the importance of gaining a competitive advantage in world markets and followed suit

(Dahlgaard, 2011). Current ideology was put on its head as products and services became passé and customer needs and demands took priority. Hence *"innovative competence" (Weberg 2012, p. 275)* became the new focus, resulting in the waning of traditional leadership models.

Quality driven processes never disappeared and still remain a benchmark today however, a plethora of new factors have come into play (i.e. new innovation driven mechanisms and business models) in the modern world in order for companies to remain economically competitive *(Dervitsiotis, 2007 & 2011; Prahalad & Krishnan, 2008)*.

1.3 RELEVANCE TO CURRENT TIMES

Stephen Hawking stated that, *"The 21st century will be the century of complexity" (Waltuck 2012, p. 15)*. It has become evident that business and economic environments have changed dramatically and companies have endeavoured to be innovative by adjusting operations to stay ahead of the competition. However, a prevailing aftermath of these changes has resulted in excessive complexity and a mediocre, if any profit growth resulting in despondency among leadership *(Gottfredson & Aspinall, 2005)*.

Keen (2000) stated that being besieged by change at all levels has become the norm in business today. Change has become a non-debatable necessity. For leaders to successfully rise to the challenge of ceaseless innovation and reinvention, transformation is needed for growth. The old leadership archetype worked in the past, but struggles to stand up to the demands of 21st Century leadership needs. The solitary champion who single handily revolutionises an entire organisation has become a fable, as expectations today no doubt outpace the capabilities of most people. Instead the focus has shifted to a multifaceted leadership approach with a focus on relationships. *Keen (2000, p. 15)* defined a modern leader as, *"someone who conducts the orchestra in a way that harmonises the brilliance of each instrument to produce an inspirational symphony in which the whole is bigger than the sum of the parts."*

Waltuck (2010) further observed that the biggest mistake leaders have made was to view complex challenges as technical issues that could be fixed and easily controlled. Any change involving humanity is intrinsically complex and that traditional hierarchical command and control leadership does not work anymore. *Richardson (2008)* agreed, stating that complexity thinking is about limits. He said that there are limitations to what leaders can know and what they can accomplish via pre-determined and planned approaches. This was further supported by *Bain and Company (2005)* who said 68% of executives interviewed admitted that excessive complexity raised operating costs and crippled growth *(Rigby 2005)*. *Gottfredson and Aspinall (2005, p. 64)* additionally stated, "*Complexity begins in the product line and then spreads outward through every facet of a company's operations.*"

Simon (1962) defined a complex system as consisting of copious components (various departments in an organisation) that interact in an entangled way. *Smith and Lewis (2011)* said that these new complex internal systems and external situations (increased products and services, processes, staffing, training and changing customer needs) create paradoxical demands on leaders. A number of researchers *(Fjeldstad et al 2012; Schraagen et al 2010)* agreed that traditional business methods do not apply anymore due to unpredictable future environments. This has resulted in companies embracing complex flexible system structures where the organisation becomes decentralised, team-based with a dispersed power structure *(Geer-Frazier, 2014)*.

1.4 BRIEF OVERVIEW

Heywood, Spungin and Turnbull (2007) proposed that companies do not behave in a linear manner. Therefore, changing organisational, cultural and operating systems can lead to unexpected repercussions that create added complexity and confusion. *Gottfredson and Aspinall (2005)* questioned whether this pursuit of innovation has not been taken too far. They asserted that as companies continually launch new products and line extensions, operational complexity and the management of that complexity magnifies while margins diminish.

Therefore an enormous challenge for leadership today is coping with the proliferating complexity of an ever changing, interconnected and interdependent global economy. Innovative performance for long-term survival has now become a priority for leaders to increase the odds of longevity for large corporations in turbulent times. Holistically viewed, the world that includes organisations, and as co-creators of this complex world, change will only occur once everyone changes *(Keene 2000)*.

1.5 THE RESEARCH AIMS

The aim of this research is to:

1.   Define complexity thinking and investigate possible contributing factors.

2.   Investigate complexity thinking in relation to leadership and leadership roles.

3.   Investigate the affect complexity thinking has on innovation.

4.   Identify actions and tools that could assist leadership in fostering innovation and actively manage complexity thinking in the future.

2. LITERATURE REVIEW

2.1 COMPLEXITY THINKING DEFINED AND CONTRIBUTING FACTORS

Dervitsiotis (2012) together with *Heywood, Spungin, and Turnbull (2007)* identified two kinds of complexity. First is strategic complexity that results when the company adds new products, production and distribution units. New nodes are crated to integrate with other external entities ranging from new suppliers to new regulators coupled with resulted interactions within the current internal environment. Second, operating complexity results when internal misalignments such as a lack of teamwork between leadership and workers ensue that negatively affect many key performance metrics including productivity *(Dervitsiotis 2012; Heywood, Spungin, &*

Turnbull 2007). This shall be discussed under the Leadership heading.

To gain a better understanding of what complexity thinking actually means, one needs to consider a variety of associated definitions that have been put forward and expand the umbrella of complexity thinking ideology. *Keene (2000)* referred to Complexity Theory and defined this as an area between order and chaos occupied by a system. She saw this as the zone of complexity. *Richardson and Cilliers (2001)* talked about the Science of Complexity, defining a complex system as one that incorporates numerous entities that demonstrate an elevated incidence of non-linear interactivity. *Browning and Sanders (2012)* similarly viewed complexity as a large system containing a variety of parts that interact in unclear, different ways that reinforce unpredictability and uncertainty of the effects of these activities.

Mason (2011) expanded on these views and added that predicting any outcome is impossible within complex systems due to these intricate interactions. He aligned himself with Keene, agreeing that complex systems exist on the edge of chaos, but added that these individual components do not have a master controller as they never fall out of complete control, even though they are not and do not have fixed or rigid roles within a particular system. Hence the unlimited variety of outcomes to any changes are infinite. *Johnson (2007)* similarly viewed complexity as the result of various varied interactions that can even produce undesired results. *Mason (2011)* further believed complex systems to be adaptive in a manner that is beneficial to that system, very much like our mental ability to adapt and learn from life experiences *(Waldrop 1992)*.

Holland (2014) concurred that complex adaptive systems are forever rearranging and changing during the process of gaining experience. He cited a rainforest, world markets and multi-celled organisms as complex systems. Take the Internet that consists of users, servers and websites, all interlinked in a complex web exhibiting what Holland referred to as "emergence" which he described as, "*the action of the whole is more than the sum of actions of the parts*" *(Holland 2014, p. 2)*.

An interesting analogy is supplied by *Taborsky (2014)* who described a junk heap of car parts as an unorganised complex object, while a working motor vehicle with its various parts that interact in varying ways and through different meaningful relationships, as an organised complex object. Even though the pile of junk car parts displayed a similar level of complexity to that of a working car, the difference is in the way either fulfills a function. He adds a cunning twist advocating that if the junk car parts heap were an artistic creation by a famous artist, then it would have purpose and no longer be disorganised. But as a mere heap of car parts it simply remains an unorganised complex object.

Complexity Leadership Theory (CLT) on the other hand, studies the interactive connectivity of complex systems entrenched within the environment of larger established systems *(Uhl-Bien, Marion & McKelvey 2007)*. Scientists similarly agree that nature is a complex, adaptive and non-linear system, i.e. various autonomous agents perpetually interacting and changing with each other. To merely study one segment of any complex dynamic system would therefore only result in an incomplete understanding of that whole system. Therefore, if we see complex systems as being adaptive, researching simple interactions will deliver unexplainable results. However, *Zenouzi and Dehghan (2012)* believed that even though such patterns are challenging to forecast, they are not random.

Another example of complexity thinking in corporations is the increase and excessive bombardment of marketing messages through various mediums, from social media to mobile phones. Instead of winning over customers, organisations are now alienating them with these unrelenting and unwanted efforts to engage *(Spenner & Freeman 2012)*.

Dervitsiotis (2012) professed that initially most organisations have limited complexity due to few strategic goals and simple day-to-day tasks being handled by a small group of founders. As the organisation grows and evolves internally and externally, new business functions, systems, world events, employees, suppliers, government interactions and technology, all lead to increased interconnectivity and complexity. This was echoed by *Porter (1995)* who viewed the level of complexity as a direct result of the interactions of the various parts within an organisation, including operational members such as clients, suppliers and wholesales, and the extended environmental regulations.

According to *Woermann (2011, p. 2)*, practitioners and academics defined complexity as something that lacks a simple explanation. However, she added an insightful statement, "*To equate complexity with original simplicity is to recognise complexity by decomplexifying it.*" According to *Rouse et al (2011)*, from the above research is became clear that attempting to forecast absolute outcomes is a flawed and unrealistic mind set in today's unstable and unpredictable world.

If anything, complexity science clearly teaches us that even a small sample of factors causing a specific complex situation will be limiting in accuracy and problematic, at the very least. Rather than view complexity in a negative context, leadership needs to realise that one cannot suppress, control or foster ownership of all consequences of things arising from complexity. Therefore a mind shift is needed to accept the 'messiness' and focus on changing diversity into opportunity.

2.2 LEADERSHIP ROLES WITHIN COMPLEX SYSTEMS

During the 20th Century leadership models were characteristically top-down, bureaucratic and highly effective in organisations focusing on physical production, rather than knowledge oriented companies. Today, complexity science advocates a completely different approach to leadership focusing on learning, innovation and adaptation *(Uhl-Bien & Marion, 2008)*.

O'Connell (2014) wrote that in the past 80 years, there have been a plethora of frameworks and theories resulting in a complex web of leadership definitions that have resulted in continuing debates between scholars regarding the most applicable definitions and most able approaches to effective leadership. In fact, *Bennis (2007)* viewed this absence on a singular definition of leadership as a cliché, while *Goffee and Jones (2006)* argued that any attempt to create a clear-cut list of leadership attributes would be futile.

During the early ages, a clan culture predominated where the masses where treated as slaves with limited rights and lead by one great man. This was known as Theory X leadership style based on authoritarian control over a demotivated workforce. Transactional leadership took time and as the workforce became more educated through training during the industrial age – the focus started shifting to a Theory Y leadership style where employees were led forward through shared visions and an internal work culture of quality and perfectionism. Today we have moved into a breakthrough (iconoclastic) leadership phase *(Zenouzi & Dehghan 2012)*. Figure 1 outlines the leadership styles and development throughout history.

Style	Variables	Attractors	
Great Man	Leader	1.	Brain: skilled hunters, Blue blood
		2.	Objective : Perform Great mission and survive
	Organization	Tribes, clans, Failure to follow leads to death	
	Environment	1.	Brute force accepted, fear-based
		2.	Long-term power derived from survival skills
		3.	Feudalistic mindset to human at late development
Transactional	Leader	1.	Brain: Controlling, measuring still Feudalistic mindset
		2.	Objective : Reduce cost, increase production
	Organization	1.	Workers were inefficient, unskilled with agricultural mind
		2.	Organize, control, command, measure and decide for results
		3.	Lazy and inefficient workers are being developed and getting ready for participation
	Environment	1.	Mass Production at minimal costs
		2.	Stability is a must, do what it takes to get the job done
		3.	Labor unions start getting power.
Transformational	Leader	1.	Brain: Systemizing brain, virtually realizing "promised land"
		2.	Objective : Insight spiritual Visions
	Organization	Theory Y employees, Flexible and participative organization	
	Environment	Post industrialized, "Brain Power" Era, Demanding speed and innovative solutions.	

Figure 1 - Zenouzi & Dehghan (2012, p. 50)

Bennis (2012) postulated that the 21st century landscape has changed radically and leaders are faced with and expansive set of constant new information (technology and complexities steered by globalisation) that needs to be unceasingly appraised and re-appraised without any final analysis. Hence learning to lead has become increasing complex while at the same time circumstantial and temporal, adjusting as the situations, individuals and groups change *(Osborn, Hunt & Jauch, 2002; Porter & McLaughlin, 2006)*. Therefore leadership growth and ability to mature in a long-term career remains paramount today *(Anderson 1993; Day 2012; Kegan 1994; Kegan & Lahey, 2010; Lord & Hall, 2005)*.

Hitt (1998) questioned whether the peak of this new economic age has been reached, while *Bettis and Hitt (1995)* and *Child and McGrath (2001)* agreed that these new international, competitive complex landscapes with knowledge and innovation as basic prerequisites are crucial for leaders and organisational longevity today. Reinvention, strategic interruptions, volatility, blurring of boundaries, sharing of knowledge, innovating thinking and increasing competition are but a sprinkling of requirements that have added to the interconnected and erratic complexity of leadership development today *(Drath et al., 2008; Martin 2007; Uhl-Bien et al., 2007)*. *Bennis (1998)* however, perceived this as an inescapable, yet more natural evolution of leadership, while *Avolio (2007, p. 31)* succinctly believed that current authentic and transformational leadership theories should "*advocate a fuller and more integrative focus that is multilevel, multicomponent, and interdisciplinary and that recognises that leadership is a function of the leader, the led, and the complexity of the context.*"

Various scholars focused on differing aspects of coping with complexity leadership today. According to *Drath et al. (2008)*, *Hooijberg et al. (1997)*, and *Schneider and Somers (2006)*, leadership traits to be mastered include; collectiveness, affiliation and cooperation and being receptive to complex challenges. *Bierly, Kessler and Christensen (2000), Boal and Hooijberg (2000), Denison et al. (1995)*, and *Jaques (1989)* added managerial acumen, flexibility, ability to absorb learning, perceptiveness, prudence, interpersonal and social intellect, critical timing as well as behavioural and cognitive complexity.   *Denison et al. (1995)* further asserted that adeptness in balancing of multitudinal roles that can be complex, connected, contrasting, competing and conflicting is equally important.

Brown (2012), Drath (2001b), Jacobs and Jaques (1987), Marion and Uhl-Bien (2001), O'Connell (2014) and *Senge (1990)* all said that not only must leaders be proficient in these competencies, but they also need to promote and foster these same competencies within their staff and organisations. *Uhl-Bien, Marion, and McKelvey (2007)* further inferred that leaders must change their thinking from old to new ideas. They observed that social resources such as business IQ and the capacity to learn and adapt quickly to change are vital for success.

Leaders who are held prisoner by physical resources will fail today. *Lians (2013)* agreed that traditional strategies no longer work and that high probability thinking is something of the past. Therefore aligning the strategies, culture and structure to the current environment is imperative. In fact *Stevenson (2012)* referred to this 'old thinking' as being mechanistic due to the leaders' inability to escape the enslavement of linear thinking.

David (2013) explained that this decision-making on new issues is based on past successful or ineffective experiences. *Scharmer (2010)* concurred that leaders need to look at the future very differently from the past that will naturally result in needed chaos. *Schneider and Somers (2006)* agreed, adding that only when this edge of chaos has been reached do complex systems reach their zenith of adaptability so that evolution may occur. The focus for leadership in complex situations is to enable, rather than control *(Geer-Frazier 2014)*. *Bajer (2009) and Uhl-Bien, Marion, and McKelvey (2007)* all acknowledged that whereas previous leadership thinking focused on controlling behaviour, today's complex adaptive systems require the development of leadership cultures where everyone strives to add value, work as a team and create change.

A panel at the 2011 IBM Think Forum *(Geer-Frazier 2014)* suggested that leaders abstain from individual biases and judgmental thinking, while empowering staff to do the same. Second, they should strive to transcend limitations in knowledge and constantly keep abreast of times. They should embrace group talents and collective intelligences. Finally they can then accept that autocratic leadership and a one person in charge position will not work anymore today.

These views are echoed by *Collins (2001)* who emphasised simplicity as one of the characteristics of great leaders. He viewed a culture of discipline, confronting the real facts, not overreacting to new technologies, and choosing the right people for the right job as crucial qualities for innovative leaders to cultivate success.

In contrast to the above, *Marion (1999)* contended that leaders mistakenly define their experiences in terms of cause and effect, calculated forecasts, cost cutting and balance. Hence complexity is not the problem. Outdated leadership ideologies are at fault as they cloud thinking and restrict modern-day leaders from shifting old beliefs to new possible modes of evaluation and understanding of organisational behaviour *(Uhl-Bien & Marion 2008)*. In fact *Anderson (1999)* stated that when companies implement strategic complex adaptive systems, they need to develop systems that can quickly adapt and evolve effective solutions.

Bradbury and Lichtenstein (2000) believed that complexity science answers what a leader really is, namely a resultant after-effect of related interactions between various role players and events through transformation, competition and collaboration within the organisational environment *(Morrison 2014)*. Thus leadership exceeds charisma, symbolism and skill, additionally developing from influential interactions. *Seers (2004)* also recognised that only focusing on the distinctive behaviour of competent executives is inadequate as a definitive explanation of the essence of leadership.

Lichtenstein et al (2006) likewise acknowledged true leadership surpasses basic individual competencies – cooperation, sharing of common interests, institutional history and knowledge, tension, external and internal responses to pressure are all part of the ever increasing pressures of leading today.

Accelerating these interdependent mechanisms among varying individuals within organisations in order to reach a unified desired outcome is known as Complexity Leadership Theory *(Drath 2001a; Meyer et al. 2005)*. It must be noted that this theory does not curtail the importance of leaders within companies, but rather rises above lone leaders by essentially being a system phenomenon. *(Marion & Uhl-Bien 2001, 2003; Uhl-Bien et al. 2007; Hazy 2006)*. Therefore leaders are capable of laying the foundations that enable the conditions for the change, but not necessarily the single isolated cause of said change *(Lichtenstein et al 2006)*.

In summary, a description of the effect of complexity thinking on leaders is given by *Heckscher (1994, p. 24)* "*There is a growing sense that effective organisation change has its own dynamic, a process that cannot simply follow strategic shifts and that is longer and subtler than can be managed by any single leader. It is generated by the insights of many people trying to improve the whole, and it accumulates, as it were, over long periods.*"

2.3 COMPLEXITY THINKING AND ITS AFFECTS ON INNOVATION

The Times of London (2006) said complexity results when the pursuit of innovation is taken too far, eventually culminating in a stagnation of profits. *Cross (2010)* built on this, seeing it as employees straining to come to grips with increased product offerings that require extra space, marketing, training, support, work and hence increased costs that result in a lower return on investment. If anything, he advocates reductionism to combat complexity and promote innovation. *Richardson (2008)* elaborated that complexity thinking with its resultant unpredictability could become so overbearing and time consuming, that it restricts innovation due to limiting what leaders can learn and achieve in a predetermined plan.

In addition to the above, companies have become customer centric, resulting in a more complex environment that is challenging for today's leader to manage *(Cross 2010)*. *Maylor, Turner and Murray-Webster (2013)* concurred with *Cross (2010)* that project complexity and management systems are on the increase. They further highlighted that leadership needs to grasp the urgency of managing this complexity to improve processes, training and staffing. Only then will frustrations, failures and unnecessary costs be reduced.

This is augmented by *Dervitsiotis (2012)* who stated that not only does leadership need to foster a better understanding of where complexity originates in daily operations, but they must also identify the long-term impacts of these complex changes in strategy and the environment in order to promote effective innovation. *Cross (2010)* shared a classic example of innovation gone astray mentioning a study done on banks that offered a complex array of between ten and nineteen different bank cards. He promotes 'lean' and questioned why they could not simply have one basic smart card that could be adapted to each customer's needs.

Pablo et al (2012) argued that innovative, companies will be faced with many challenges, resulting in two barriers to innovation, those that arise from, and those that stop organisations from taking part in innovative processes. Revealed barriers deal with the difficulty of achieving the innovation process and the resultant learning of that process, i.e. the company awareness of the problems that accompany innovation processes. While deterring barriers are those obstacles that prevent innovation from taking place, i.e. impossible to overcome.

Galia and Legros (2004, p. 1189) agreed that certain obstacles cannot be effectively solved until they are encountered and insightfully stated that "*innovative firms face problems and more innovative firms have more problems.*" *Baldwin and Lin (2002)* and *Tourigny and Le (2004)* offer a twist, suggesting that difficulties in achieving innovation should not be seen as negative, but rather as a positive indication of how effectively an organisation overcomes them and hence builds on its success. *Schneider and Somers (2006, p. 355)* further added that complex adaptive systems will be "*most adaptive when near the edge of chaos*" and this is vital for change and evolution to occur.

Following on this school of thought, the Complexity Leadership Theory view of an innovation driver suggests that when tension arises from the interaction of agents within an organisation, this challenges and pressures their personal knowledge base *(Carley & Hill 2001)*. These confrontations to the agent's agenda can, under ideal circumstances, promote and result in the conversion of the agents emotional views, therefore realigning their schema *(Kauffman 1993; Marion & Uhl-Bien 2001)*. These tension associated compromises often produce unexpected, new and fresh innovations, ideas and schema from a limiting current knowledge base *(Uhl-Bien, Marion & McKelvey 2007)*. *Lichtenstein et al (2006)* defined adaptive leadership as the resultant positive change resulting from these new understandings.

Additionally, *Conti (2009, 2010)* believed that the world has changed to such an extent; leaders can no longer afford to only focus on quality products and processes. They need to include quality innovative processes that scrutinise new value driven opportunities and foster an efficient, constant and continual high quality adaptation process to remain optimally fit in an ever changing and emerging modern world.

Dervitsiotis (2010, 2011, 2012) asserted that this strategic complexity requires bi-focal leadership to achieve short-term operational successes that produce critical earnings (those that sustain the running costs of a company) which in turn concurrently expose new possibilities and innovations for long-term excellence *(Christensen 1998; Govindarajan & Trimble, 2010)*. Dervitsiotis cited Apple, Google, Samsung and BMW as companies with bi-focal leadership that has achieved such results. He concurs that a key to survival today is the quality of a company's innovation processes. These are however dependant on the vision of innovative leaders who display characteristics such as flexibility, trustworthiness, and openness to experimentation, risk taking and accepting of failure and a willingness to learn.

Donaldson (1995) added a twist to current research by contending that there is an overabundance of examples of management science that has splintered into competing archetypes. This he asserted has resulted in innovation for the wrong reasons, i.e. personal career advancement only. Thus the focus has shifted from a positive holistic organisation knowledge gain and promotion view to a negatively self-serving perspective.

Browning and Saunders (2012) advocated that innovative organisations could be lean, even though such environments have a tendency to be novel and complex. They agreed that "*cutting out the fat*" *(2012, p. 5)* is a formidable task, especially when considering the traditional lean environment compared to a complex one, as in Figure 2.

TRADITIONAL LEAN VS. NOVEL & COMPLEX ENVIRONMENTS

Environmental Characteristics	
Traditional Lean	**Novel and Complex**
• Stable and routine processes	• Dynamic and unfamiliar processes
• High-volume production	• Low-volume production
• Stable workforce	• Workforce turnover
• Traditional learning curve	• Learning curve disruptions
• Eliminated buffers	• Purposeful buffers

Figure 2 - Browning & Sanders (2012, p. 8)

Research done by *Browning and Saunders (2012)* on Lockheed Martin's F-22 jet clarified that within complex and novel environments, striving for competitive and stable lean settings that cultivate understanding are possible, provided five cautionary procedures are followed;

1. Timing: Apply lean principles when disruptions will be minimal. If a process is already operating effectively, do not attempt to add lean changes.

2. Insight: Seek to identify and understand all novel and complex resultant effects of the resultant lean change in order to eliminate unexpected surprises.

3. Knowledge: Understand that changing an isolated low-level activity into an efficient, leaner activity may not improve the overall process, i.e. increasing vehicle performance by adding a turbo charge is pointless if the vehicle still remains stuck in peak hour traffic at the end of the day.

4. Analyse: Compare the value versus the waste produced within the complex environment, embracing the ideology that waste reduction is the main attribute of lean. Be mindful to always explicitly differentiate between wasteful fat and real muscle.

5. ROI: Be cautious by limiting lean practices that may inhibit any return on investment, i.e. do not take the lean practices too far that they become wasteful.

2.4 ACTIONS AND TOOLS TO MANAGE COMPLEXITY THINKING

A number of schools of thought exist on managing complexity thinking. *Cross (2010)* proposed three general steps a leader should follow for organisations to become leaner and eradicate complexity. First, they should change employee awareness by shifting their thinking to understand what they currently believe may not always be correct. Second, they should institute and practice exercises that phase out waste. Third, actualise a 5-S approach to eradicate complexity, i.e. *sort* everything into two piles – what they need (essential to run the business) and trash or wasteful items practices, services, etc. (non-essential). Second, *straighten* up everything in the need pile by packing it where it belongs and/or streamlining processes and systems, and/or prioritising these in terms of importance. *Shine* these items by re-branding, painting or lighting them in a new way. **Standardise** by highlighting their importance and making these part of the company brand and vision. Finally **sustain** and keep this product or service by maintaining constant high performance levels.

Geer-Frazier (2014) postulated that in order for companies to adapt to changes, cognisance of internal and external dynamic environments by leadership is of paramount importance. Building on this, a panel at the *IBM Think Forum (2011)* focused on leaders enabling staff through collaboration, rather than controlling them. They stressed that leaders should avoid and not succumb to individual biases and foster the same behaviour from their staff. They further highlighted the importance of leadership tapping into the collective intelligences of the group, rather than relying on possible limiting self-knowledge. *Bajer (2009, p. 38)* agreed that companies should *"attempt to develop leadership cultures where everyone in an organisation is actively working together to create changes and add value."*

Gottfredson and Aspinall (2005) felt that many organisations were puzzled by poor results after fine-tuning their operations. This they blamed on the company never identifying its Innovation Fulcrum, i.e. identifying products/service range, sales turnover and the point where the balance between operating complexity and customer satisfaction breaks down. In order to identify this baseline, leaders need to establish the standard minimal basic operating criteria needed before complexity sets in, i.e. the basic indispensable resources, bottom-line processes, expenditure and earnings required to maintain this service. Once identified, services and products can now be added one at a time. When earnings begin to decrease due to complexity of offerings, the Innovation Fulcrum has been has been surpassed. Therefore the amount and kind of services/products before this happens is known as the Innovation Fulcrum. However, in changing times, this will shift as your customer needs change *(Tarantino 2006)*.

The premise offered by *Heywood, Spungin and Turnbull (2007)* was that in order to bolster competitive advantage, leaders may purposely add complexity. However, the predicted benefits of this increased complexity needs to be justified through increased value creation from the related cost reductions. They also felt that senior leadership wrongly emphasised strategic complexity, whereas the less precarious operational complexity that focuses on reducing complexity in daily organisational tasks is more efficacious.

Dervitsiotis (2012) believed that complexity should be managed using a systematic 5-phase approach. Firstly the area where the complexity exists needs to be identified, i.e. at a certain hierarchy level in the company, a particular process or even a specific function such as customer support. Secondly, remove, disperse or trim superfluous complexity. This can be accomplished by dispersing complexity in one area to various skilled staff, or even by creating a new department. Thirdly, analyse and revise the organisational design. This could include extending the premises, adding a new component based on practical needs, or even redesigning the organisational architecture.

Fourthly, perfect and enhance organisational and production processes in order to achieve optimal performance. *Rummler and Brache (1995)* added that a leader needs to continually strive to achieve the best blend of human skills and technology to maintain continual advancement. Finally, cultivate and improve internal processes (quality and service) and employee competencies (knowledge, communication, problem solving and creativity). *Brown and Duguid (2000)* and *Dervitsiotis (2011)* further believed that through teamwork and open dialogue, all staff members have the potential to identify problem areas, and improve and solve these though step-by-step accumulative smaller innovations.

Govindarajan and Trimble (2010) asserted that in order to develop innovation excellence, a leader must be able to meticulously sense emergent opportunities by accurately deciphering all signs of change within the environment. The leader must also be able to act rapidly, economically and effectively to deliver the innovation to market, while maintaining an overall balance between the supply and demand, accumulative and chaotic innovations, plus internal and external projects.

Today complexity of projects and management systems are on the increase, hence in the interest of minimising risk and gaining possible benefits, it is imperative to manage this complexity effectively. According to *Maylor, Turner and Murray-Webster (2013)*, the more complex a project is, the less the possibility of achieving innovative success. Hence they developed the Complexity Assessment Tool (CAT).

The Complexity Assessment Tool

Areas of complexity	Do you agree with this statement? (Y/N)	Do you expect this situation to remain stable (i.e., NOT to change)? (Y/N)
• Structural Complexity (1–21)		
• Sociopolitical Complexity (22–32)		
• Emergent Complexity (defined by expectations for stability)		

Structural Complexity

1	The vision and benefits for the work can be clearly articulated.
2	Success measures for the work can be defined in agreement with the client.
3	The technology is familiar to us.
4	The commercial arrangements are familiar to us.
5	The scope can be well defined.
6	Acceptance criteria for quality and regulatory requirements can be well defined.
7	A schedule and resource plan can be well defined.
8	The supply chain is in place.
9	Lines of responsibility for tasks and deliverables can be defined.
10	Accurate, timely, and comprehensive data reporting is possible.
11	Existing management tools can support the work.
12	Sufficient people with the right skills are available.
13	Managers have adequate control of human resources (i.e., direct reporting).
14	Key people are wholly allocated to the work.
15	Integration across multiple technical disciplines is not required.
16	The budget is sufficient for the task.
17	The budget can be used flexibly.
18	The work will be carried out in a single country/time zone/language/currency.
19	The work is independent of other projects and business-as-usual operations.
20	The pace is achievable.
21	Resources (e.g., test facilities, equipment) will be available when needed.

Sociopolitical Complexity

22	The work has clear sponsorship consistent with its importance.
23	The business case for the work is clear.
24	The goals for the work align with the organization's strategy.
25	Your own senior management supports the work.
26	Team members are motivated and function well as a team.
27	Managers are experienced in this kind of work.
28	The work involves no significant organizational/cultural change.
29	The work will be unaffected by significant organizational/cultural change.
30	The external stakeholders (i.e., not immediate team members) are aligned, supportive, and committed to the project and have sufficient time for the work.
31	The external stakeholders (i.e., not immediate team members) have a realistic, shared understanding of the implications of the work.
32	The core team has the authority to make decisions.

Figure 3 - Maylor, Turner & Murray-Webster (2013, p. 48)

This tool assists leaders in the early detection of complexities so that they can be managed in order to diminish the adverse repercussions on the team and organisation. The Complexity Assessment Tool consists of 32 statements, divided in 3 areas (structural, socio-political and emergent) of complexity that include 160 themes. All statements cover a wide scope of projects and can also be custom-fitted to individual organisational needs, Figure 3 on the previous page.

Maylor, Turner and Murray-Webster (2013) acknowledged that leaders in their study group (consisting of private and public entities) reacted favourably to the tool, as it offered an analytical and methodised approach to deliberating about a current project, thereby drawing attention to concerns brushed aside and/or neglected previously. Therefore, participants do not benefit directly from the Complexity Assessment Tool as such, but indirectly from the sense making discussions that follow by promoting a wider, integrated and commonplace understanding between the participants.

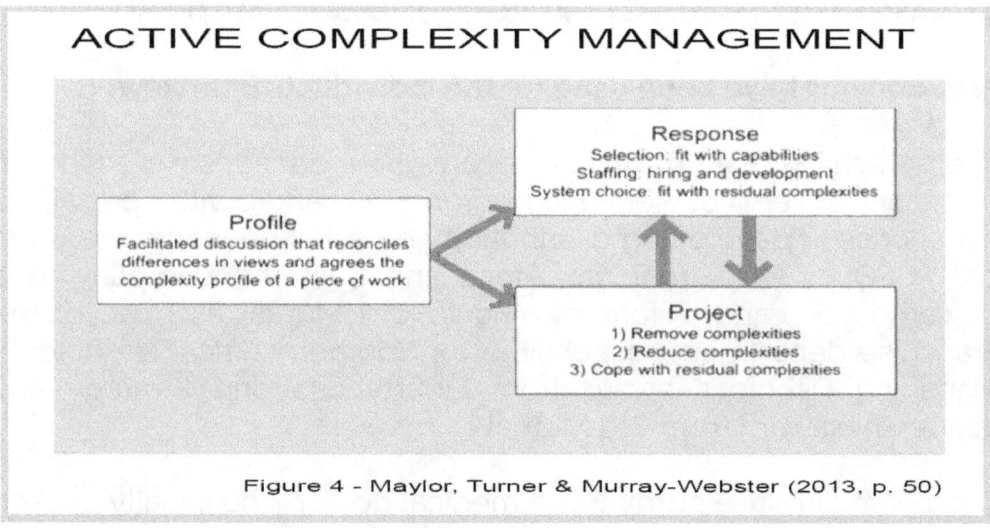

Figure 4 - Maylor, Turner & Murray-Webster (2013, p. 50)

The ramifications of using the Complexity Assessment Tool is that complexity can be monitored and handled so that projects can be chosen according to their complexity levels at the same time enabling leaders to allocate ideal staff, resources and applicable process in order to remove and/or reduce the impact of said complexities, as in Figure 4. However, it must be noted that residual complexities can linger. Therefore the Complexity Assessment Tool should be seen as encouraging mechanism that aids leaders in organisations to better support and hinder complexity in projects. *"Structural complexity is hard. The rest of it, now that's proper hard"* *(Maylor, Turner & Murray-Webster 2013, p .51).*

2.5 REFLECTION ON LITERATURE REVIEW

From the literature review a clearer understanding of what complexity thinking is, as well as its effects on leadership and innovation has been ascertained. In terms of tools that can assist in managing complexity, the Complexity Assessment Tool appears to be the most comprehensive mechanism to assist leaders. Now investigation into the real-world environment through 5 individual case studies of experienced CEO's will take place to attempt augment the above research and to see to what extent they agree/disagree that complexity thinking inhibits innovation.

3. RESEARCH

3.1 CASE STUDY: SUBJECT BACKGROUND INFORMATION

Pseudonyms have been used for the individuals interviewed.

The person in **Case Study A** has nearly three decades experience in the financial services sector and property market with specialised experience in developing distribution and sales networks. He is the past CEO of AIDA in South Africa and built the company to a powerhouse brand before moving to Old Mutual as head of the Franchise department responsible for Southern Africa. He holds a Managing Director's award from Liberty Life and Strategy and Leadership award from Old Mutual.

The person in **Case study B** is a medical doctor who initially worked in health services for 14 years followed by 16 years of managing various hospitals for a multi-national private hospital group. He is currently based in Cape Town heading up their flagship private hospital for the Netcare group.

The person in **Case study C** is the most internationally experienced subject of the group, having initially served as business development manager for a dairy company in infant nutrition in Holland before moving on to Spain and Portugal. He built businesses in the Philippines and Singapore, followed by three years as general manager in the Netherlands before moving to Rumania where he built a factory and set up the market. He moved across to the animal feed and nutrients market working for Nutreco, spending five years in Bucharest and another five years in Moscow, where he concurrently oversaw the building of the largest animal feed factory in the world in southern Russia while leading this 500 million Euro giant. He now resides in South Africa where he is pursuing a new venture. Subject C initially held the role of development manager in infant nutrition in a dairy company, moving to feed and feed ingredients with Nutreco where he built and set up markets in Eastern Europe ending up as GM in Russia building the largest animal feed factory in the world.

Subject D was a past business manager in the ITC (information technology and communication) business for Bytes System Integration and Oracle. Today he is managing account executive of Business Connexion in Southern Africa who supplies ITC solutions to southern Africa's largest organisations.

The subject of **Case study E** has 29 years of experience in management and leadership positions within the ICT industry. He has worked for two multi-national companies, and currently the vice president of delivery for T-Systems in South Africa and Africa. He serves on the board and is part of Europe and Middle East leadership team with extensive experience as a customer and service provider.

3.2 METHODOLOGY

This research uses a qualitative approach to meet the research objectives. The literature review includes further books, journals, surveys and relevant academic research on the subject of complexity thinking and leadership roles within complex modern organisations.

It has been of paramount importance to research real world experience and investigate in depth, the current thinking on the complexity thinking; hence the study has taken a pragmatic approach *(Robson 2011)*. The focus has been on qualitative research *(Saunders, Lewis & Thornhill 2009)* using the research aims as a broad outline for personal interviews that were undertaken with C level (high ranking executives with 'Chief' titles) executives at their offices in their natural business setting, generating ample representative data that has assisted in evaluating their experiences, attitudes and concerns *(Dingwall et al, 1988)* gained through actual practice *(Meredith 1998)*. All interviews where recorded and transcribed and this research formed the final segment of a dissertation for a Masters degree in Innovation & Change at the University of York St John in the United Kingdom.

The fundamental research strategy is a case study with interviews of five senior corporate executives of five different multi-national and international companies in South Africa (hospital group, telecommunications & ICT solutions, animal nutrition, financial institution and property group). The organisations were chosen with the specific aim of researching a broad spectrum of industries, ideologies and leadership styles to gain an objective representation of views. The intention of this research is not only to contribute to current research, but also the further collection and generation of data to assist in understand real-world problems relating to complexity thinking *(Bickman & Rog 2008)*.

It was an observational inquiry investigating current views *(Yin 2009)* where the leaders have been specifically selected for their experience and standing in the South African and international business scene. All subjects are in their late forties and fifties and have had to adapt to the changes in the economic, cultural and political environment over the last three decades in order to remain innovate and competitive. They have openly shared their insights concerning the research questions, in their ever changing, complex business environments.

During the interview process, a flexible data gathering strategy was used *(Robson 2011)*. It has been a cross sectional research, initially planned over a period of five weeks, with one week per subject for the interview, follow-up and any further questioning. The questions were open ended and constructed from research completed in the literature review, with the intention of collecting meaningful and astute answers that validated, expanded on, or contradicted current research. At times their answers also allow for further probing in order to explain and build on their responses *(Saunders, Lewis & Thornhill 2009)*.

As there is no typical approach for scrutinising qualitative data *(Saunders, Lewis & Thornhill 2009)*, the interviews have been transcribed and repetitive themes, keywords and salient points highlighted via (thematic) content analysis *(Yin 2009, Bynum et al 2009)*. A combination of archival records, direct observation, participant observation, documentation and physical artefacts was considered in triangulating the information received from the interviews *(Yin 2009)*.

3.3 LIMITATIONS

According to *Farquar (2012)* and *Remenyi et al. (1998)*, case studies can fall short due to an absence of objectivity, rigour and accuracy. The case study only represents five senior C level executives of large corporations. However, industries are varied, and each subject has managed at least two different companies in his lifetime.

Although the sample is small, they represent a fair cross-section of the business world. Before embarking on the study there was concern that a strong possibility existed that this could result in five completely different viewpoints. The subjects did have a general consensus on many of the questions, however there are some additional views that were not expected.

Although none of the subjects were given access to any of the literature used in the study at any stage, previous studies, in-house training and courses may have influenced their answers to align with current research. Finally, as this book is the result of a full Masters Degree study, this final research had to remain within the boundaries of a master's dissertation word count and accepted structure, the number of interview questions where thus limited to 18. Although it can be argued that more questions may have produced a far wider field of study, repetitive themes where part of this initial batch of questions and it was found that subjects who did volunteer any extra information still kept within the basic field of research as intended. Therefore in hindsight, I feel that the questions where ample and a good overall representation of the research topic.

4. DATA AND ANALYSIS

4.1 PRESENTATION OF SECONDARY DATA

All five interviews were recorded and transcribed. The interview questions were included in the dissertation to the University of York St John and adhered to the ethics requirements of the university. In line with the ethics requirements, the original transcripts have beed left out of this book to preserve the anonymity of the research subjects.

The criteria for asking the specific questions was based on and extracted from the literature review and research done to date, in order to determine whether the case study subjects agreed or disagreed with the current findings within their own business environments. Each question has been further summarised in tabular point form with horizontal rows representing similar views. Certain themes were also reworded and posed as a different question at another point in the interview in order guide the subjects back to research aims, should they have deviated from the specifics of a previous question; hence certain tables contain two or more questions that pertain to a theme.

4.2 ANALYSIS AND LINK WITH LITERATURE REVIEW

On seeking a definition of complexity thinking in Question 1, Subject A's interview as a whole endorsed *Heywood, Spungin, and Turnbull's (2007)* views of highlighting strategic and operational complexity and the stumbling blocks associated with these as the foundation of complexity thinking. He conjointly concurred that misaligned communication and lack of synergy between leadership and the workforce was a further contributing factor tin defining complex systems within an organisation. He cited his CEO successes within a previous smaller leadership team as pivotal in fending off complexity and increasing brand awareness due being able to implement innovative idea speedily, in alignment with *Dervitsiotis (2012)*.

QUESTION 1:
How would you define complexity thinking within organisations?

Subject A	Subject B	Subject C	Subject D	Subject E
Misaligned communication	Differing feedback cycles			
Lack of synergy between leadership and workforce				
Strategic and Operational Complexity		Information overload and Increase in compliance		Balancing multitudinal roles
	Non - Linear interactivity seen as origin of chaos			
			Individual state of mind/ level of consciousness	

Horizontal green rows represent similar views by various subjects, but worded differently

Subject B validated *Richardson and Cilliers (2001)* incidence of non-linear interactivity, highlighting *Browning and Sanders (2012)* view that complexity occurs as a result of the differing feedback cycles of assorted departments within an organisation. Subject B was the only subject to view this non-linear complex relationship as the origin of chaos in alignment with *Keene (2002)* and *Mason (2011)* definition on complexity theory and felt that it was synonymous with complexity thinking. Subject C agreed with *Bennis (2012)* and cited excessive and readily available information together with increasing compliance regulations as the main contributors to complexity in organisations. Subject D gave this question serious thought, offering an insightful definition by suggesting that complexity thinking is dependent, not only on how and individual perceives a situation, but additionally on their state of mind at that given point in time. This is very much in line with *Waldrop (1992) and Mason's (2011)* complex adaptive systems views. It is only through repetition, that complexity eventually becomes simple.

He offered a simple; yet spot on analogy of a new golfer learning a golf swing. The initial instruction and run down by the golf pro of how to swing that club is complex. But after a few weeks it becomes second nature. At this point additional tips are easier to assimilate and adapt *(Waldorp 1992)*. He also mentioned that someone might suggest swinging the club left handed rather than right. The first swing may be an improvement and a possible reason to change, but questioned whether the associated complexity of changing and the resultant one probable improvement outweigh the other 173 facets not considered? This is very much in alignment with *Johnson (2007)* who questioned whether these adaptive procedures wouldn't result in undesired consequences.

In addition to *Porter's (1995)* views that complexity thinking resulted from interactions between operational members and the company, Subject D highlighted that today's leadership roles are multi-faceted, i.e. a CIO (Chief Information Officer) needs to also be a CTO (Chief Technical Officer) as does a CFO (Chief Financial Officer) need to understand legal and compliance related topics; hence an increase in complexity. *Denison et al (1995)* referred to this as being adept in balancing multitudinal roles.

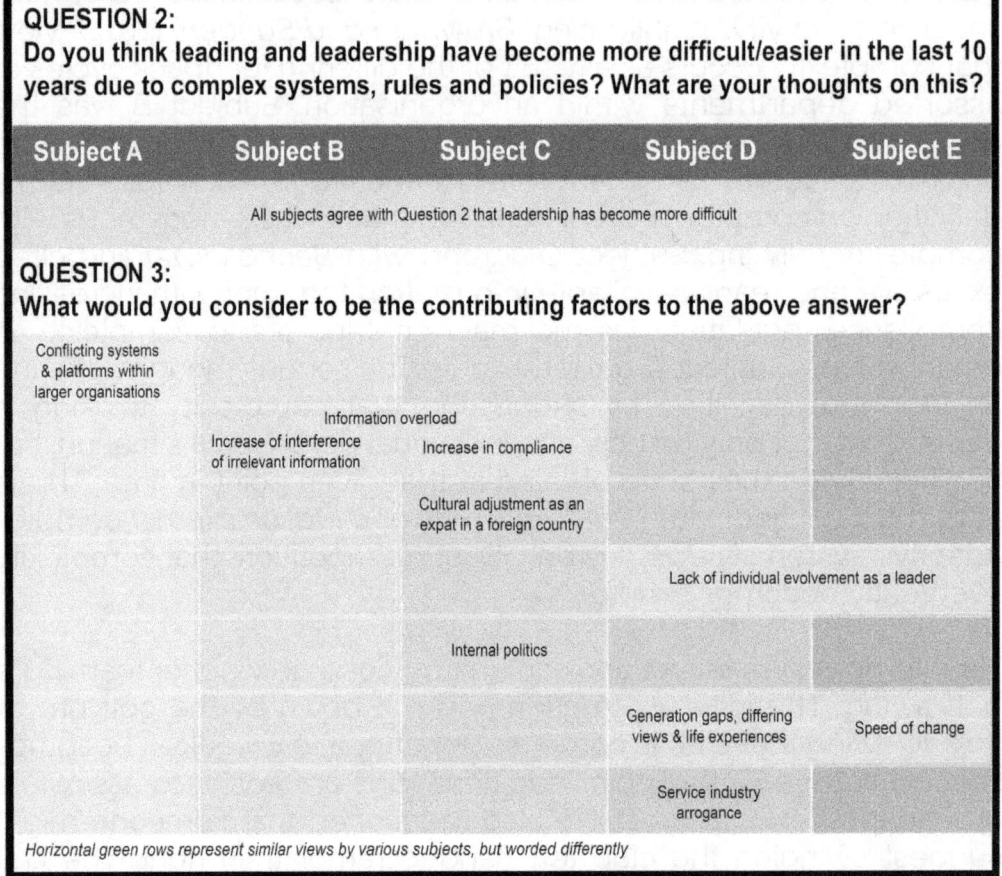

QUESTION 2:
Do you think leading and leadership have become more difficult/easier in the last 10 years due to complex systems, rules and policies? What are your thoughts on this?

Subject A	Subject B	Subject C	Subject D	Subject E
All subjects agree with Question 2 that leadership has become more difficult				

QUESTION 3:
What would you consider to be the contributing factors to the above answer?

Subject A	Subject B	Subject C	Subject D	Subject E
Conflicting systems & platforms within larger organisations				
	Information overload			
	Increase of interference of irrelevant information	Increase in compliance		
		Cultural adjustment as an expat in a foreign country		
			Lack of individual evolvement as a leader	
		Internal politics		
			Generation gaps, differing views & life experiences	Speed of change
			Service industry arrogance	

Horizontal green rows represent similar views by various subjects, but worded differently

In answer to whether leadership has become more difficult in the last decade and what possible contributing factors are, subject A, in alignment with *Porter (1985)* and *Dervitsiotis (2012)* works viewed systems and platforms within large corporations as stumbling blocks, stating that these severely slowed down, and eventually negatively influence leaders decision making process, compared to smaller companies where communication and process was easier. These bureaucratic mechanisms and inward focus are similar to *Kotter and Hesket's (2011)* unadaptive culture that they see as undermining change. Similarly, subject C concurred that internal politics *(Mintzberg 1985, Changing Minds 2002 and Deal & Kenny 2000)* has a huge impact on decision-making, hence complicating leading today.

Subject B felt that managers become distracted by irrelevant information that in turn makes current problems appear more complex than what they really are. Hence instead of simplifying the process, leaders now complicate them. Although all subjects agreed that leading has become more convoluted, Subject C concurred with subject B that information overload is a major contributing factor as cited by *Bennis 2012, Osborn, Hunt and Jauch (2002)* and *Porter and McLaughlin (2006)*. He added cultural adjustment as an expat in a foreign country as a further contributing factor that could hinder innovation in leadership. *Hofstede's (2001)* Cultural Dimensions model may well be of practical use here.

Subject D and E saw this not so much as a complexity problem within organisations, but within the leader not personally evolving. Both felt leaders have become managers who manage the current flow of a situation, rather than surround themselves with the right people. *Collins (2001)* was the first to express this view, followed by *Waterman et al (2008)* who also stressed the importance of appointing capable people. Additionally subject D felt that younger leaders are more complex by nature having experienced so much more at a much younger age (in terms of exposure to technology and information) than senior leaders. They extend the boundaries of today's leaders, which complicates the relationship between the two and is aligned with views echoed at the 2011 IBM Think Forum *(Geer-Frazier 2014)* and the research results of others *(Anderson 1993); (Day 2012); (Kegan 1994); (Kegan & Lahey 2010); (Hall 2005)*. In addition, subject E stated that the speed of change *(Deal & Kenny 2000)* plays a role in making leadership more difficult today.

QUESTION 4:
In your experience, what actions and tools could assist leadership in being productively innovative in today's complex business environment?
QUESTION 12:
What role does risk taking play in being innovative in today's organisations?

Subject A	Subject B	Subject C	Subject D	Subject E
See the bigger picture & take a risk to achieve it	All risk taking and staying long enough to face consequences	Promote risk taking rather than a 'comfort zone'	You will never know what you don't know if you don't take risks	Risk bringing out an 80% ready rpoduct - just to be first - then update it.
Significantly simplify internal decision making process and speed up				
			First identify talent then give training in order to build future leaders	Pro-active innovation Future thinking

QUESTION 5:
In your opinion, what actions and tools could assist leaders in managing complexity thinking in the future?

Subject A	Subject B	Subject C	Subject D	Subject E
Understand culture and attitudes of staff				
		Freedom to be innovative	Allow freedom of growth by challenging boundaries	
	Identify & use relevant business models			
	Leaders need on the ground understanding of operational issues			Understand that technology is a business enabler

Horizontal green rows represent similar views by various subjects, but worded differently

---

Question 12 was incorporated in this answer, as everyone agreed cited risk as a tool that could assist leaders. Subject A felt that seeing the bigger picture and following through is a risk in itself. Subject B asserted that productively innovative leaders need to take risks, and remain long enough in their positions to face the consequences of these risks. Besides also advocating risk as a tool in being productively innovative, Subject C suggested that the lack of innovation is due to an adversity in leaders to taking risks and preferring to remain in a comfort zone. Insight, clear understanding and effective application of the Complexity Assessment Tool (CAT) by *Maylor, Turner & Murray-Webster (2013)* may be a step in the right direction to promoting more calculated innovations by leaders. Subject D chose his words carefully explaining it as, "*You will never know what you don't know if you are not prepared to take a risk.*" While subject E emphasised that risk is all about being first to market, even if the product is only 80% ready, citing Microsoft, Samsung and Apple as examples of hugely successful companies that follow this practice. This aligns with *Browning and Saunders (2012)* view on timing in order to remain competitive within complex environments.

Subject D stressed that training in itself was not enough. He accentuated the importance of leaders taking the responsibility of actively identifying future leadership talent and guiding them through mentorship and training in order to become innovative and productive future leaders as similarly advocated by *Brown (2012), Drath (2001b), Jacobs and Jaques (1987), Marion and Uhl-Bien (2001), O'Connell (2014) and Senge (1990)*. Additionally Subject E emphasised '*proactive innovation*' where leaders similarly predict and innovate possible future solutions as expressed by *Dahlgaard (2011)* and the Total Quality Management (TQM) Principal.

To manage future complexity thinking, Subject A agreed that leaders need to promote an all-inclusive understanding of people's attitudes, cultures and beliefs as stressed by *Bierly, Kessler and Christensen 2000; Bajer 2009; Boal and Hooijberg 2000; Denison et al. 1995* and *Jaques 1989*. However, he did express frustration at excessive political correctness, performance appraisals and assessments within larger organisations and questioned whether these alienated staff rather than brought them together as researched by *Schafer (2014)*. Additionally Subject B believed that leaders should consult with operational managers at strategic planning sessions to understand the real issues at hand, before implementing complex innovations based on limited operational experience. Subject E expanded on this mentioning that leaders need to understand that technology is a business enabler *(Mason 2011)*. Subjects C and D similarly agreed that innovative freedom and challenging of personal growth is imperative in developing productive future leaders and long-term excellence in accordance with the views of *Christensen (1998)* and *Govindarajan and Trimble (2010)*.

QUESTION 6:
Quality and quality driven processes played an important role in past business practices. Given today's complex ever changing environment, what elements/processes do you feel are needed to remain competitive in the future?

Subject A	Subject B	Subject C	Subject D	Subject E
Find out what client wants not what you want to sell Creativity & innovation			Minimum benchmark must always be quality	ZERO Outage, Deviation & Distance
		Internet & spread of communication from clients necessitates high quality		
	Feedback forms pointless is not acted upon			

Horizontal green rows represent similar views by various subjects, but worded differently

Subjects A, D and E agreed that quality adaptable innovation process are additionally essential to maintain optimal business fitness, in accordance with the views of *Conti (2009 & 2010)*. Subject A expressed this as, **"great is no longer good enough, it's got to be excellent,"** while Subject B referred to it as constantly moving the benchmark higher.

Subject E shared his company's philosophy of 'zero outage, "zero deviation and zero distance." In other words quality is a key to his business where leaders are encouraged to prevent issues before they occur, foster close customer relationships and ensure that all promises are be met at agreed upon prices and times without deviation. As a global player this company believes that quality is the cornerstone of their business and cultivates this belief in their leadership team.

Subject C built on this view in alignment with *Child and McGrath (2001)* that innovation is a basic requirement in today's competitive complex landscape, and emphasised the fact that through technology (Internet) bad service experiences are spread speedily around the world. Additionally he added that quantity does not always equate to quality, especially in staffing in governments and hence the shift to staff reduction and employing better quality people *(Collins 2001)*. Subject B argued that the use of feedback forms to improve quality is futile if leadership won't action comments made by virtue that it has no bearing on bottom line profits.

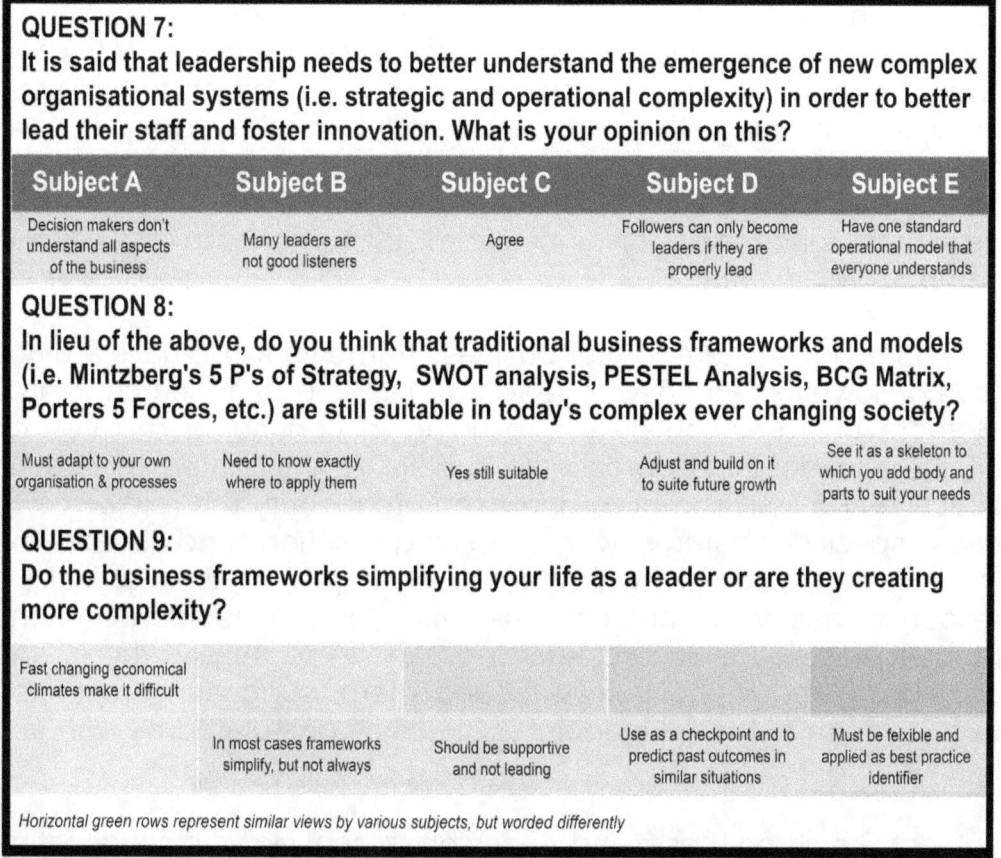

QUESTION 7:
It is said that leadership needs to better understand the emergence of new complex organisational systems (i.e. strategic and operational complexity) in order to better lead their staff and foster innovation. What is your opinion on this?

Subject A	Subject B	Subject C	Subject D	Subject E
Decision makers don't understand all aspects of the business	Many leaders are not good listeners	Agree	Followers can only become leaders if they are properly lead	Have one standard operational model that everyone understands

QUESTION 8:
In lieu of the above, do you think that traditional business frameworks and models (i.e. Mintzberg's 5 P's of Strategy, SWOT analysis, PESTEL Analysis, BCG Matrix, Porters 5 Forces, etc.) are still suitable in today's complex ever changing society?

Must adapt to your own organisation & processes	Need to know exactly where to apply them	Yes still suitable	Adjust and build on it to suite future growth	See it as a skeleton to which you add body and parts to suit your needs

QUESTION 9:
Do the business frameworks simplifying your life as a leader or are they creating more complexity?

Fast changing economical climates make it difficult				
	In most cases frameworks simplify, but not always	Should be supportive and not leading	Use as a checkpoint and to predict past outcomes in similar situations	Must be felxible and applied as best practice identifier

Horizontal green rows represent similar views by various subjects, but worded differently

All interviewees agreed that learning to lead has become more complex and agreed with *Avolio (2007)* views that leadership theories should be more unified to embrace various levels, components and disciplines not only by leadership, but by the staff and organisation as well. Subject A highlighted personal experience of *Porter's (1995)* views that lack of effective leadership interaction and understanding of operational issues adds to complexity. Subject B stressed that for a leader to grow in the long-term *(Anderson 1993; Day 2012; Kegan 1994; Kegan & Lahey 2010 and Lord and Hall, 2005)*, an important additional trait is lacking today, and that is that *"leaders need to learn to listen"* in order to effectively innovate.

Subject D stressed that *"leaders of tomorrow are the followers of today,"* therefore concurring with *Bajer (2009) and Uhl-Bien, Marion, and McKelvey (2007)* that leaders need to change their thinking from old to new ideas and that strategic leadership needs to extend beyond influencing all players in a company to work together and see the end goal (*Johnson, Scholes & Whittington, 2011*) in order to be innovative in the future. Subject E agreed with *Bettis and Hitt (1995)* and *Child and McGrath (2001)* views that in order to maintain organisational longevity one needs certain basic prerequisites in order to survive. His company promotes a simple fundamental operational model driven by key strategies, namely zero outage, deviation, touch and distance from customers, to maintain a competitive advantage.

Each interviewee agreed that business frameworks do have a place today. However, in answer to *O'Connell's (2014)* research that a plethora of frameworks exist resulting in continuing debates on effective leadership approaches, Subject A highlighted that to be effective and less complex, one needs to identify the relevance to each specific strategy within an organisation and adapt the framework accordingly, with the goal of simplifying life. Subject B's response was very much in line with this, as he identified the problem as leaders not knowing where to apply them and developing too much theory around them, suggesting restricted thinking from outdated leadership styles as postulated by *Uhl-Bien and Marion 2008*.

Subject C built on these, and *Anderson's (1999)* views by suggesting that the frameworks should be used as a tool to understand the complexity and in turn cut out irrelevant items so that they become supportive and not leading, i.e. develop systems that evolve and adapt efficiently.

Subject D similarly suggested that various aspects of different frameworks can be used during various stages of development within an organisation, i.e. at start-up there are probably many commonalities across the board allowing a broader range of models to be used that are then refined and adapted as the business grows. His analogy was that a business model is a checkpoint of work done by someone else. It has a "predicted outcome based on someone else's best practice that they experienced." It is a roadmap for following a specific route. Therefore if a leader has an identical strategy then a past framework can deliver the same outcome and simplify the current situation. However in most cases the leader needs to use one piece from different frameworks to create their own.

Subject E unknowingly added to Subject D's views by saying that a framework as a "*best practice*" is merely a "*skeleton for a strategy*" onto which the leader has to add the various body parts from other models, creating their own specific model at times. *Johnson, Scholes & Whittington (2011)* premise that leaders use a "strategic toolkit" ranging from one to nine different tools is another solution that frameworks should be adapted and used where they are relevant within a specific organisation.

QUESTION 10 : One school of thought argues that there is an overabundance of examples of management science that has splintered into competing archetypes resulting in innovation for the wrong reasons, i.e. personal career advancement only. Thus the focus has shifted from a positive holistic organisation knowledge gain and promotion view to a negatively self-serving perspective. Do you agree with this assessment? How do you feel about this?

Subject A	Subject B	Subject C	Subject D	Subject E
Not just personality but circumstances too 'once bitten - twice shy'				
	Mercenary temporary mindset due to head-hunters			
			Generation gaps & thirst for knowledge makes leaders move	Limited life span normal leaders must move on
		Lack of skills and entitlement attitudes		

Horizontal green rows represent similar views by various subjects, but worded differently

---

Donaldson (1995) contended that innovation for the wrong reasons has resulted in excessive examples of management science, fragmenting into rivalling archetypes where leaders only seek self-serving advancement. **Subject A built on** *Seers' (2004)* views, in that he believed focussing on personality as the sole distinctive behaviour was inadequate as a variety of additional environmental factors also influenced leadership style. He did suggest that **"once bitten, twice shy"** experiences could well promote self-serving behaviour. Very much in alignment with *Pablo et al's (2012)* deterring barriers that hinder innovation.

Subject B agreed that there is an increasingly typical mind set resulting in a **"mercenary attitude unheard of until now."** Sadly, rather than being an elite unit, leaders have now become part of a temporary agency promoted through head hunters. Subject C highlighted the Russian situation and compared it to the uniqueness of the South African environment and blamed black economic empowerment for this trend *(Albertyn 2011; Griffiths & Prozesky 2010; Steyn & Foster 2008)*. Not only do lack of skills and knowledge result in more frequent career changes, but also the accompanying entitlement attitude cultivates this self-serving view.

Subject D suggested that the immediate self-gratification trends of the current generation could play a role *(Zenouzi & Dehghan 2012)*. Although he believed it had more to do with personality types and quoted 'performance ratings' as an influencing factor. The majority average rating of 3 was vital for maintaining an organisation followed by the 4's that *"consistently pushed boundaries"*. He blamed those with the top score of 5 (the ones that constantly challenged the leadership) who's thirst for knowledge (the driving factor of innovation) were not being satisfied in the current company as examples of people that will jump jobs regularly in search of that satisfaction. Hence they may appear to be self-serving when in fact they are bored and need more stimulation.

Subject E agreed that the *"quick buck, in and out"* leaders can crumble an organisation, but he also believed that leaders with integrity, stability and a good sense of direction, even if only employed for a shorter period, can make a difference. His argument followed that of *Cross (2010)* that the banking system is an example of innovation gone haywire with the complex array of products they offer. However, he gave the example of the new 38-year old CEO of a national banking group in South Africa who turned the organisation around by identifying all the emergent opportunities *(Govindarajan & Trimble 2010)*, additionally applying technology and empowering his staff. After five years the CEO he had done all he could and handed the reigns over to a younger 35-year old who is now adding his own innovative ideas resulting in this bank becoming the leader in the banking industry. So there are exceptions to the rule.

QUESTION 11:

It has been said that strategic complexity requires bi-focal leadership (innovative leaders who display characteristics such as flexibility, trustworthiness, and openness to experimentation, risk taking and accepting of failure and a willingness to learn) to achieve short-term operational successes. Following this style of exposes new possibilities and innovations for long-term future leadership successes. Examples of such companies would be Apple, Google and Samsung. Give your viewpoint on this?

Subject A	Subject B	Subject C	Subject D	Subject E
Bi-focul leaders are unique and hard to find				
Traditional mindset difficult to change	Industry specific		Business as usual versus constant challenge of growth	
	Over-familiarity results in command & control issues			
		Combination of risk taking & respecting company values		
				Adaptability & team work

QUESTION 13:

What other traits would you consider to be crucial for leaders to be innovative in today's complex organisational structures?

Entrepreneurship & non-conformist	Be different & win over those around you	Freedom of handling within bigger boundaries	Be daring, but with a safety net	Learn from others through open dialogue

Horizontal green rows represent similar views by various subjects, but worded differently

In Questions 11 and 13, although Subject A agreed with *Dervitsiotis (2010, 2011, 2012)* views on bi-focal leadership, and sees such individual's as unique, he does argue that one individual (even those contracted through consulting firms) will have a difficult time trying to re-invent a thirty to fifty year-old traditional mind set, even if they are flexible, trustworthy and open for experimentation as postulated by Dervitsiotis.

Subject B aligned himself with the views of *Conti (2009, 2010)* suggesting that in order to remain optimally fit a leader must continually scrutinise all opportunities and constantly adapt. He suggested that what works in one company, may not necessarily work in another. In a fire Department as in a hospital, an autocratic approach is more suitable due to life and death situations. In his current hospital environment the bi-focal leadership style has led to familiarity. This has resulted in further systems and checks being added to the current procedure list, (adding complexity and rigidness) which in turn has stifled innovation.

Subject C saw the juggling of risk versus company values as the challenge for bi-focal leadership today. Whereas Subject D insightfully refers to the insurance industry as a classic example of innovative bi-focal leadership due to the constant challenge of growth. In the past they focused solely on a life cover whereas today investments and other tax benefits have been included into these policies. This is in alignment with the competitive, yet stable and lean environments as postulated by *Browning & Saunders (2012)*. Subject E displays good bi-focal leadership skills by following the principles of *Bajer (2009)* where his entire leadership team works together on topics that are currently relevant, yet are also flexible enough to change focus on the spur of the moment if needs be.

Everyone agreed that some form of entrepreneurship is imperative for leaders to be innovative especially effective communication within the company as in *Brown and Duguid (2000)* and *Dervitsiotis (2011)* open dialogue, to identify and solve challenges.

QUESTION 14:

Do you feel that past successes and experience are crucial in coping with today's ever changing business environment? If so cite some examples.

Subject A	Subject B	Subject C	Subject D	Subject E
Past experiences, i.e military principles still apply today	Experience enables you to scan the environment and identify possible opportunities	Experience enables you to be open for new development & opportunities	Past experiences are cruicial to climb the corporate ladder	The past paves the way to the future

Horizontal green rows represent similar views by various subjects, but worded differently

---

All subjects agreed unanimously that past experiences are paramount, although subjects A, B and D could still display old style mechanistic linear thinking as postulated by *Stevenson (2012)*. Especially if one considers subject A's analogy that leadership of the battlefield is identical to that of the corporate boardroom. Subject's C and E appeared to be more in alignment with the thinking of *Bennis (2012)* that environments need to be constantly reappraised, at the same time being acutely aware of the circumstantial and temporal changing situations within individuals and groups *(Osborn, Hunt & Jauch, 2002 and Porter and McLaughlin, 2006)*.

QUESTION 15: Some researchers advocate that today's chaos as a result of complexity thinking and ever changing environments are necessary and force a leader to enable rather than control. Other researchers feel that the 'one person in charge' stance does not work anymore and that leaders need to empower staff to learn, embrace group talents and use their collective intelligences. Should you agree that there is indeed chaos today, what are your comments on this?

Subject A	Subject B	Subject C	Subject D	Subject E
Bring discipline to the chaos	You need to 'manage' rather than 'enable' the chaos	Chaos is fine - but everyone must have the same vision	Chaos is about the incubation of ideas	'Organised' chaos creates harmony, versus 'total' chaos that complicates

Horizontal green rows represent similar views by various subjects, but worded differently

All subjects agreed that chaos exists and that it is crucial to manage this complex chaotic environment effectively to be productively innovative *(Maylor, Turner & Murray-Webster, 2013)*. Subject A referred to this as bringing discipline to the chaos which closely aligned with Subject E's reference to 'organised' chaos that he viewed as controlled chaos that creates harmony. Subject C expanded on this view by adding that everyone needs the same vision in order to focus the chaos which paired with subject B's views that leaders need to manage, rather than enable complexity – expanding on *(Geer-Frazier 2014)* views that criticised controlling leadership. Subject D interestingly referred to chaos as the "*incubation period for ideas.*"

Everyone's views supported *Bajer (2009)* and *Uhl-Bien, Marion, and McKelvey (2007)* in that they all acknowledged that endorsing group talents and teamwork is key to managing chaos today.

QUESTION 16: As organisations becomes more complex, especially in terms of systems and policies, it has been argued that, traditional command and control leadership is failing. What is your view on this?

Subject A	Subject B	Subject C	Subject D	Subject E
Open Dialogue Give staff a chance to make up and change	It is organisation specific	In full agreement	Leaders enable staff & managers control staff	Leaders need to bring together and harmonise the experts

Horizontal green rows represent similar views by various subjects, but worded differently

All subjects agreed with the complexity science views that today leadership needs to focus on learning, adaptation and innovation in accordance with *Uhl-Bien and Marion (2008)*. Subject A referred to changing staff awareness and thinking *(Cross 2010)*, believing this is possible through open dialogue *Brown & Duguid (2000)* and *Dervitsiotis (2011)*.

Subject B believed that leadership style is organisation specific, and in accordance with the views of *Conti (2009 & 2010)*. Subject D aligned himself with the views of the *IBM Think Forum (2011)* stating that command and control leadership is in fact management, and true leadership is about enabling staff through collaboration. Subject E built on this, using an orchestra as an analogy. Each musician has their own speciality and expertise, and is made up of a complex array of people and instruments that the conductor (leader) needs to harmonise. This view aligns with *Bajer (2009)* that highlighted the importance of leadership tapping into the collective intelligences (expertise) of the group, instead of relying on probable restrictive self-knowledge.

Subject A was the odd one out of the group by aligning himself with the views of *Heywood, Spungin and Turnbull (2007)* who advocated adding complexity to a current model. He gave fuel stations as an analogy. Years ago they only supplied fuel. Today they have convenience stores, cash machines, food franchises and more attached to them. Something simple has become a more complex machine, however this has been justified through added value creation that has boosted competitive advantage and profits.

QUESTION 17: Researchers state that complexity thinking is about limitations to what we can know and what we can accomplish via pre-determined and planned approaches. Hence excessive complexity can raise running costs and cripple growth when taken too far. One solution to combating complexity thinking is'reductionism', i.e. cutting the amount of products and services and focusing on a core speciality, i.e. making customer choices simpler. What are your thoughts on this?

Subject A	Subject B	Subject C	Subject D	Subject E
	Have a base product offering a few variations	Decrease complexity/ product portfolio per person	Identifying window of opportunity in order to gain leverage	Focus on key products i.e. niche market
Agree, but you can still add complexity in terms of new products & services				

Horizontal green rows represent similar views by various subjects, but worded differently

Subject B's analogy of the Land Rover having a base model and creating a few variations falls in line with *Cross (2010)* who advocated the 5S approach of sorting and straightening everything out (reduction). Shining it up and standardising the Land Rover model while sustaining a high quality product. Subject E had very similar views citing Apple and the iPad as an example.

Subject C went beyond decreasing product and suggested decreasing the complexity per person, similar to the views of *Dervitsiotis (2012)*. He further suggested selling off departments that are not your core focus, citing Philips as an example of a company that sold off the lighting section as their core focus has now moved to medical equipment. They cut off the fat in order to become lean *(Browning & Saunders 2012 and Cross 2010)*.

Subject D felt that reductionism could be achieved by *"identifying the window of opportunity associated with getting the leverage against your competitors before they enter that same space"*. This view aligns with *Govindarajan and Trimble (2010)* who asserted that leaders need to accurately decipher and sense all signs of change while acting rapidly to bring this innovation to the market.

5. CONCLUSION

On completing the literature review and case studies, Stephen Hawking's *(Waltuck 2012)* view of the 21st century as a time teeming with complexity appears to rings true. Attempting to formulate a succinct definition of complexity thinking is not a clear-cut process as research has indicated that various factors play a role in contributing to complexity. However, predominant themes that arose include; communication, as a leading problem, whether between strategic and operational process as professed by *Heywood, Spungin, and Turnbull (2007)*, as well as ineffective feedback cycles as suggested by *Browning and Sanders (2012)* and Subject B. This results in misaligned communication between various levels of staff and departments within the organisation.

Two further factors that cropped up repeatedly included information overload *(Bennis 2012; & Subject C)* coupled with increasing compliance issues that hinder innovation and complicate the efficient functioning of a company. Finally, leadership uncertainty in understanding the current set of environmental circumstances, coupled with the inability to apply a multifaceted approach to these constant-changing circumstances also played a role *(Keen 2000; Subject D)*.

Complexity thinking could therefore be defined as the result of leadership limitations in effectively streamlining and communicating pertinent task/organisation related information to various levels of staff and departments. This results in misaligned communication that in turn encourages the implementation of complex systems and processes being put into play to combat these constraints. This ultimately results in increasing the complexity of achieving actual harmonious and productive workflow within the organisation as a whole *Porter (1985)* and *Dervitsiotis (2012)*. Simplistically, this aligns with *Collins' (2001)* and *Waterman et al's (2008)* views that the focus must be on employing the right people for the right job.

In terms of complexity thinking in relation to leadership and leadership roles, all case studies were in agreement with *Uhl-Bien, Marion, and McKelvey (2007)* that leaders must shift their thinking from old to new ideas and adapt expeditiously to change.

Although subject A focused on internal politics as expanding complexity *(Mintzberg 1985, Changing Minds 2002; Deal & Kenny 2000)* the international leader, subject C, cited expat and different cultural issues as a major contributor *(Hofstede's 2001)*. This goes along with *Bennis' (2012)* views that the speed of change and continual new information (Subject C and D) increasingly complicates leadership. In addition, the premise that some leaders are not evolving at an equal pace to others (Subject D and E) would indicate that complexity thinking is the resultant outcome *(Anderson 1993; Day 2012; Kegan 1994; Kegan & Lahey 2010; Lord & Hall, 2005)*. The conclusion here would be in alignment with *Heckscher (1994)* and Subject E that today single leadership is something of the past. Instead today leaders need to surround themselves with specialists in their fields, and manage these specialists effectively, so that the insights generated by many improve the whole. Subject E's analogy of a leader as a conductor harmonising an orchestra is apropos.

On the question of whether complexity thinking has affected innovation, all subjects were in agreement with *Dervitsiotis (2012)* that leaders needs to urgently *(Cross 2010)* cultivate an improved understanding of where and how complexity originates and its effects on long-term strategy in order to promote effective innovation. The subjects further agreed that risk taking was an essential leadership trait and that the efficient management of complex chaotic environments is crucial to being productively innovative *(Maylor, Turner & Murray-Webster 2013 & Schneider & Somers 2006)*. Furthermore, the entire case study agreed that some form of entrepreneurship is critical for innovative leadership, particularly bi-focal leadership that promotes effective communication and open dialogue, to identify and solve challenges *(Brown & Duguid 2000; Dervitsiotis 2011)*.

The consequence of the above views has curiously led to two opposing views on the affect complexity thinking has on innovation; Subject A concurred with *Heywood, Spungin and Turnbull (2007)* that adding complexity to a simple model improves efficiency and productivity as in the example of a 'basic' fuel station developing into the complex, yet effective 'one-stop' convenience solution of today as seen along all major highways. On the other hand, Subject B and E aligned themselves with the 5S approach (sort, straighten, shine, standardise and sustain) of *Cross (2010)* citing the standardising the Land Rover model, Apple and the iPad while conjointly maintaining a high quality product. One could therefore conclude that whichever direction the complexity thinking process takes, as long as it is efficiently and productively innovative and adds to the value proposition of the organisation, it is effective. Whereas if it does not achieve this, then complexity thinking indeed hinders innovation amongst leadership.

6. RECOMMENDATIONS

On completing the literature search and case studies, identifying actions and tools that could effectively aid leaders in promoting innovation and adeptly manage complexity thinking in the future include: first shifting employee awareness by altering their thinking to comprehend what they currently believe may not always be correct. This can be achieved through the use the 5S approach thereby establishing and practicing exercises that phase out waste *(Cross 2010)*. Second, is enabling staff through collaboration *(IBM Think Forum 2011)* with a focus on learning, adaptation and innovation *(Uhl-Bien and Marion 2008)*. Third, a blending human skills and technology to maintain continual advancement *(Rummler & Brache 1995)* by cultivating and improving internal processes (quality and service) and employee competencies (knowledge, communication, problem solving and creativity).

Fourth is promoting innovative freedom and cultivating personal growth to develop productive future leaders and long-term excellence *(Christensen 1998; Govindarajan & Trimble 2010)*. Next, is the identification of the Innovation Fulcrum, i.e. the point where the balance between operating complexity and customer satisfaction breaks down *(Gottfredson & Aspinall 2005)*.

Sixth is to meticulously sense emergent opportunities by accurately deciphering all signs of change within the environment. Then acting rapidly, economically and effectively to deliver the innovation to market *(Govindarajan & Trimble 2010)*. Seventh is an early detection of complexity by implementing the Complexity Assessment Tool (CAT) *(Maylor, Turner & Murray-Webster 2013)*.

Eight, is an application of business models as roadmaps and understanding that current frameworks should be seen as a "*skeleton for a strategy*" (Subject E) onto which the leader has to add the various body parts from other models, creating their own specific model applicable to their specific circumstances *(Anderson 1999)*. Finally, the acceptance that although past leadership experience is paramount, today's environments need to be constantly reappraised, while additionally remaining acutely aware of the circumstantial and temporal changing situations within individuals and groups *(Osborn, Hunt & Jauch, 2002; Porter & McLaughlin, 2006)*.

7. REFLECTIONS ON THE RESEARCH STUDY

I started this research believing that it was a given that complexity thinking inhibits innovation amongst leadership, and that it was only a question of to what extent. Today I acknowledge the repeated referrals by researchers that as leaders a plethora of factors influence complexity thinking. Pros and cons will always exist, but ultimately the simple solution begins not only with our staff, but we ourselves, as leaders need to alter our views by continually re-evaluating our environment and personal thinking and involve our staff in this growth process.

Only then can we embrace the magnitude of this question and truly proceed innovatively and productively forward. Complexity thinking plays an important role and is a reality of the world we live in today. It is our personal interpretation as leaders of complexity thinking and how we apply it within our own organisations and to our staff that eventually determines to what extent this complexity either inhibit or advances innovation amongst leadership within multinational organisations.

"In the future, are others going to look at what you left behind and question the point of it all? Or are you going to leave a legacy?"

(Wolfgang Riebe)

CHAPTER 7
SIMPLE SOLUTIONS TO
COMPLEX PROBLEMS

INTRODUCTION

"It's not the magic that makes it work; it's the way we work that makes it."

(Lee Cockerell)

In this chapter I am going to focus on simple solutions and keep them generic so that the majority of organisations can benefit from them. As this entire book is based on research, my personal conclusion is that two people stand head and shoulders above everyone else in terms of practical simplicity. Jim Collins (Collins, 2001) and Lee Cockerell (Cockerell, 2008). Without a doubt Disney has been a forerunner on service and sales, and especially a 'magical experience' for everyone that walks through their gates. Hence my focus will be on Cockerell's insights and to share and expand on his views of the way in which companies make something work. I did not expand of research any of Cockerell's work within my dissertation and only discovered him after completing the studies. No doubt there are many other exceptional people that I will discover later on too – all part of my growth. Hence this chapter will mainly focus on the contributions and insights shared by Lee Cokerell (Cockerell, 2008).

And eventually after all the heavy academic research, the final chapter written in 'simple' English and based on 'simple' tips that are practical and sustainable!

My first tip to identify whether you are suffering from complexity issues within your organisation is to complete the Complexity Assessment Tool by Maylor, Turner & Murray-Webster (2013, p. 48). I believe this is a necessity, as we all perceive the world from our own personal experiences – and you may not believe there to be a complexity problem, when in fact there is. Hence I believe everyone needs to take an objective test, regardless of personal views. It may be an enlightening eye opener for those in denial!

As a trainer and speaker I have so many companies that ask me to 're-train' employees and focus on an attitude adjustment so that they become team players and integrate into the organisational culture once again. In my younger years I believe I was naïve and would attempt such an impossible task. Today I laugh at the challenge, as I believe that academics and research may support a hypothesis on paper, but practical experience and reality is a completely different kettle of fish. To sit in an office on a steady salary and research differing opinions, case studies and views and then come up with a logical conclusion based on this research, does not answer why some people remain arseholes and others don't. Sorry, I just have a big issue with this and find that in my short life I have seen too many 'entitled' people in companies that ride the system and will not change. That's another research project on its own as to why this selfish self-satisfying and greedy attitude is becoming so prevalent in today's society.

Hence I look up in awe and support Jim Collins' view of 'First Who, then What' as the only logical solution to most attitude problems today. Yes, government (which in general is already incompetent) has implemented laws protecting your rotten apples, so this makes Collins' suggestion difficult for existing companies – hence I cover the majority of suggestions by Cockerell as an alternative solution.

Please do not misunderstand me on this point. Yes government has policies and regulations in place to protect employees from unscrupulous employers – with that I have absolutely no issue. If anything, you need to treat your staff impeccably and help them grow – but only if they deserve it. A salary is not a right, there has to be value exchange. The problem comes in that every employee today has a right to do what they want, even if they do not agree with your vision and mission. Once employed you sit with this troublemaker and idiotic laws prevent you from getting rid of them. And hello, the current system isn't working anymore!

Bottom line – if you are starting a new company = chose the right people! Have the right assessments done, make sure the potential candidates agree and think in line with your vision and mission. Spend the money on having the right people do the right assessments so that the right people are chosen. In the property industry there is a belief that you make your profit on a property when you buy it, not when you sell it. This makes complete sense. And the same applies to any organisation, if you start with rotten apples, it is going to be virtually impossible toe get rid of them – they will affect everyone else. In my research I now have come to an understanding why complexity exists in companies. It is the continual attempt to cope with, and keep the arseholes in line that has resulted in layers and layers of new policies, rule and process coming into play. The simple solution is to get rid of them. End of argument! Now you can start fresh.

No matter what you want to do, if the attitude of your staff (this includes leaders and followers) is wrong – you WILL NOT move forward. Putting policies into place to control all of this WILL negatively affect your productivity (Morieux, 2015) and have many knock-on effects down the line. If you have a problem accepting this view, let me put it even simpler. If you continually eat junk food and don't exercise, you will become fat, unhealthy and prone to sickness. In a race you will run out of breath and lag behind the fitter competitors. Bad employees are like bad food – they hold you back.

Of course Collins expressed himself in a way more polite manner than I just did, but the reality remains the same, chose the right people - 'First Who', and only then strategise and achieve your goals - 'Then What' (Collins, 2001).

What if you are sitting with a team full of rotten apples? Laws prevent you from firing them!

Having expressed my frustration above at the reality of today, I have to add that some of Cockerell's suggestions, in my opinion, feed and nurture the troublemakers in an organisation. Hence I acknowledge my bias and will only focus on his action steps that I personally believe to be fair, objective and realistic, plus that I personally believe to be representative of leadership who themselves strive for fairness and objectivity, but are also exasperated by the complexity of sustaining the agitators within an organisation.

1. All employees are significant!

Not only your staff, but the leadership too needs all the information and resources currently available to learn and apply what they need in order to successfully complete all required tasks. If you hold back, you will have animosity and targets won't be reached. If you openly supply all that is needed and they don't achieve, then you have provable ammunition to give them the opportunity to fit in or fire them.

Everyone must have the right to be heard and you need to have an open door policy so that this can happen. Issues occur spontaneously, so a chain of command process to be heard is not acceptable. Everyone must know that they can speak to you at anytime and anywhere. However, not everyone has a right to push their own beliefs down everyone else's throat with the expectation that others must confirm. If as an example, you choose to follow a particular religion - that is your right. But you do not have the right to make others change their behaviour to accommodate you. If you want to argue the point and insist that this is your right, then you must understand that the other people around you should then be afforded that exact same right. And if this is the case, then they too have the right not to accommodate your personal requests.

Where companies are losing the plot is that suddenly everyone's rights are being addressed, to the detriment of the 'right' and goals of the company – hence the complexity and the drop in productivity. At the end of the day the workplace needs to be a 'neutral zone' where everyone fits in and respects each other equally and where no one can force any personal beliefs that are not part of the organisation vision and mission. This is the crux of being heard and having an open door policy. From day one you need to make it clear that any and all ideas and suggestions in terms of improving work relations, productivity, future plans, improvements on procedures, etc. will be openly heeded – but the focus must be for the improvement of everyone concerned.

Everyone must have a responsibility and be held accountable which know that they form part of a well-oiled machine where each and every person plays a vital part in keeping that machine running. It is also imperative that they all realise and believe that by constantly re-assessing themselves being team players and viewing the greater purpose of the company that they comprehend that any improvement on any aspect of their work or department benefits the entire organisation.

2. Stop the 'sheeple' mentality

Bring responsibility for actions back into your workplace and make sure each and every person clearly understands their duties and responsibilities. If you have a responsibility you have importance! Don't we all want to feel important? However, hand in hand with responsibility comes accountability. Once this is understood, information flow, authority, decision making and answers to questions are much easier and efficiently handled as your departments operate effectively and speedily due to everyone fully understanding their roles.

3. Your staff represents your organisation

If this is the case, why would you go for second best? So many companies merely employ someone because they need to fill a post, even if the person is not ideal. What kind of thinking is that? No wonder problems are created. You need to learn to wait until you find the right person for that post, rather than a clone or unlikely fit. If you are struggling to find the right person – search in different places. Move away from the standard head-hunters and recruiting agents if they are not finding the right fit for you. Yes it is essential to involve your current employees and advertise the post internally as well, but be careful of the above and consider that this individual needs to integrate well into the current team. Always make sure that this person can be trained and nurtured, and if you do make a mistake, replace them swiftly, and in decent manner. Therefore when employing someone in the first place, make sure not to make unrealistic promises, nor to have them either, and have a solid contract that allows you to get rid of them if things don't work out within a fair period of time.

4. Create magical moments

If you have purpose in life you feel wanted and life does become magical. Now imagine you have an entire team with that viewpoint? This will rub off and everyone, including your customers. The simplest way to begin creating magic is to offer purposeful and practical training so that they can work independently and grow as human beings. More important is that you lead by example. Sadly, the majority of companies I have consulted for and trained at have that one manager that everyone hates! Guess what? Someone didn't hire the proper person for the job! As a leader you need to coach and mentor you staff through leading by example. If you cannot do that, then maybe the problem doesn't lie with your staff! In today's ever changing world the most important skill you need to focus on is to train everyone for the unexpected by training them in multiple ways to achieve goals and accomplish their tasks.

5. Negate problems & issues

If you have no open communication with staff and customers, you may never hear of the problems, and when you do, the damage is done. We all make mistakes, as we are human! Although the right attitude amongst your staff can turn an irate customer into a lifelong follower, we need to be well aware that mistakes should never be repeated. This is only possible by keeping your ears to the ground, earning trust from those in your team, having constant and open communication with everyone, including your customers, and basically knowing what is going on in your organisation and department. More importantly it is also imperative that everyone knows their accountability and responsibility, so that when a problem does occur, the blame is not passed around, but that the responsible individual has the power to rectify it with the client, and then learn the lesson not to allow it to happen again. The same individual also needs to have the trust to be able to come to you and acknowledge what has happened, plus have the training to have been able to put processes into place to rectify the issue at hand. Hence constant education, training and remaining up to date with technical advancements is a must.

6. Be on the inside track

Know what is going on in your company/department. You cannot sit on your high chair, bark orders and expect to know what is going on. Walk the floor, speak to everyone, stay in contact with your customers and please DO NOT email and phone clients with these automated feedback questionnaires on your current service that are one-sided. If you do that to me, I will never deal with you again! If your customer service is great because your employees are the right fit – then you don't need to follow up on customer service and stupid questionnaires. These all distract from the business at hand and slow down productivity. If you make a point of personally experiencing everything in your organisation from an employee and a customer perspective, then you will know where attention is needed. Just do it!

7. Acknowledge all of your staff

I really don't care if you woke up from the wrong side of the floor this morning. That does not give you the right to be rude, arrogant or disrespectful to anybody. I heard a great story from a past CEO of a retail chain at a conference where he spoke about people being rude to beggars in the parking lot. Yes they are annoying, but vulgarity and rudeness is not called for as that beggar also has a family and children who look up to and respect him/her. So what gives you the right to disrespect that person? This visual picture has stayed in my mind ever since and today it makes me think twice before reacting, or being rude to anyone.

Back to the issue at hand, know the names of your staff members as well as your good customers. Make it personal and stop the Whataspp and email nonsense. This is NOT personal. If a good customer or a staff member has a birthday, an email, or a birthday card doesn't do it anymore! At the very minimum it should be a personal warm wish between you and them, or at worst a personal phone call. Be genuine, talk about family and personal matters. Make this one time where the business does not come into play. Consider this simple truth... everything is about turnover and money. Very few companies, especially larger organisations focus on 'personal' caring service. Just care and show that you do. It will make a HUGE difference. Included in that caring is showing an interest in that person's family too. It all boils down to, not just communication, but meaningful communication. And by meaningful I do not mean social media and email, but by looking someone in the eyes and actually paying 100% attention to them. Similarly, if someone does something great – acknowledge this publicly. Praising someone in front of their peers will inspire the team to become greater too. We all want to be acknowledged – this is a primal basic instinct. No complexity here – just a simple life truth! So start doing it more! And never forget the social side by making time for fun too!

8. Be the forerunner

How many companies that were top performers 30 years ago still exist today? Why is that? They simply stuck their head in the ground and didn't grow, nor keep up with advancing technology and trends. Never think you are better than your competitors. You need to constantly learn and share with your team. You need to have the best people around you to keep you informed and ahead of the others. Whereas in the past an autocratic leadership style work, today you will die! You have to grow with your team and learn together. You have to acknowledge your competitors and be acutely informed as to what they are doing. Remember, you can be on top today, and tomorrow you can be gone. If you don't expand your horizons and keep up with the latest developments, your business won't last. If you have a bad team who are not passionate about what you are doing, this is going to be tough to do. But if you have the right people who respect you and you lead by example, then the passion and energy amongst you will already put you ahead of the others. Additionally this passion will be the driving force to want to continually stay ahead because your team love what they do! A word of caution though, subscribing to industry publications and hanging out with the clique does not necessarily mean you are being fed the right information either. Look for changes, ideas and innovations where others are not! Be an innovator rather than a follower – that is the secret to survival.

9. Watch your words

We are all humans and besides gossiping, we all have said a bad thing or two about others. As a leader focus intently on what you say and listen to your employees. Preach positive verbal communication and set high standards. Count to ten before reacting to or answering a negative person. Think before you speak and always remember that as a leader people watch you the whole time. No one said it's easy, but if you remain aware and realise that what you do affects your entire team – you can instil a positive attitude that in turn will benefit everyone and your organisation. If you believe in vibrational medicine and energy – negative sounds (words) attract more negativity. Make the magical spells in your company be positive word usage so that the resultant follow-up magic of that verbal spell becomes positive too!

10. Promote attributes of greatness

If you ask me what the most important value, or characteristic in another human being should be, then I would say it must be honesty. If you are not honest, you cannot expect your team to be either. Teaching decent, ethical values grounded in honesty is imperative in building trust and a success within an organisation as well as amongst the staff. If there is trust, then responsibility follows and people become accountable.

For those of you that have read to the end of this final chapter, I am assuming there will be one of two possible mindsets right now. One – you agree fully and happy that someone actually has said it the way it is. Two – you completely disagree with me and think I am an idiot.

Either way, whatever you believe, let me conclude this book with a FACT.

A business can only be successful if it makes a profit. The only non-debatable elements in any organisation are assets and liabilities, profit and loss – it's all about making a profit. Anything that is not in alignment with these elements is detrimental to the business. So anyone that has an opinion and who demands that their personal issues are adhered to, is taking away from the core mission of said business. Their self-serving, subjective demands are taking time away from reaching the company goal, to satisfying their own biased needs. As a society we have allowed these individuals to control how you run your businesses that in turn has resulted in the deluge of complex policies and regulations. No one else is to blame, but the leadership who have allowed this to happen.

I repeat, treat your employees with fairness and treat them well, but never favour one person or group's biases over another and to the detriment of the productivity of your organisation. By doing this you are allowing complexity to rule. By sticking to decent, ethical and humane policies that treat everyone equally and that require personal belief systems (which are only opinions) to be left at home, you organisation is well on the road to function according the basic and simple core values on which it was founded. Along the way make sure you remain humble, have fun, train your employees, acknowledge greatness and inspire everyone by leading through example.

And now, eventually to explain my M^2 = cc formula on the book cover. Magical Moments (M^2) equals Corporate Clarity (cc). In other words, by creating magical moments for everyone in your organisation, simplicity can take over and corporate clarity becomes a reality! That's as simple as it gets!

*"The past has taught me to proactively plan for
the future while striving to make the most of now."*

(Wolfgang Riebe)

REFERENCES

Adair, J 2003, *Effective Strategic Leadership: The Complete Guide to Strategic Leadership*, New Revised Edn. Pan Macmillan: London.

Adams, JS 1963, 'Toward an Understanding of Inequity', *Journal of Abnormal and Social Psychology*, vol. 67, no. 4, pp. 422 - 436.

Agle, BR & Caldwell, CB 1999, 'Understanding Research on Values in Business', *Business & Society*, vol. 38, no. 3, pp. 326 – 287.

Aiken, C & Keller, S 2009, 'The Irrational Side of Change Management', *McKinsey Quarterly,* no. 2, pp100 – 109.

Albertyn, C 2011, 'Law, Gender and Inequality in South Africa', *Oxford Development Studies*, vol. 39, no. 2, pp. 139 – 162.

Alexander, SA, Reicher, SD & Platow, MJ 2011, *The New Psychology of Leadership:* Identity, influence and Power. Psychology Press: New York.

Alimo-Metcalfe, B & Alban-Metcalfe, J 2006, 'More (Good) Leaders for the Public Sector', *International Journal of Public Sector Management,* vol. 1, no. 4, pp. 293 - 315.

Allison, G 1971, Essence of Decision: Explaining the Cuban Missile Crisis. Little Brown: Boston.

Alvesson, M & Sveningsson, S 2008, *Organizational Culture: Cultural Change Work in Process.* Routledge: New York.

Amabile, T 1996, *Creativity and Innovation in Organisations.* Harvard Business School: Boston.

Amabile, TM 1998, 'How To Kill Creativity', *Harvard Business Review,* vol. 76, no. 5, pp. 76 – 87.

Amabile, TM, Conti, R, Coon, H, Lazenby, J & Herron, M 1996, 'Assessing the Work Environment for Creativity', Academy of *Management Journal*, vol.39, no. 5, pp. 1154 – 1184.

Anderson, B 1993 *Leadership: Uncommon sense The Leadership Circle.* Available from: <http://leadershipcircle.com/wp content/uploads/2011/05/07_SpiritOfLeadership .pdf>. [4March 2015].

Anderson, P 1999, 'Complexity theory and organization science', *Organization Science*, vol. 10, no. 3, pp. 216 - 232.

Ang,S & Van Dyne, L 2008. *Handbook of Cultural Intelligence: Theory, Measurment & Applications.* M.E. Sharpe: New York.

Ansoff, I H 1988, *Corporate Strategy,* 2nd edn. Penguin Books: New York.

Arnold, J 2004, 'The Congruence Problem in John Hollands Theory of Vocational Decisions', *Journal of Occupational and Organizational Psychology*, vol. 77, no. 1, pp. 95 - 113.

Arvey, RD, Rotundo, M, Johnson, W, Zhang, Z & McGue, M 2006, 'The determinants of Leadership Role Occupancy: Genetic and Personality Factors', *Leadership Quarterly*, vol. 17, no. 1, pp. 1 - 20.

Ashkanasy, NM, Wilderom, CPM & Peterson, MF 2011, 'The Handbook of of Organizational Culture and Climate, 2nd edn', Sage: Thousand Oaks.

Avolio, BJ & Luthans, F 2006, *The High Impact Leader: Moments Matter in Accelerating Authentic Leadership Development.* McGraw-Hill: New York.

Baddeley, S & James, K 1987, 'Owl, Fox, Donkey or Sheep: Political Skills for Managers', *Management Education & Development,* vol. 18, no. 1, pp. 3 – 19.

Bain & Company 2005, 'Insights: management tools and trends'. Available from: http://www.bain.com/publications/business-insights/management-tools-and-trends.as px>.[13 January 2015].

Bajer, J 2009, 'Today, either everyone is a leader, or nobody is', *Strategic HR Review*, vol. 8, no. 5, pp. 38 - 39.

Baldwin, J & Lin, Z 2002, 'Impediments to advanced technology adoption for Canadian manufacturers', *Research Policy*, vol. 31, no. 1, pp. 1 - 8.

Bass, BM & Riggio, RE 2005, Transformational Leadership, 2nd edn. Lawrence Erlbaum Associates: London.

Bass, BM 1985, *Leadership and Performance Beyond Expectation.* Free Press: New York.

Bass, BM 2008, *The Bass handbook of leadership: Theory, research, & managerial applications*, 5th edn, Free Press: New York.

Beal, GM, Rogers, EM & Bohlen, JM 1957, 'Validity of the Concept of Stages in the Adoption Process', *Rural Sociology,* vol *22* no. 2, pp. 166 -168.

Beer, M & Nohria, N 2000, *Breaking the Code of Change.* Harvard Business School: Boston.

Belbin, M 2010, *Team Roles at Work, 2nd edn*. Routledge: London.

Belbin, M 2012, *Belbin Team Roles.* Available from: <http://www.belbin.com>. [30 August 2014].

Bennis, WG & Nanus, B 1997 *Leaders: The Strategies for Taking Charge, 2nd edn.* Harper Collins: New York.

Bennis, WG 2007, 'The challenges of leadership in the modern world: An introduction to the special issue'. *American Psychologist*, vol. 62, no. 1, pp. 2 - 5.

Bennis, WG 2012, *The crucibles of authentic leadership*, D.V. Day, J. Antonakis (Eds.), *The nature of leadership,* Thousand Oaks: Sage.

Bensimon, EM, Neumann, A & Birnbaum, R 1989, *Making Sense of Administrative Leadership: The 'L' Word in Higher Education.* ASHE-ERIC Higher Education Report No. 1. Washington, D.C.: The George Washington University, Graduate School of Education and Human Development. Available from: <http://bf.memphis.edu/vp/theor eticalframework.pdf>. [8 October 2014].

Bereel, AC 2009, *Leadership and Change Management.* Sage: Los Angeles.

Bertocci, DI 2009, L*eadership in Organisations.* University Press: Lanham.

Bettis, RA & Hitt, MA 1995, 'The new competitive landscape', *Strategic Management Journal*, vol. 7, no. 13, pp. 7 - 19.

Bickman, L & Rog, D (Eds.) 2008, *The SAGE Handbook of applied social research methods*, 2nd edn, Thousand Oaks: Sage.

Bierly, PE, Kessler, EH & Christensen, EH 2000, 'Organizational learning, knowledge and wisdom. *Journal of Organizational Change Management,* vol. 13, no. 6, pp. 595 - 618.

Boak, G 2010, *Understanding Innovation and Change*. Robert Kennedy College: Zurich. [30 May 2014].

Boal, KB & Hooijberg, R 2000, 'Strategic leadership research: Moving on', *The Leadership Quarterly,* vol. 11, no. 4, pp. 515 - 549.

Bolden, R, Gosling, J, Marturano, A & Dennison, P 2003, Cenbtre for Leadership Studies: *A Review of Leadership Theory & Competency Frameworks*. University of Exeter: Exeter.

Bonanno, GA 2009, *The Other Side of Sadness: What the New Science of Bereavement Tells Us About Life After Loss.* Basic Books: New York.

Bonn, I 2001, 'Developing strategic thinking as a core competency', *Management Decision,* vol 39 no. 1 pp 63-70.

Bower, M 1966, The Will to Manage. McGraw-Hill: New York.

Boytazis, R & McKee A 2005, *Resonant Leadership: Renewing Yourself and Connecting with Others Through Mindfulness, Hope, and Compassion*. Harvard Business School Press: Boston.

Bradbury, H & Lichtenstein, B, 2000, 'Relationality in organizational research: Exploring the space between', *Organization Science,* vol. 11, no. 5, pp. 551 - 564.

Bridges, W 2009, *Managing Transitions.* Nicholas Brealey: London.

Brotherton, P 2013, 'Leadership: Nature or Nurture?', *American Society for Training & Development,* vol. 67, no. 2, pp. 25.

Brown, DL 2012, I*n the minds of followers: Follower-centric approaches to leadership*, D.V. Day, J. Antonakis (Eds.), *The nature of leadership,* Sage: Thousand Oaks.

Brown, JS & Duguid, P 2000, *The social life of information*, HBS Press: Cambridge.

Browning, TR & Sanders NR 2012, 'Can innovation be lean?', *California Management Review*, vol. 54, no. 4, pp 5   19.

Bryman, A 2004, 'Qualitative research on leadership: A critical but appreciative review', *The Leadership Quarterly*, vol. 15, no. 6, pp. 729 - 769.

Buchanan, D & Badham, R 2008, *Power, Politics, and Organizational Change: Winning the Turf Game, 2nd edn.* Sage: London.

Buchanan, DA & Huczynski, AA 2010, *Organizational Behaviour*, 8th edn. Pearson Education: Harlow.

Burnes, B & Cooke, B 2013, 'Kurt Lewin's Field Theory: A Review and Re-evaluation', *International Journal of Management Reviews*, vol 15, no. 4, pp 408 – 425.

Burnes, B 2004, 'Kurt Lewin and the Planned Approach to Change: A Re-appraisal', *Journal of Management Studies*, vol 41 no. 6, pp 977 – 1002.

Burns, J. M. (1978). *Leadership*. Harper & Row: New York.

Busco, C, Frigo, MK, Giovannoni, E & Maraghini, MP 2012, ' Control vs. creativity: Strive Toward a Twofold Purposeful Imbalance to Keep Management Control from Killing Creativity and Innovation', *Strategic Finance*, vol. 94, no. 2, pp. 29 – 37.

Bynum LA, Clayton RW, Hayek M, Moeller M & Williams Jr. WA 2009, 'Chandler as a biographer: content thematic analysis of Chandler's biography of Henry Varnum Poor', *Journal of Management History*, vol. 15, no. 3, pp. 272 - 283.

Cable, D 2012, 'The New Oath to Organisational Change', *Business Strategy Review*, vol 23 no. 3, pp 45 – 47.

Cameron, K & Quinn, RE 2006, *Diagnosing and Changing Orgaizational Culture: Based on the Competing Values Framework*. Jossey-Bass: San Francisco.

Capowski, G 1994, 'Anatomy of a leader: Where are the leaders of tomorrow?', *Management Review*, vol 83 no. 3, pp 10 – 14.

Carley, KM & Hill, V 2001, Structural change and learning within organizations in E.R. Larsen (ed.) *Dynamics of Organizations: Computational Modeling and Organization Theories.* MIT Press: Menlo Park.

Carlyle, T 1888, *On Heroes, Hero-Worship and the Heroic History.* Frederick A. Stokes & Brother: New York. Available from: <http://www.questia.com/read/1444983/on-heroes-hero-worship-and-the-heroic-in-history> [8 October 2014].

Carnall, C 2007, *Managing Change In Organizations,* 5th edn. Pearson Education: Harlow.

Carneiro, RL 1981, American Museum of Natural History: Herbert Spencer as an Anthropologist. *The Journal of Library Studies*, vol. 5, no. 2, pp. 153 - 210.

Changing Minds 2002, *Mintzberg's Political Games.* Available from: <http://changingminds.org/explanations/behaviors/games/mintzberg_game.htm>. [5 September 2014].

Chapman, MR 2006, In Search of Stupidity: Over 20 years of High Tech Marketing Disasters, 2nd edn. Apress: Berkely.

Child, J & McGrath, RG 2001, 'Organizations unfettered: Organizational form in an information-intensive economy', *Academy of Management Journal*, vol. 44, no. 6, pp. 1135 - 1148.

Christensen, C 1998, *The innovator's dilemma,* HBP: Boston.

Cockerell, L 2008, *Creating Magic: 10 Common Sense Leadership Strategies from a Life at Disney.* Doubleday: New York.

College, RK & University, YS 2014, *Master of Arts & Post Graduate Diploma Leading Innovation & Change:* Programme Handbook.

Collins, JC & Porras, JI 2004, *Built to Last,* 3rd edn. Harper Collins Publishers: New York.

Collins, JC 2001, *Good to Great: Why Some Companies Make the Leap... and Others Don't,* Harper Collins Publishers: New York.

Collins, JC 2005, 'Level 5 Leadership: The Triumph of Humility and Fierce Resolve', *Harvard Business Review,* vol. 83, no. 7/8, pp. 136 - 146.

Conti, T 2009, *Systems thinking: The new frontier in quality management.* Proceedings 53rd EOQ Conference, Dubrovnik. Available from: <http://www.tandfonline.com/doi/abs/10.1080/14783363.2012.728849#.VLZ_HV qOd5g>. [14 January 2015].

Conti, T 2010, 'The dynamics of value generation and their dependence on an organization's internal and external value systems', *Total Quality Management & Business Excellence,* vol. 21, pp. 9 - 10.

Conway, M 2009, Strategic Thinking: What It Is and How To Do It. Available from: <http://www.slideshare.net/mkconway/strategic-thinking-what-it-is-and-how-to-do-it14
88155>. [4 May 2014].

Cooper, GL 2005, *Leadership and Management in the 21st Century: Business Challenges of the Future.* Oxford: Oxford University Press: Oxford.

Covey, S 2013, *Leadership Essentials.* Rosetta Books: New York.

Cross, B 2010, 'Service complexity: Managing a house of cards (Really)', *Ivey Business Journal,* vol. 74, no. 3, pp. 8.

Dahlgaard, SM 2011, 'The quality movement: Where are you going?', *Total Quality Management & Business Excellence,* vol. 22, no. 5 - 6, pp. 493 - 516.

Das, T.K. & Kumar, R 2010, 'Interpretive Schemes in Cross-National Alliances: Managing Conflicts andDiscrepancies', *Cross Cultural Management: An International Journal,* vol. 17, no. 2, pp. 15 – 169.

David Ng, FS 2013, 'Leadership learning through the lens of complexity theory', *Human Systems Management,* vol. 2, no. 1, pp. 43 - 55.

Dawson, J 2013, 'How to Make Change in the Workplace Work for You', *America's Health Care Financial Managers,* vol 28 no. 7, pp 8 – 10.

Day, DV & Antonakis, J (Eds.) 2012, *The nature of leadership,* Sage: Thousand Oaks.

De Bono, E 1990, *Lateral Thinking: Creativity Step by Step.* Harper & Row: New York.

De Wit, B & Meyer, R 2005, *Strategy Synthesis: Resolving Strategy Paradoxes to Create Competitive Advantage.* Thomson Learning: London.

Deal, TE & Kennedy, AA 2000, *Corporate Cultures: The Rites & Rituals of Corporate Life.* Perseus Books: New York.

Den Hartog, DN, House, RJ, Flanges, PJ, Ruiz Quintanilla, SA & Dorfman, PW 1999, 'Culture-Specific and Cross-Culturally Generalizable Implicit Theories: Are Attributes of Charismatic/ Transformational Leadership Universally Endorsed?', *Leadership Quarterly* vol. 10, no. 2, pp. 219 – 257.

Denison, DR & Spreitzer, GM, 1991, 'Organizational Culture and Organizational Devleopment: A Competing Values Approach', *Research in Organizational Change and Development,* vol. 5, pp. 1 – 12.

Denison, DR 1990, Corporate Culture and Organizational Effectiveness. Wiley: New York.

Denison, DR 2007, Denison: *Culture & Leadership Diagnostics.* Available from: <http://former.denisonconsulting.com/diagnostics/organizational-culture>.   [8 October 2014].

Denison, DR, Hooijberg, R & Quinn, RE 1995, 'Paradox and Performance: Toward a Theory of Behavioral Complexity in Managerial Leadership', *Organization Science,* vol. 6, no. 5, pp. 524 - 540.

Dervitsiotis, K 2007, 'On becoming adaptive: The new imperative for survival and success in the 21st century', *Total Quality Management & Business Excellence,* vol. 18, no. 1 - 2, pp. 21 - 38.

Dervitsiotis, K 2010, 'Developing full-spectrum innovation capability for survival and success in the global economy', *Total Quality Management & Business Excellence,* vol. 21, no. 2, pp. 157 - 168.

Dervitsiotis, K 2011, 'The challenge of adaptation through innovation based on the quality of the innovation process', *Total Quality Management & Business Excellence,* vol. 22, no. 5 - 6, pp. 553 - 566.

Dervitsiotis, K 2012, 'An innovation-based approach for coping with increasing complexity in the global economy', *Total Quality Management & Business Excellence,* vol. 23, no. 9 - 10,   pp. 997 - 1011.

Dharmaraj, C, Sivasubramanian, M & Sudhahar, CJ 2010, 'Car Industry: SWOT Analysis', *SCMS Journal of Indian Management,* vol. 7 no. 2, pp. 67 – 79.

Dibella, AJ 2007, 'Critical Perceptions of Organisational Change', *Journal of Change Management,* vol 7 no. 3/4, pp 231 – 242.

Dingwall, R, Murphy, EA, Watson, P, Greatbatch, D & Parker, S 1998, 'Catching Goldfish: quality in qualitative research', *Journal of Health Services Research and Policy,* vol. 3, no. 3, pp. 167 - 172.

Dorfman, PW & Howel, JP 1988, 'Dimensions of National Culture and Effective Leadership Patterns: Hofstede revisited', *Advances in International Comparative Management,* vol. 3, pp. 127- 150.

Drath, W 2001a, *The Deep Blue Sea: Rethinking the source of leadership,* Jossey-Bass: San Francisco.

Drath, W 2001b, 'Beyond leaders and followers', *LIA,* vol. 28, no. 2, pp. 5.

Drath, WH, McCauley, CD, Palus, CJ, Velsor, EV, O'Connor, PMG, & McGuire, JB 2008, 'Direction, alignment, and commitment: Toward a more integrative ontology of leadership, *The Leadership Quarterly,* vol. 19, no. 6, pp. 635 - 653.

Drucker, PF 2006, *The Practice of Management,* Reissue edn. Harper Collins Publishers Inc.: New York.

Dudovsky, J 2013, Research Methodology: *Leadership Contimuum Theory by Tannerbaum & Schmidt.* Available from: <http://research-methodology.net/leadership-continuum-theory-by-tannerbaum-and-schmidt/>. [21 August 2014].

Earley, CP & Ang, S 2003, *Cultural Intelligence: Individual Interactions Across Cultures.* Stanford University Press: Stanford.

EFQM, W 2013, The *EFQM Excellence Model.* Management, European Foundation for Quality. Available from: <http://www.efqm.org/the-efqm-excellence-model>. [19 June 2014].

Esteban, Q 2014, 'Leading People Through Change', *Strategic Finance,* vol 96 no. 5, pp 15 – 16.

Farquar, JD 2012, *Case study research for business*, SAGE: London.

Fiedler, FE 1972, 'The Effects of Leadership Training and Experience: A Contingency Model Interpretation', *Administrative Science Quarterly*, vol. 17, no. 4 pp. 453 - 470.

Fjeldstad, D, Snow, CC, Miles, RE & Letti, C 2012, 'The architecture of collaboration', *Strategic Management Journal,* vol. 33, no. 6, pp. 734 - 750.

Flamholz, EG & Randle, Y 1998, *Changing the Game: Organizational Transformation of the First, Second, and Third Kinds.* Oxford University Press New York.

Ford, JD, Ford, LW & D'Amelio, A 2008, 'Resistance to Change: The Rest of the Story', *Academy of Management Review,* vol *33* no. 2, pp 362 – 377.

Funny Junk, 2014: *Star Trek Funny pictures.* Available from: <http://funnyjunk.com/Star+trek/funny-pictures/4995022/>. [23 July 2015]

Galia, F & Legros, D 2004, 'Complementarities between obstacles to innovation: evidence from France', R*esearch Policy*, vol. 33, no. 8, pp. 1185 - 1199.

Gardiner, JW 1993, *On Leadership.* The Free Press: New York.

Gardner, G 1977 'Is There a Valid Test to Herzberg's Two-Factor Theory?', *Journal of Occupational Psychology*, vol. 50, no. 3, pp. 197 - 204.

Gardner, H 1983, *Frames of Mind: The Theory of Multiple Intelligences.* Basic Books: New York.

Geer-Frazier, B 2014, 'Complexity leadership generates innovation, learning, and adaptation of the organisation', *Emergence: Complexity & Organisation*, vol. 16, no. 3, pp. 105 - 116.

George, B 2005, Management Skills. John Wiley & Sons: San Francisco.

Gladwell, M 2008, *Outliers: The Story of Success*. Penguin: London.

Goffee, R & Jones, G, 2006, 'Extraordinary leadership', *Business Strategy Review*, vol. 17, no. 2, pp. 30 - 33.

Goffin, K & Mitchell, R 2010, *Innovation Management: Key Aspects of innovation Management, 2nd edn*. Palgrave Macmillan: Basingstoke.

Goffin, K 2007, *Interview: Professor Keith Goffin, Innovation Management: Strategy Implementation Using the Pentathlon Framework*. Cranfield School of Management: Cranfield.

Goleman, D 1996, *Emotional Intelligence: Why it can Matter More than IQ*. Bloomsbury: London.

Goleman, D, Boyatzis, R & McKee, A 2003, *The New Leaders: Transforming the Art of Leadership*. Time Warner: London.

Gottfredson, M & Aspinall, K 2005, 'Innovation vs. Complexity: What Is Too Much of a Good Thing?', *Harvard Business Review*, vol. 83, no. 11, pp. 62 – 72.

Govindarajan, V & Trimble, C 2010, *The other side of innovation, HBP: Boston.*

Grabel, I 2013 'Global financial governance and development finance in the wake of the 2008 financial crises', *Feminist Economics*, vol. 19, no. 3, pp. 32 - 54.

Graeff, C 1983, 'The Situational Leadership Theory: A Critical View', *Academy of Management Review*, vol. 8, no. 2 pp. 285 - 291.

Graham, S, Blanchard, K, Huntsman J, Lennick, D, Kiel F 2012, *Leading Teams with Integrity: Advice from Leadership Experts*. FT Press: Upper Saddle River.

Grant, R 2008, *Contemporary Strategy Analysis*, 6th edn. Blackwell Publishing: Oxford.

Gravenhorst, K, Werkman, R & Boonstra, J 2003, 'Kubler-Ross' 5-stage model (Kubler-Ross 2003)', *Applied Psychology: An International Review,* vol 52 no. 1, pp 83 – 105.

Grey, SP & Stechly, WA 2010, *Leading Good Schools to Greatness: Mastering What Great Principals Do Well*. Corwin: California.

Griffiths, D & Prozesky, MLC 2010, 'The Politics of Dwelling: Being White/Being South African', *Africa Today*, vol. 56, no. 4, pp. 22 - 41.

Hackman, JR & Oldham, GR 1980, *Work Redesign*. Addison-Wesley: Reading.

Hamel, G & Prahalad, C 1994, *Competing for the Future*. Harvard Business School Press: Boston.

Hamel, G 1998, 'Strategic Innovation and the Quest for Value', *Sloan Management Review,* vol 39 no. 2 pp 7 – 14.

Hamington, M 2010, 'The Will to Care: Performance, Expectation, and Integration', *Hypatia*, vol. 25 no. 3, pp. 675 - 695.

Hammer, M & Champy, J 2001, *Reengineering the Corporation: A Manifesto for Business Revolution*. Nicholas Brealey: London.

Handy, C 1993, *Understanding Organisations: How Understanding the Ways Organizations Actually Work can be Used to Manage Them Better, 4th Edn*. Oxford University Press: Oxford.

Handy, CB 1976, *Understanding Organizations, 4th e d n*. Penguin Books: Harmondsworth.

Hansen, M & Birkenshaw, J 2007, 'The Innovation Value Chain', *Harvard Business Review*, vol 85 no. 6, pp 121 – 130.

Harrison, R 1972, *'Understanding Your Organisation's Character'*, vol. 5, no. 3, pp. 119 – 128.

Hart, C 2003, Management And Accounting Web, *Beer, M. and N. Nohria. 2000. Cracking the code of change. Harvard Business Review (May-June): 133-141*. Available from: <http://maaw.info/ArticleSummaries/ArtSumBeerNohria2000.htm>. [23 June 2014].

Hatch, MJ 1993, 'The Dynamics of Organizational Culture', *Academy of Management Review*, vol. 18, no. 4, pp. 657 – 693.

Hayes, J 2010, *The Theory & Practice of Change Management*, 3rd edn. Palgrave Macmillan: New York.

Hazy, JK 2006, 'Measuring leadership effectiveness in complex socio-technical systems', *Emergence: Complexity and organisation, vol. 8, no. 3*, pp. 58 - 77.

Heckscher, C, 1994, *Defining the post-bureaucratic type* in A. Donnellon and C. Heckscher (eds) *The Post-Bureaucratic Organization: New Perspectives on Organizational Change*, Sage: Newbury Park.

Heinzmann, R 2009, FLVS Motivation Group: *Theories of Motivation*. Available from: <http://flvsmotivation.pbworks.com/w/page/7154171/February%3A %C2%A0Theories%C2%A0of%C2%A0Motivation>. [26 August 2014].

Henderson, B 1973, Boston Consulting Group: The Experience Curve Reviewed. Available from: <http://www.bcg.com/documents/file13904.pdf>. [23 June 2014].

Henderson, B 1979, *Henderson on Corporate Strategy*. Harper Collins.

Heracleous, L 1998, 'Strategic Thinking or Strategic Planning', *International Journal of Strategic Management: Long Range Planning*, vol 31 no. 3 pp 481 – 487.

Hersey, P & Blanchard, K & Johnson, DJ 2001, *Management of Organisational Behaviour, 8th edn*. Prentice Hall: New Jersey.

Herzberg, F 1968, *Work and the Nature of Man*. Corby Lockwood & Staples: London.

Herzberg, F 1983, One More Time: How Do You Motivate Employees?', *Harvard Business Review*, vol. 63, no. 6, pp. 247.

Heywood, S, Spungin, J & Turnbull, D 2007, 'Cracking the complexity code', *McKinsey Quarterly*, no. 2, pp. 84 - 95.

Hiatt, JM & Creasey, TJ 2012, *Change Management: The People Side of Change*. Prosci Learning Centre Publications: Loveland.

Hiatt, JM 2006, *ADKAR: A Model for Change in Business, Government and our Community.* Prosci Inc.: Loveland.

Higgs, M 2003, 'How can we make sense of leadership in the 21st century?', *Leadership and Organization Development Journal,* vol. 24, no. 5/6, pp. 273 - 284.

Hitt, MA , Keats, BW & DeMarie, SM 1998, Navigating in the New Competitive Landscape: Building Strategic Flexibility and Competitive Advantage in the 21st Century. *Academy of Managment Executive,* vol 12 no. 4, pp. 22 – 42.

Hitt, MA 1998, 'Twenty-first-century organizations: Business firms, business schools and the academy', *Academy of Management Review*, vol. 23, no. 2, pp. 218 - 224.

Hoch, J & Morgeson, F 2014, 'Vertical and Shared Leadership processes: Exploring Team Leadership Dynamics', *Academy of Management Annual Meeting Proceedings*, pp. 1607 - 1612.

Hoffman, EA 2008, 'A Wolf in Sheep's Clothing: Discrimination Against the Majority Undermines Equality, While Continuing to Benefit Few Under the Guise of Black Economic Empowerment', *Syracuse Journal of International Law & Commerce*, vol. 36, no. 1, pp. 87 – 115.

Hofstede G, 2014, *MIC: Joint Master International Communication.* Available from: <http://www.masterinternationalcommunication.eu/links/geert-hofstede-consortium/professor-dr-geert-hofstede/>. [14 September 2014].

Hofstede, G & Minkov, M 2010, 'Long-versus Short-Term Orientation: New Perspectives', *Asia Pacific Business Review*, vol. 16, no. 4, pp. 493 – 504.

Hofstede, G 1984, *Cultural Consequences: International Differences in Work Values.* Sage: London.

Hofstede, G 2001, Culture's Consequences: Comparing Values, Behvaiours, Institutions and   Organisations Across Nations, 2nd edn, Sage Publications: London.

Hofstede, G, Hofstede GJ & Minkov M 2010, Cultures and Organizations: Software of the Mind, 3rd edn. McGraw-Hill: New York.

Hofstede, G, Hofstede GJ 2014, *Culture: Organizational Level.* Available from: <http://www.geerthofstede.nl/culture>. [17 August 2014].

Hofstede, G, Neuijen, B, Ohayv, DD & Sanders, G 1990, 'Measuring Organizational Cultures: A Qualitative and Quantitative Study across Twenty Cases', *Administrative Science Quarterly,* vol. 35, no. 2, pp. 286 – 316.

Holbeche, L 2006, *Understanding Change: Theory, Implementation and Success.* Elsevier Butterworth-Heinemann: London.

Hooiberg, R, Hunt, JG & Dodge, GE 1997, Leadership Complexity and Development of the Leaderplex Model. *Journal of Management,* vol 23 no. 3, pp. 375 – 408.

Hooijberg, R, Hunt, JG & Dodge, GE 1997, 'Leadership complexity and development of the leaderplex model. *Journal of Management*, vol. 23, no. 3, pp. 375 - 408.

Horwitz, EJ & Klontz, BT 2013, 'Understanding and Dealing with Client Resistance to Change', *Journal of Financial Planning,* vol *26* no. 11, pp 27 – 31.

House, RJ & Wigdor, LA 1967, 'Herzberg's Dual-Factor Theory of Job Satisfaction and Motivation: A Review of the Evidence and Criticism', *Personanel Psychology,* vol. 20, no. 4, pp. 369 - 389.

House, RJ, Hanges, PJ, Javidan, M, Dorfman, PW & Gupta, V 2004, *Culture, Leadership and Organizations: The Globe Study of 62 Societies.* Sage: London.

Howard, G 1988, 'Validating the Competing Values Model as a Representation of Organizational Cultures', *International Journal of Organizational Analysis*, vol. 6, no. 3, pp. 231 – 250.

Huether, D 2011, The Critical Path: *Theory X vs. Theory Y.* Available from: <http://thecriticalpath.info/2011/08/22/theory-x-vs-theory-y/>. [21 August 2014].

Hughes, RL & Beatty, K 2005, *Becoming a Strategic Leader.* Jossey-Bass: San Fransisco.

Hunt, J 2010, London Business School. Why It's So Hard To Delegate. Available from:<http://www.zoominfo.com/s/#!search/profile/person?personId=74199995&targe
tid=profile>.[27 August 2014].

IBM Think Forum 2011, 'A conversation on bringing science to leadership', Available   from:

<http://www.youtube.com/watchv=aEcEdJaxr0c&list=UU28uMrop1YYpzHN8 ukzOXA&index =71&feature=plcp>. [9 January 2015].

Idhammer, C 2014, 'Why some reliability and maintenance improvement initiatives fail to deliver: Hedgehog or Fox?', *PPI: Pulp & Paper International,* vol 56 no. , pp. 11 – 12.

Iles, V & Sutherland, K 2001, *Organisational Change: A Review for Health Care Managers, Professionals and Researchers. NCCSDO:* London.

Isaacs, ED 2013, 'Foxes, Hedgehogs and Life After Graduate School', *Vital Speeches of the Day,* vol 79 no. 3 pp. 63 – 67.

Isaksen, S & Tidd, J 2006, *Meeting the Innovation Challenge: Leadership for Transformation and Growth.* John Wiley & Sons: Chichester.

Jacobs, TO & Jaques, E 1987, *Leadership in complex systems* In Zeidner, J (Ed.), *Human   productivity enhancement,* Vol. 2. Praeger: New York.

Jacques, E 1978, *General Theory of Bureaucracy,* 3rd edn. Heinemann Educational Publishers: London.

Jamrog, J, Vickers, M & Bear, D 2006, 'Building and Sustaining a Culture that Supports Innovation', *Human Resource Planning*, vol. 29, no. 3, pp. 9 – 19.

Janis, IL 1982, *Victims of Groupthink.* Wadsworth: Boston.

Jaques, E 1989, *Requisite organisation*, Cason Hall: Arlington.

Jennings, MM 2006, *The Seven Signs of Ethical Collapse: How to Spot Moral Meltdowns in Companies... Before It's Too Late.* St Martin's Press: New York.

Johnson, G 2001, *Exploring Public Sector Strategy:* Pearson Education: Harlow.

Johnson, G, Scholes, K & Whittington, R 2011, *Exploring Strategy: Texts and Cases,* 9th edn, Prentice Hall: Harlow.

Johnson, J, Scholes, K & Whittington, R 2005, *Exploring Corporate Strategy, 5th edn.* Pearson Education Limited: Harlow.

Johnson, J, Scholes, K & Whittington, R 2008, *Exploring Corporate Strategy, 8th edn.* Pearson Education Limited: Harlow.

Johnson, J, Whittington, R & Scholes, K 2012, *Fundamentals of Strategy, 2nd edn.* Pearson Education: Harlow.

Johnson, N 2007, *Simply Complexity: A Clear Guide to Complexity Theory,* Oneworld: Oxford.

Juarez, AC 2013, eHow: Models of Organisational Culture, Structure, Process & Control. Available from: <http://www.ehow.com/info_8621096_models-culture-structure-process-control.html>. [5 October 2014].

Judge, TA & Cable DM 1997, 'Applicant personality Organizational Culture and Organizational Attraction', *Personnel Psychology,* vol. 50, no. 2, pp. 359 – 394.

Jurevicius, O 2013, Strategic Management Insight: BCG Growth-oShare Matrix. Available from: <http://www.strategicmanagementinsight.com/tools/bcg-matrix-growth-share.html> [28 june 2014].

Kanter, RM, Stein, BA & Jick, T S 1992, *The Challenge of Organisational Change.* Free Press: New York.

Kaplan, RS & Norton, DP 2001, *The Strategy-focused Organization: How Balanced Scorecard Companies Thrive in the New Business Environment.* Harvard Business School Press: Boston.

Kar, A 2007, *Business Fundas: The GE-McKinsey Matrix and its Limitations for Business Portfolio Analysis.* Available from: <http://business-fundas.com/2010/the-ge-mckinsey-matrix-and-its-limitations-for-business-portfolio-analysis/>. [2 July 2014].

Kar, A 2012, *Business Fundas : Comparison of Business Strategy Frameworks.* Available from: <http://business-fundas.com/2012/comparison-of-business-strategy-frameworks/>. [24 May 2014].

Kasi 2010, *MBA Tutorials:* GE/McKinsey Matrix. Available from: <http://www.mba-tutorials.com/strategy/1159-ge-mckinsey-matrix.html>. [2 July 2014].

Katzenberg, JR & Smith DK 1993 & 2006, *The Wisdom of Teams: Creating the High Performance Organization.* Harper Collins: New York.

Katzenberg, JR & Smith DK 2005, 'The Discipline of Teams', *Harvard Business Review,* vol. 83, no. 7/6, pp, 162 - 171.

Kauffman, S, 1993, *The Origins of Order: Self-Organization and Selection in Evolution,* Oxford University Press: New York.

Keene, A 2000, 'Complexity theory: the changing role of leadership', *Industrial and Commercial Training*, vol. 32, no. 1, pp. 15 - 18.

Kegan, R & Lahey, L 2010, *Adult development and organizational leadership*, Nitin Nohria, Rakesh Khurana (Eds.), *Handbook of leadership theory and practice: A Harvard Business School centennial colloquium*, Harvard Business Press: Boston.

Kegan, R 1994, *In over our heads. The mental demands of modern life*, Harvard University Press: Cambridge.

Keller, S & Price, C 2011, *Beyond Performance: How Great Organizations Build Ultimate Competitive Advantage.* John Wiley & Sons: New Jersey.

Klemp, GO 2001, 'Leadership Competencies: Putting It All Together' in J Raven and J Stephenson (eds) *Competence in the Learning Society.*   Peter Lang International Academic Publishers: New York.

Koo, CM, Koh, CE & Nam, K 2004, 'An Examination of Porter's Competitive Strategies in Electronic Virtual Markets: A Comparison of Two On-line Business Models', *International Journal of Electronic Commerce, vol 9* no. 1, pp 163 – 180.

Kotter JP 1996, *Leading Change.* Harvard Business School Press: Boston.

Kotter, JP & Cohen D 2002, *The Heart of Change.* Harvard Business School: Boston.

Kotter, JP & Hesket, JL 2011, *Corporate Culture and Performance*, Free Press: New York.

Kotter, JP 1990, *A Force for Change: How Leadership Differs from Management.* Free Press: London.

Kotter, JP 1999, *What Leaders Really Do.* Harvard Business School Press: Boston.

Kotter, JP 2001, 'What Leaders Really Do', *Harvard Business Review*, vol 79 no. 11, pp 85 – 96.

Kotter, JP 2011, *Kotter International: Video Interview on Change Management vs. Change Leadership - W h a t's th e Difference?*   Available   from: <http://www.forbes.com/sites/johnkotter/2011/07/12/change-management-vs-change-leadership-whats-the-difference/>. [5 June 2014].

Kotter, JP 2013, 'Change Leadership', *Leadership Excellence*, vol 30 no. 1, pp 6 – 7.

Kubler-Ross, E 2003, *On Death & Dying.* Scribner: New York.

Kuhlmann, A 2010, 'Reinventing Innovation', *Ivey Business Journal*, vol 74 no. 3, pp 28 – 30.

Kuriger, CC 2006, 'Workplace Change and Worker Fears. *Army Logistician*, vol *38* no. 4, p 38.

Lamotte, G & Carter, G 2000, Balanced Scorecard Collaborative: *Are the Balanced Scorecard and the EFQM Excellence Model Mutually Exclusive or do they Work Together to Bring Added Value to a Company?* Available from: <http://www.consultingmg.com/web/es/doc/efqmcmi.pdf>. [30 June 2014].

Lawrence, E 1999, *Strategic Thinking. Public Services Commission of Canada.* Available from: <http://www.hrbartender.com/images/thinking.pdf>. [5 July 2014].

Lawson, E & Price, C 2003, 'The Psychology of Change Management', *McKinsey Quarterly*, Special Edition no. 4, pp. 30 – 41.

Leonard, D & Swap, W 1999, *When Sparks Fly: Harnessing the Power of Group Creativity.* Harvard Business School Press: Boston.

Leslie, JB & Velsor, EV 1998, A Cross-National Comparison of Effective Leadership & Teamwork, Centre for Creative Leadership: Greensboro.

Lester, A, Borden, D & Fiedler, F 1977, 'Validation of Contingency Model Leadership Training: Leader', *Academy of Management Journal*, vol. 20, no. 3 pp. 464 - 470.

Lewin, K 1951, *Field Theory in Social Science.* Harper & Row: New York.

Lewis, RD 2006, *When Cultures Collide: Leading across cultures. 3rd edn.* Nicholas Brealey Publishing: Boston.

Lians, T 2013, 'Edge of emergence, relativistic complexity and the new leadership', *Human   Systems Management*, vol. 32, no. 1, pp. 3 - 15.

Lichtenstein, BB, Uhl-Bien, M, Marion, R, Seers, A, Orton, JD & Schreiber, C 2006, 'Complexity   leadership theory: An interactive perspective on leading in complex adaptive systems', *Emergence:Complexity and Organisation*, vol. 8, no. 4, pp. 2 - 12.

Liedtka, J 1998, 'Strategic Thinking: Can It be Taught?', *International Journal of Strategic Management: Long Range Planning*, vol 31 no. 1 , pp 120 – 129.

Livermore, D 2009, '*Leading with Cultural Intelligence*' (video file). Available from: <http://davidlivermore.com/cq/>. [12 August 2014].

Livermore, D 2010, *Leading with Cultural Intelligence: The New Secret to Success.* AMACOM: New York.

Locke, EA & Latham GP 1984, *Goal Setting: A Motivational Technique That Works.* Prentice Hall: New Jersey.

Locke, EA & Latham, GP 2009, 'Has Goal setting Gone Wild, or Have It's Attackers Abandoned Good Scholarship?', *Academy of Management Perspectives*, vol. 23, no. 1, pp. 17 - 23.

Loehle, C 1996, *Thinking strategically: Power Tools for Personal and Professional Advancements.* Cambridge University Press: Cambridge.

London School of Hygiene & Tropical Medicine 2001, *Managing Change in the NHS.* NHS Service Delivery and Organisation R&D Programme. Available from: <http://www.netscc.ac.uk/hsdr/>. [22 June 2014].

Longenecker, C 2014, 'The Best Practice of Great Leaders', *Industrial Management*, vol. 56, no. 4, pp. 20 - 25.

Lord, RG & Hall, RJ 2005, Identity, deep structure, and the development of leadership skill. *The   Leadership Quarterly*, vol. 16, no. 4, pp. 591 - 615.

Lowell, B 2008, McKinsey & Company, *Enduring Ideas: The 7-S Framework.* Available   from:

<http://www.mckinsey.com/insights/strategy/enduring_ideas_the_7-s_framework>. [26 July 2014].

Lydamore, V 2014, E-How: *Situational Leadership Pros & Cons*. Available from: <http://www.ehow.com/info_7851680_situational-leadership-pro-cons.html>. [21 August 2014].

Lynn M, & Gelb, B 1996, 'Identifying Innovative National Markets for Technical Consumer Goods', *International Market Review*, vol. 13, no. 6, pp. 43 - 57.

Maccoby, M 2000, 'Understanding the Difference between Management and Leadership', *Research Technology Management*, vol. 43, no. 1, pp. 57 - 59.

Margerison, CJ & McCann, D 1995, *Team Management: Practical New Approaches, 2nd edn*. Management Books: Oxford.

Marion, R & Uhl-Bien, M, 2003, 'Complexity theory and Al-Qaeda: Examining complex leadership', *Emergence: Complexity Issues in Organizations and Management*, vol. 5, no. 1, pp. 54 - 76.

Marion, R & Uhl-Bien, M. 2001, 'Leadership in complex organizations', *Leadership Quarterly*, vol. 12, no. 4, pp. 389 - 418.

Markides, C 2012, 'Think Again: Fine Tune Your Strategic Thinking', *Business Strategy Review*, vol 23 no. 4, pp 80 – 85.

Marques, JF 2007, 'On Impassioned Leadership: A Comparison Between Leaders from Divergent Walks of Life', *International Journal of Leadership Studies*, vol. 3, no. 1, pp. 98 - 125.

Martin, A 2007, 'The future of leadership: Where do we go from here?' *Industrial and Commercial Training*, vol. 39, no. 1, pp. 3 - 8.

Maslow, AH 1987, *Motivation and Personality*. Longman: New York.

Maslow, AH 1993, *The Farther Reaches of Human Nature*. Viking Press: Arkana.

Mason, WH 2011, '*Complexity Theory*', Available from: <http://www.referenceorbusin ess.com/fmanagement/Bun-Comp/Complexity-Theory.html>. [11 February 2015].

Mayfield, P 2014, 'Engaging with Stakeholders is Critical when Leading Change', *Industrial & Commercial Training*, vol 46 no. 2, pp 68 – 72.

Maylor, HR, Turner, NW & Murray-Webster, R 2013, 'How hard can it be?: Actively managing complexity in technology projects', *Research Technology Management*, vol. 56, no. 4, pp. 45 -   51.

McClelland, DC 1988, *Human Motivation*. Cambridge University Press: Cambridge.

McDonald, M & Payne, A 1996, *Marketing Planning for Services*. Butterworth-Heinemann: Oxford.

McGregor, D 2006, *The Human Side of Enterprise*. McGraw-Hill: New York.

McKinsey 2008, 'The GE-McKinsey Nine-Box Framework', *McKinsey Quarterly*, issue 4, p 142.

McNamara, C 2000, Managementhelp.org, *Organizational Culture and Changing Culture.* Available from: <http://managementhelp.org/organizations/culture.htm>. [10 August 2013].

Meredith, J 1998, 'Building operations management theory through case and field research', *Journal of Operations Management*, vol. 11, no. 3, pp. 239 - 256.

Meyer, A , Gaba, V, & Colwell, K, 2005, 'Organizing far from equilibrium: Nonlinear change in organizational fields', *Organization Science*, vol.16, no. 5 , pp. 456 - 473.

Miller, L, Rankin, N & Neathley 2001, *Competency Frameworks in UK Organisations.* CIPD: London.

MindTools.com 2014, *Hofstede's Cultural Dimensions: Understanding Workplace Values Around the World.* Available from: <http://www.mindtools.com/pages/article/newLDR_66.htm>. [17 August 2014].

Miner, JB 2005, *Organizational Behaviour: Essential Theories of Motivation and Leadership.* ME Sharpe Inc: New York.

Mintzberg, H 1985, 'The organisation As Political Arena', *Journal of Management Studies*, vol. 22, no. 2, pp. 133 – 154.

Mintzberg, H 1994, 'Strategic Planning', *Harvard Business Review,* vol 72 no. 1, 1pp 07 – 114.

Mintzberg, H 1997, 'The Strategy Concept I: Five Ps for Strategy', *California Management Review,* vol 30 no. 1, pp 11 – 24.

Mintzberg, H 1998, *Strategic Safari: The Complete Guide Through the Wilds of Strategic Management.* The Free Press: New York.

Mintzberg, H 2003, *The Strategy Process.* Pearson Education: Upper Saddle River.

Mitchell, T, Biglan, A, Oncken, GR & Fiedler, FR 1970, 'The Contingency Model: Criticism and Suggestions', *Academy of Management Journal*, vol. 13, no. 3 pp. 253 - 267.

Moore, K & Lenir, P 2011, Forbes: *Mintzberg's Better Way to Do Corporate Strategy.* Available   from: <http://www.forbes.com/sites/karlmoore/2011/06/21/emergent-strategy-demands-emergent-learning/>. [20 June 2014].

Moore, R 2008, 'Why Leaders Fail: When the Best Strategies Can't Get It Done', *Cost Engineering,* vol 50 no. 11, pp 3 – 4.

Morrison, A & Wensley, R 1991, 'Boxing Up or Boxed In?: A Short History of the Boston Warwick Business School Consulting Group Share/Growth Matrix', *Journal of Marketing Management*, vol 7 no. 2, pp 105 – 129.

Morrison, K 2014, 'Complexity theory, school leadership and management: questions for theory and   practice', *The Leadership Quarterly*, vol. 25, no. 2, pp. 183 - 203.

Nadler, D & Tushman, M 1995, *Types of Organizational Change: From Incremental Improvement to Discontinuous Transformation.* Jossey-Bass: San Francisco.

Nadler, D, Shaw, R & Walton, A 1994, *Discontinuous Change: Leading Organizational Transformation.* Jossey-Bass: San Francisco.

Nanus, B & Nanus, W 1997, *Leaders: Strategies for Taking Charge, 2nd edn.* Collins Business Essentials: New York.

Needle, D 2004, *Business in Context: An Introduction to Business and its Environment, 4th edn.* Thomson Learning: London.

Nelson, C 2004, IBM Developer Works: Overcoming Cultural Challenges in Adopting Iterative Development. Available from: <http://www.ibm.com/developerworks/rational/ library/content/RationalEdge/oct04/nelson/>. [10 September 2014].

Norton, MI, Sommers, SR, Apfelbaum, EP, Pura, N & Arlely, D 2006, 'Color Blindness and Interracial Interaction: Playing the Political Correctness Game', *Psychological Science*, vol. 11, no. 11, pp. 949 - 953.

O'Connell, PK 2014, 'A simplified framework for 21st century leader development', *The Leadership Quarterly*, vol. 25, no. 2, pp. 183 - 203.

O'Reilly, CA, Chatman, J & Cladwell, DF 1991, 'The Impact of Normative Social Influence and Cohesiveness on Task Perception and Attitudes: A Social Information processing Approach', *Journal of Occupational Psychology,* vol. 58, no. 4, pp. 193 – 206.

OCAI Online 2010, Organizational Culture Assessment Instrument (OCAI) online. Available from: <http://www.ocai-online.com>. [10 September 2014].

Olson, DA 2009, 'Are Great Leaders born, or Are They Made?', *Frontiers of Health Services Management*, vol. 26, no. 2, pp. 27 - 30.

Oreg, S & Berson, Y 2011, 'Leadership & Employee's Reaction to Change', *Personnel Psychology,* vol 64 no. 3, pp 627 – 659.

Oreg, S 2003, 'Resistance to Change: Developing an Individual Differences Measure', *Journal of Applied Psychology,* vol 88 no. 4, pp 80 – 693.

Oreg, S, Vakola, M & Armenakis, A 2011, 'Change Recipients' Reactions to Organizational Change: A Sixty-Year review of Quantitative Studies', *Journal of Applied Behavioral Science,* vol 47 no. 4, pp 461 – 524.

Osborn, RN, Hunt, JG & Jauch, LR 2002, 'Toward a contextual theory of leadership. *The Leadership Quarterly*, vol. 13, no. 6, pp. 797 – 837.

Otley, DT 1999, 'Performance Management: A Framework for Management Control System Research', Management Accounting Research, vol. 10 no. 4 pp. 363 - 382.

Pablo,D, Lammarino, S, Savona, M & Von Tunzelmann, N 2012, 'What hampers innovation? Revealed barriers versus deterring barriers', *Reaserach Policy,* vol. 41, no. 2, pp. 482 - 488.

Paul, J, Costley, DL, Howell, JP & Dorfman, PW 2002, 'The Mutability of Charisma in Leadership Research', *Management Decisions*, vol. 40, no. 1/2, pp. 192 - 200.

Pedler, M, Burgoyne, J & Boydell, T 2004, *A Manager's Guide to Leadership.* McGraw Hill: London.

Peretomode, O, 2012, 'Situational and Contingency theories of Leadership: Are They the Same?', *IOSR Journal of Business and Management*, vol. 4, no. 3 pp. 13 - 17.

Peters, T & Waterman, RH 1982, *In search of Excellence: Lessons from America's Best Run Companies*. Harper Collins: New York.

Peters, T 1994, *To Succeed, Learn to Love Politics, then Forget Them. The Baltimore Sun*. Available from: <http://articles.baltimoresun.com/1994-05-02/business/1994122138_1_office-politics-love-politics-politics-means>. [5 September 2014].

Peters, T 2011, 'McKinsey &S Model: It Continues to benefit Leaders', *Leadership Excellence*, vol. 28, no. 10, pp. 7.

Peters, T 2011, A Brief History of the 7-S Model. 9 January 2011. *Tom Peters: Blog*. Available from: <http://tompeters.com/2011/03/a-brief-history-of-the-7-s-mckinsey-7-s-model/>. [26 July 2014].

Porter, LW & McLaughlin, GB 2006, 'Leadership and the organizational context: Like the weather?' *The Leadership Quarterly*, vol. 17, no. 6, pp. 559 - 576.

Porter, M, 1985, *Competitive advantage,* Free Press: New York.

Porter, M, Argyres, N & McGahan, AM 2002, An Interview with Michael Porter. *The Academy of Management Executive, vol 16* no. 2, pp 43 – 52.

Porter, ME 1980, *Competitive Strategy.* Free Press: New York.

Porter, ME 2008, 'The Five Competitive Forces that Shape Strategy', *Harvard Business Review, vol 86 no 1,* pp 79 – 93.

Potter, D, 2010, *Cultural Change: Differentiated Culture.* Available from: <http://www.culturalchange.co.uk/?p=16>. [4 October 2014].

Prahalad, CK & Krishnan, MS 2008, *The new age of innovation,* McGraw-Hill: New York.

Quinn, RE & Rohrbaugh, J 1983, 'A Spatial Model of Effectiveness Criteria: Towards a Competing Values Approach to Organizational Analysis. *Management Science*, vol. 29, no. 3, pp. 363 - 377.

Quinn, RE 1988, *Beyond Rational Management: Mastering the Paradoxes and Competing Demands of High Performance*. Jossey-Bass: San Francisco.

Rafferty, AE & Griffin, MA 2004, 'Dimensions of Transformational Leadership: Conceptual and Empirical Extensions', *The Leadership Quarterly, vol.* 15, no. 3, pp. 329 - 354.

Rankin, N 2008 'Competencies in the Workplace' *IRS Employment Review* 906 IRS. Available from: <http://www.xperthr.co.uk/survey-analysis/survey-competencies-in-the-workplace/88527/>. [19 September 2014].

Ravasi, D & Schultz, M 2006, 'Responding to Organizational Identity Threats: Exploring the Role of Organizational Culture', *Academy of Management Journal*, vol. 49, no. 3, pp. 433 – 458.

Rawlinson, R 2007, 'Think laterally for success', *Manager: British Journal of Administrative Management,* Issue 60, pp 10 – 12.

Raynor, ME 2007, 'What is Corporate Strategy Really?', *Ivey Business Journal: Improving the Practice of Management,* vol 71 no. 8, , pp 1 – 3.

Razeghi, A 2008, *The Riddle.* Jossey-Bass: San Francisco.

Reades, C 2003, 'Going the Extra Mile: Local Managers and Global Effort', *Journal of Managerial Psychology*, vol. 13, no. 3, pp 208 - 228.

Reingold, J & Underwood, R 2005, 'Was Built to Last Built to last?', *Research Technology Management,* vol 48 no. 1, pp. 64.

Remenyi, D, Williams, B, Money, A. & Swartz, E 1998 *Doing Research in Business and Management: An Introduction to Process and Method,* Sage Publications: London.

Richardson, K & Cilliers, P 2001, 'Special editors' introduction: What is complexity science? A view from different directions', *Emergence*, vol. 3, no. 1, pp. 5 - 23.

Richardson, KA 2008, 'Managing Complex Organizations: Complexity Thinking and the Science and Art of Management', *Emergence: Complexity & Organization*, vol. 10, no. 2, pp. 13 - 26.

Richardson, M & Evans, C 2007, 'Strategy in action Applying Ansoff's Matrix', *Manager: British Journal of Administrative Management,* issue 59, pp i – iii.

Riebe, W 2013, *Millionaire Speaker Secrets.* Mind Power Publications: Cape Town.

Rigby, D 2005, '*Management tools and trends 2005*'. Available from: <http://www.bain.com/management_tools/Management_Tools_and_Trends_20 05.pdf>. [13 January 2015].

Robson, C 2011, *Real World Research,* 3rd edn, Wiley: Chichester.

Rogers, EM 2003, *Diffusion of Innovations,* 3rd edn. Free Press: New York.

Rosenzweig, P 2007, *The Halo Effect.* Free Press: New York.

Rosenzweigh, P 2007, *The Halo Effect: And the Eight Other Business Delusions That Deceive Managers.* Free Press: New York.

Rothlin, P & Werder, P 2008, *Burnout! Overcoming Workplace Demotivation.* Kogan Page: London.

Rouse, WB, Boff, KR, Sanderson, P & Beautement, P 2011, 'Making complexity work in practice', *Information Knowledge Systems Management*, vol. 10, no. 1 - 4, pp. 345 - 372.

Rummler, GA & Brache, AP 1995, *Improving Performance,* 2nd edn, Jossey-Bass: San Francisco.

Ruvolo, CM, Petersen, SA, LeBoeuf, JNG 2004, 'Leaders are Made, Not Born: The Critical Role of a Developmental framework to Facilitate an Organizational Culture of Development', *Consulting Psychology Journal: Practice & Research*, vol. 56, no. 1, pp. 10 - 19.

Safi, AE 2010, *Argument in Support and Against of Hostede Work, Individual Paper.* Available from: <https://unitn.academia.edu/abedsafi>. [19 August 2014].

Saunders, M, Lewis, P & Thornhill, A 2009, *'Research methods for business students',* 5th edn, Pearson Education: Harlow.

Schachter, E 2014, 'Change Leadership: The 5 Must-Do's for CEOs About to Hire a Change Agent', *Leadership Excellence, vol 31* no. 3, p 23.

Schafer, J 2014, *Cowering behind the walls of political correctness.* Psychology Today. Available   from: <https://www.psychologytoday.com/blog/let-their-words-do-the- talking/201404/cowering   -behind-the-walls-political-correctness>. [25 February 2015].

Scharmer, O 2010, *'The blind spot of institutional leadership: How to create deep innovation through moving from egosystem to ecosystem awareness',* World Economic Forum Annual Meeting   of the New Champions 2010, pp. 2-13, Available   from: <http://www.ottoscharmer.com/docs/   articles/2010_DeepInnovation _Tianjin.pdf>. [9 January 2015].

Schein, EH 1990, 'Organizarional Culture', *American Psychologist,* vol. 45, no. 2, pp. 109 – 119.

Schein, EH 1990, *Career Anchors: Discovering Your Real Values.* Joessey-Bass Pfeiffer: San Francisco.

Schein, EH 2010, *Organizational Culture & Leadership, 4th edn.* Jossey-Bass: San Francisco.

Schein, EH 2014, *Culture University: Culture Fundamentals - 9 Important Insights from Edgar Schein.* Interviewed by Tim Kuppler. Available from: <http://www.cultureuniversity.com/culture-fundamentals-9-important-insights-from-edgar-schein/>. [4 September 2014].

Schneider, A & Wishnie, P 2014, 'Changing with the times: How to adjust to the new economic realities', *Podiatry Management,* vol. 33, no. 8, pp. 65 - 70.

Schneider, B & Alderfer, CP 1973, 'Three Studies of measure of Needs Satisfaction in Organisations', *Administrative Science Quarterly,* vol. 22, no. 4, pp. 658 - 669.

Schneider, M & Somers, M 2006, 'Organizations as complex adaptive systems: Implications of complexity theory for leadership research', *The Leadership Quarterly,* vol. 17, no. 4, pp. 351 - 365.

Schraagen, J, Veld, M & De Koning, L 2010, 'Information sharing during crisis management in hierarchical vs. network teams', *Journal of Contingencies and Crisis Management,* vol. 18, no 2, pp. 17 - 127.

Seers, A 2004, *Leadership and flexible organizational structures,* in G. B. Graen (ed.),   *Newfrontiers   of leadership, LMX Leadership: The Series,* Information Age Publishing: Greenwich.

Selznick, P 1984, *Leadership in Administration: A Sociological Interpretation.* University of California Press: Berkeley.

Senge, P & Crainer, S 2008, 'Senge and Sensibility', *Business Strategy Review,* vol 19 no. 4, 7pp1 – 75.

Senge, P 2006, *The Fifth Disciplne: The Art and Practice of the Learning Organisation.* Random House Business: London.

Senior, B & Flemming, J 2006, *Organizational Change*, 3rd edn. Prentice Hall: Harlow.

Sherman, HJ & Schultz R 1998, *Open Boundaries: Creating Business Innovation Through Complexity,* Perseus Books: Reading.

Shulver, M & Lawrie, G 2007, *2GC* Active Management: *The Balanced Scorecard and the Business Excellence Model. European Institute for Advanced Studies in Management.* Available from: <http://2gc.eu/files/resources/2GC-CP-EFQM-090327.pdf>. [19 June 2014].

Silva, A 2014, What Do We Really Know About Leadership?', *Journal of Business Studies*, vol. 5, no. 4, pp. 1 - 4.

Simon, HA 1962, 'The architecture of complexity', *Proceedings of the American Philosophical Society*, vol. 106, no. 6, pp. 467 - 482.

Sirkin, HL, Keenan, P & Jackson, A 2005, 'The hard side of change', *The Harvard Business Review*, vol. 83, no. 10, pp. 108 - 118.

Smith, WK & Lewis, MW 2011, 'Toward a theory of paradox: a dynamic equilibrium model of organizing', *Academy of Management Review*, vol. 36, no. 2, pp. 381 - 403.

Spenner, M & Freeman, K 2012, 'To keep your customers, keep it simple', *Harvard Business Review*, vol. 90, no. 5, pp. 108 - 114.

Stansbury, J 2009, 'Reasoned Moral Agreement: Applying Discourse Ethics Within Organizations', *Business Ethics Quarterly*, vol. 19, no. 1, pp. 33-56.

Steele, C & Francis-Smythe J 2007, Career Anchors - An empirical Investigation. *Proceedings of the British Psychological Society's 2007 Occupational Psychology Conference, Bristol, England. Available from: <https://eprints.worc.ac.uk/265/1* CareerAnchorsEmp.pdf>. *[26 August 2014].*

Steers, RM, Mowday, RT & Shapiro, DL 2004, 'The Future of Work Motivation Theory', *Academy of Management Review*, vol. 29, no. 3, pp. 379 - 387.

Stevenson, BW 2012, 'Application of systemic and complexity thinking in organizational development', *Emergence: Complexity & Organization*, vol. 14, no.2, pp. 86 - 99.

Steyn, M & Foster, D 2008, 'Repertoires for Talking White: Resistant Whiteness in Post-   Apartheid South Africa', *Ethnic & Racial Studies*, vol. 31, no. 1, pp. 25 - 51.

Stogdill, RM & Bass, B 1990, *Bass and Stogdill's Handbook of Leadership, 3rd edn.* Free Press: New York.

Stogdill, RM 1974, Handbook of Leadership: A Survey of Theory and Research. Free Press: New York.

Straker, D 2013, Changing Minds.org, *Leadership vs Management.* Available from: <http://changingminds.org/disciplines/leadership/articles/manager_leader.ht m#man>. [20 May 2014].

Strategic Direction 2008, 'Leaders Are Made Not Born: Essential Steps in Leadership Development', *Strategic Direction*, vol. 24, no. 4, pp. 10 - 13.

Suderman, J 2012, 'Using the Organizational Cultural Assessment (OCAI) as a Tool for New Team development', *Journal of Practical Consulting*, vol. 4, no. 1, pp. 52 – 58.

Sullivan, M 1993, Reengineering the Corporation. *Magill's Book Reviews.*

Swe, S 2013, Organisational Change: Trompenaar's Four Corporate Cultures. Available from: <http://www.selwyn.org/selwyn/node/27>. [5 october 2014].

Taborsky, P 2014, 'Is complexity a scientific concept?', *Studies in History and Philosophy of   Science*, vol. 47, pp. 51 - 59.

Tannenbaum, R & Schmidt ,WH 1958 'How to Choose a Leadership Pattern', *Harvard Business Review,* vol. 36, no. 2 pp. 95 - 101.

Tannenbaum, R & Schmidt, WH 1973 'How to Choose a Leadership Pattern', *Harvard Business Review,* vol. 51, no. 3 pp. 162 - 180.

Tannenbaum, R & Schmidt, WH 1986 'How to Choose a Leadership Pattern', *Harvard Business Review*, vol. 64, no. 4 pp. 129.

Taormina, RJ & Gao, JH 2013, 'Maslow and the Motivation Hierarchy: measuring Satisfaction of the Needs', *American Journal of Psychology*, vol. 126, no. 2, pp. 155 - 177.

Tarantino, D 2006, 'Do You Know Your Innovation Fulcrum?' *Physician Executive*, vol. 32, no. 2, pp, 56 - 58.

Teng Kok, JL 2013, 'Lessons on the S'pore Spirit', *The Straits Times 16 September.* Available   from   <http://www.straitstimes.com/premium/forum-letters/story/lessons-the-spore-spirit-20130916>. [8 August 2014].

The Telegraph 2011, 'Sunday Telegraph 50th anniversary: Key events of the last 50 years'. Available from: <http://www.telegraph.co.uk/news/sunday-telegraph-at-50/8300828/Sunday-Telegraph-   50th-anniversary-key-events-of-the-last-50-years.html>. [24 February 2015].

The Times 2006, *'Innovation V complexity: what is too much of a good thing?; Case Study'*, available at: <http://go.galegroup.com.ezproxy.yorksj.ac.uk/ps/retrieve.do?sgHitCountType=None&sort=DASORT&inPS=true&prodId=AONE&userGroupName=urjy&tabID=T004&searchId=R1&resultListType=RESULT_LIST&contentSegment=&searchType=AdvancedSearchForm&currentPosition=1&contentSet=GAL%7CA140771766&&docId=GALE|A140771766&docType=GALE&role=>. [11January 2015].

Thompson, J & Martin, F 2005, *Strategic Management: Awareness & Change,* 6th edn. *South Western Publishers: Boston.*

Tidd, J & Bessent, J 2009, *Managing Innovation: Integrating Technological, Market and Organizational Change,* 4th edn. Wiley, Chichester.

Tourigny, D & Le, CD 2004, 'Impediments to innovation faced by Canadian manufacturing firms', *Economics of Innovation and New Technology*, vol. 13, no. 3, pp. 217 - 250.

Trompenaars, F & Hampden-Turner, C 1997, Riding the Waves of Culture: Understanding Diversity in Global Business, 2nd edn. McGraw-Hill: New York.

Trompenaars, F & Woolliams, P 2003, Business Across Cultures. Capstone Publishing: Chichester.

Trompenaars, F 2009, Dr Fons Trompenaars on Corporate Culture. Available from: <https://www.youtube.com/watch?v=aS1K_rl8PrQ>. [5 October 2014].

Tushman, M & Romanelli, E 1985, 'Organizational Evolution: A Metamorphosis Model of Convergence and Reorientation', JAI Press, vol 20, pp 171 – 222.

Uhl-Bien, M & Marion, R. (Eds.) 2008, *Complexity & Leadership, Volume I*: Conceptual Foundations. Information Publishing Associates.

Uhl-Bien, M, Marion, R & McKelvey, B 2007, 'Complexity Leadership Theory: Shifting leadership from the industrial age to the knowledge era,' *The Leadership Quarterly*, vol. 18, no. 4, pp. 298 - 318.

Umble, M & Umble, E 2014, 'Overcoming Resistance To Change', *Industrial Management,* vol 56 no. 1, pp 16 – 21.

Vakola, M 2014, 'What's in There for Me? Individual Readiness to Change and the Perceived Impact of Organizational Change', *Leadership & Organization Development Journal,* vol *35* no. 3, pp 195 – 209.

Van Eerde, W & Thierry, H 1996, 'Vroom's Expectancy Models and Work-related Criteria: A Meta-Analysis', *Journal of Applied Psychology*, vol. 81, no. 5, pp. 575 - 586.

Waite, AM 2014, 'Leadership's Influence on Innovation and Sustainability', *European Journal of Training and Development*, vol 38, no. 1/2, pp 15 – 39.

Waldrop, MM 1992, *Complexity: The emerging science at the edge of order and chaos,* Simon and Schuster: New York.

Wallace, A, Sawheny, N, & Gardjito, W 1995, Leader Characteristics that Incline People to Willingly Follow in Japan, India, Indonesia, and the United States. *Asian Pacific International Business: Regional Integration and Global Competitiveness*. Murdoch University: Perth.

Waltuck, BA 2012, 'Complexity-based change methods', *Journal for Quality & Participation*, vol. 35. no. 3, pp. 13 - 16.

Waterman, RH, Peters, TJ, Phillips, JR & Julken R 2008, *Structure is Not organisation.* Available from: <http://tompeters.com/docs/Structure_Is-Not_Organizati on.pdf> [26 July 2014].

Weberg, D 2012, 'Complexity leadership: A health perspective', *Nursing Forum*, vol. 47, no. 4, pp.   268 - 277.

Whyte, G 1989, 'Groupthink Reconsidered', *Academy of Mangement Review*, vol. 12, no. 1, pp. 40 - 56.

Wikipedia   2006,   *P E S T A n a l y s i s.*   Available   from: <http://en.wikipedia.org/wiki/PEST_ analysis>. [7 July 2014].

Wikipedia 2014, *Ethical Leadership*. Available from: <http://en.wikipedia.org/wiki/Ethi <hcal_leadership>. [9 September 2014].

Wikiquote 2014, Talk Plato. Available from: <http://en.wikiquote.org/wiki/Talk:Plato>. [5 September 2014].

Woermann, M, 2011, *'What is complexity theory?'*, Dept. of Philosophy, Stellenbosch University. Available from: <https://www.academia.edu/823563/What_is_complexity_ theory>. [30 December 2014].

Wongrassamee, S, Gardiner, PD & Simmons, JEL 2003, 'Performance Measurement Tools: The Balanced Scorecard and the EFQM Excellence Model', *Measuring Business Excellence,* vol 7 no. 1, pp. 14 – 29.

Yeung, AK & Ready, DA 1995, 'Developing Leadership Capabilities of Global Corporations: A Comparative Study in Eight Nations', *Human Resource Management*, vol. *34, no.* 4, pp. 529 - 547.

Yin, RK 2009, *Case Study Research: Design and Methods,* 4th edn, SAGE: London.

Youngwirth, J 2010, 'Guidelines for Good Delegation', *Journal of Financial Planning*, vol. 23, no. 11, pp. 12 - 13.

Yu, T & Wu, N 2009, 'A Review of the Study of the Competing Values Framework', *International Journal of Business and Management*, vol. 4, no. 7, pp. 37 – 42.

Yukl, G 2010, *Leadership in Organisations.* 6th edn. Pearson Hall: New York.

Yukl, G 2012, *Leadership in Organizations.* 8th edn. Pearson Education Limited: Harlow.

Yüksel, I 2012, 'Developing a Multi-Criteria Decision Making Model for PESTEL Analysis', *International Journal of Business & Management,* vol 7 no. 24, pp 52 – 66.

Zaleznik, A 1977, 'Managers and Leaders: Are They Different?', *Harvard Business Review*, vol. 55, no. 3, pp. 67 - 78.

Zaleznik, A 1992, 'Managers and Leaders: Are They Different?', *Harvard Business Review*, vol. 70, no. 2, pp. 126 - 135.

Zaleznik, A 2004, 'Managers and Leaders: Are They Different?', Harvard Business Review, vol 82 no. 1, pp 74 – 81.

Zaleznik, A 2004, 'Managers and Leaders: Are They Different?', *Harvard Business Review*, vol. 82, no. 2, pp. 61 - 71.

Zenouzi, BN & Dehghan, A 2012, 'Complexity theory and general model of leadership', *Global Journal of Management and Business Research*, vol. 12, no. 21, pp. 47 - 60.

Zwilling, M 2013, Forbes: How To Delegate More Effectively In Your Business. Available from <http://www.forbes.com/sites/martinzwilling/2013/10/02/how-to-delega
te-more-effectively-in-your-business/>. [27 August 2014].

 **FREE OFFER**

FREE E-COURSES & MORE

You can also visit www.wolfgangriebe.com for many more inspirational and educational online e-courses.

* * * * * * * * * * * * * * * * * * * *

MORE INSPIRATIONAL VIDEOS ON YOU TUBE

Subscribe to Wolfgang's You Tube Channel,
https://www.youtube.com/user/inspiringtheworld
for hundreds of inspirational and entertaining videos.

* * * * * * * * * * * * * * * * * * * *

HARD COPY PRINTED BOOKS

All Wolfgangs's publication are available in Paperback and

hardcover. Visit www.wolfgangriebe.com, or the publisher at

www.mindpowerpublications.com, or most book suppliers online

About the author:

Wolfgang Riebe is a globally acclaimed magical keynote speaker who has inspired millions with his mesmerising performances and motivational speeches. A towering figure in both the magic and speaking industries, he is a best-selling author of over 60 books on magic, business, and inspiration. With over 30 years of experience, Wolfgang has captivated audiences in more than 165 countries, from Hollywood to Singapore, and has starred in over 200 television shows, including his own prime-time series.

Wolfgang's journey began in South Africa, and he has since lived in the UK, Germany, and Switzerland. In 2012, he earned his Certified Speaking Professional (CSP) designation from the National Speakers Association in America, a prestigious honour held by fewer than 750 speakers worldwide at the time. He made history as the first two-term national president of the Speakers Association for Africa and has shared his insights as a TEDx speaker. His groundbreaking research culminated in his acclaimed book, "Complexity Simplified," which has been cited by over 300 doctoral students.

Wolfgang's adventures are as diverse as his achievements. From walking with penguins in Antarctica to exploring the Arctic icecap and surviving force 12 hurricanes, he has lived a life that most can only dream of. His books reflect his passion for sharing his wisdom and helping others find meaning in their lives. Wolfgang embodies the KISS principle, believes in the magic of life, celebrates milestones, and charts paths to future success. He is a rare speaker who practices what he preaches and truly walks his talk, making him a world leader in his field.

POTATO WEDGES FOR THE HEART

INSPIRATIONAL STORIES, THOUGHTS & INSIGHTS
THAT COULD CHANGE YOUR LIFE!

Chicken Soup of the Soul is a world best seller and phenomenal book! Well, here is it's brother... Potato Wedges from the Heart!

When you picture a potato wedge, what comes to mind? Something warm, tasty and cosy?

That's what this life-changing book is... a collection of short, tasty inspirational stories collected from all over the world, by unknown authors. They will not only touch your heart, but also feed your soul. Careful consideration and deep thought has gone into the selection of stories, insights and life lessons that are shared in this book. Wolfgang also shares his interpretation of all the thoughts shared, in order to expand on the meaning and give you real value from each story.

Most stories are only one page long, yet have so much depth that just reading one insight per day will give you a new meaning to life. All stories are expanded upon with many more anecdotes, personal experiences and quotations.

If you want to put your life back into perspective, be inspired, and find the magic within yourself again, this book could just the answer!

Great for the beside to read one story per night before going to sleep!

HARD COVER: ISBN-13: 979-8533154222
PAPERBACK & PDF: ISBN-13: 978-1489533258
E-READER FORMATS: ISBN: 978-1301031252

POSITIVE THINKING
250 MOTIVATIONAL QUOTES

250 ORIGINAL QUOTATIONS
WITH PHOTO, EXPLANATION AND VIDEOS!

Enjoy a unique collection of 250 original quotes, reflections and thoughts to help you find direction and be more positive in life. As a keynote speaker, Wolfgang Riebe has inspired millions of people throughout the world and shared positive messages live on the platform, in his many publications and on social media.

This book is unique in that all motivational quotes, are accompanied by a photo and Wolfgang's explanation of each quotation and what it means to him. Numerous links to various Quick Tip videos accompany many of the quotes in order to share even more insights.

It's a first and current one-of-a-kind book of daily affirmations from a one-of-a-kind man whose vision it is to create memorable magical moments for everyone that crosses his path.

Perfect as a corporate gift to inspire clients and staff!
Great for the beside to read one quote before going to sleep.
Also ideal for waiting/reception rooms and as a coffee table book!

Available in Hard Cover, Paperback, PDF and all E-Reader formats

HARD COVER (FULL COLOUR): ISBN-13: 979-8548313478
PAPERBACK & PDF: ISBN-13: 978-1547291854
E-READER FORMATS: ISBN: 978-1370912896

500 HOME BUSINESS IDEAS

500 HOME BUSINESS IDEAS FOR EVERYONE!

The global economy is in constant turmoil. Money is becoming tight. Everyone is searching for ideas to ease the global downturn and put some extra cash in their pockets. Well, here's the answer! A book containing 500 Home Business Ideas that you can start part time from home. Some require no start up capital at all. Others require some money. Many rely on skills you may already have, or skills that are relatively easy to acquire. No matter who you are, if you are looking for an extra side-line income, and possibly even a business venture that could become a full time business, this book has something for everyone.

Please note that this book does not supply you with business plans! It supplies you with practical ideas that you need to implement on your own. These ideas can easily trigger off many other possible ventures. It's aimed at people who want to work for themselves and become independent. Whether you are just looking for that extra money every month to make ends meet, or want to start a new career, this book is definitely worth a read.

The book has been divided into 10 chapters of 50 ideas each:

Administrative Ideas You Can Do in Your Pajamas, Arts & Crafts, Design & Print, Handyman/DIY Supply & Fit , Home Services Outside The Home , Ideas With The Internet , Photo, Video & Audio, Teach Your Skill To Others, Transport: Your Car, Motor Cycle Or Bicycle , Personal Services & Treatments At Home.

Each chapter is also available as a 'stand-alone' Ebook!

HARD COVER: ISBN-13: 979-8533154222
PAPERBACK & PDF: ISBN-13: 978-1479312191
E-READER FORMATS: ISBN: 978-1311919205

LEADERSHIP SKILLS IN NETWORK MARKETING

DO YOU HAVE WHAT IT TAKES TO BE A SUCCESSFUL NETWORK MARKETER?

MLM TIPS & SKILLS TO BUILD YOUR DOWNLINE

Network marketing can be one of the most rewarding and lucrative careers in the world, as proven by thousands of people. However, there is way more to running a successful MLM business than simply recruiting a downline!

Why is it that so few people make such a huge success of such a simple concept? Simple! It's not a quick overnight 'get-rich-quick' scheme, but a professional business that needs to be run as such. You need to be a leader, manager, friend and mentor to your entire team, and lead by example.

Here's a practical book which shares with you various secrets and tips to building a successful multi-level marketing business

Is network marketing as easy as it sounds?

Leadership qualities of a good networker.

Would you like to be sponsored by you?

Women as network leaders.

Quick tips on being a successful leader.

HARD COVER: ISBN-13: 979-8531645395
PAPERBACK & PDF: ISBN-13: 978-1470085377
E-READER FORMATS: ISBN: 978-1466058248

365 QUOTES TO KEEP YOU INSPIRED

VOLUME 1
HARD COVER (FULL COLOUR):
ISBN-13: 979-8539749941
PAPERBACK & PDF:
ISBN-13: 978-1540408600
E-READER FORMATS:
ISBN: 978-1370895151

VOLUME 2
HARD COVER (FULL COLOUR):
ISBN-13: 979-8542928159
PAPERBACK & PDF:
ISBN-13: 978-1545269541
E-READER FORMATS:
ISBN: 978-1370501281

VOLUME 3
HARD COVER (FULL COLOUR):
ISBN-13: 979-8545870325
PAPERBACK & PDF:
ISBN-13: 978-1545432181
E-READER FORMATS:
ISBN: 978-1370546473

3 BOOK SERIES EACH WITH 365 INSPIRATIONAL QUOTES

Each book is a truly unique publication that not only shares 365 'unknown author' quotes, but also includes a custom photo, plus a short analysis of each quotation.

Additionally, links to various inspirational and self-help videos have been included that accompany, amplify and tie into the various topics.

You can use the books as a daily tonic and read one quote per day for a year, or you can savour as many sayings as you need per day.

Perfect as a corporate gift to inspire clients and staff!
Great for the beside to read one quote before going to sleep.
Also ideal for waiting/reception rooms and as a coffee table book!

Buy each book individually, or all three together!

Available in Hard Cover, Paperback, PDF and all E-Reader formats

PUBLIC SEMINARS & KEYNOTES

Would you like Wolfgang to speak at your organisations next meeting or event? Simply visit ***www.wolfgangriebe.com*** for more details and keynotes on offer.

www.ingramcontent.com/pod-product-compliance
Lightning Source LLC
Chambersburg PA
CBHW080653190526
45169CB00006B/2091